Competition Law in New Zealand

Competition Law in New Zealand

Anna Kingsbury

This book was originally published as a monograph in the
International Encyclopaedia of Laws/Competition Law

Founding Editor: Roger Blanpain
General Editor: Frank Hendrickx
Volume Editors: Francesco Denozza & Alberto Toffoletto

Wolters Kluwer

Published by:
Kluwer Law International B.V.
PO Box 316
2400 AH Alphen aan den Rijn
The Netherlands
E-mail: international-sales@wolterskluwer.com
Website: lrus.wolterskluwer.com

Sold and distributed in North, Central and South America by:
Wolters Kluwer Legal & Regulatory U.S.
7201 McKinney Circle
Frederick, MD 21704
United States of America
Email: customer.service@wolterskluwer.com

Sold and distributed in all other countries by:
Air Business Subscriptions
Rockwood House
Haywards Heath
West Sussex
RH16 3DH
United Kingdom
Email: international-customerservice@wolterskluwer.com

Printed on acid-free paper

ISBN 978-94-035-1634-9

e-Book: ISBN 978-94-035-1635-6
web-PDF: ISBN 978-94-035-1640-0

Printed in the United Kingdom.

The Author

Anna Kingsbury was born in Wellington, New Zealand. She obtained a Bachelor of Arts degree in History and Politics from the University of Auckland and a Bachelor of Laws from Victoria University of Wellington. She also has a Master's in Law from the University of Melbourne, a Master's in Law specialising in Trade Regulation from New York University, and a Doctorate in Juridical Science from La Trobe University, Australia. She has been admitted as a Barrister and Solicitor of the High Court of New Zealand. She has taught in the Faculty of Law at the University of Waikato, New Zealand since 1997, where she teaches Competition Law, the Law of Intellectual Property and the Law of Torts and Competition Law. She has published widely in the areas of Competition Law and Intellectual Property Law, both in New Zealand and internationally.

The Author

Table of Contents

The Author 3

List of Abbreviations 11

General Introduction 13

§1. General Background of the Country 13

§2. Economic System 14

§3. Legal System 15

§4. Historical Background of Antitrust Law 15

Part I. Structure of Antitrust Law and Its Enforcement 17

Chapter 1. Sources of Antitrust Law 17

§1. National Sources 17

§2. International Sources 18

§3. Secondary Sources 19
I. Regulations 19
II. Guidelines 19

§4. Sources' Relation and Hierarchy 20

§5. Role and Authority of Precedents 20

Chapter 2. Scope of Application 21

§1. Territorial Reach 21

§2. Special Sectors 23

§3. State-Owned Enterprises and Public Utilities 24

§4. Sensible Effect and *De Minimis* 24

Chapter 3. Overview of Substantive Provisions 25

§1. Restrictive Agreements 25

§2. Dominant Undertakings 28

§3. Business Acquisitions (Concentrations) 29

§4. Other Prohibitions 31

§5. Tests of Illegality 31
I. Per Se Prohibitions and Naked Restraints 31
II. Balancing Tests 32
III. Merger Tests 34

Chapter 4. Overview of Main Notions 35

§1. Undertaking 35

§2. Relevant Market 36

§3. Market Power/Dominant Position 37

§4. Agreements and Concerted Practices 39
I. Contracts 39
II. Arrangements and Understandings 39

§5. Restriction of Competition 41
I. Purpose and Likely Effect 41
II. Substantial Lessening of Competition 41

§6. Monopolisation and Abuse of Dominance 42
I. Market Power 43
II. Taking Advantage 44
III. Purpose 45

§7. Concentrations 46

§8. Joint Ventures 47

Chapter 5. Consequences of Violations and Enforcement Institutions 52

§1. Administrative Enforcement 52

I. Antitrust Authorities 52
A. Formation, Composition 52
B. Investigating Powers 53
C. Adjudicating Powers (Ascertaining and Sanctioning) 55
D. Other Institutional Tasks (Consultancy to Parliament/ Government) 57
II. Government Direct Enforcement Activities 58
III. Other Administrative Agencies Applying Antitrust Rules 58
IV. Administrative Fines 58
V. Administrative Injunctions and Other Restrictive Orders 59
VI. Interim Measures 59

§2. Civil Enforcement 59
I. Competent Civil Courts 59
II. Sanctions 60
A. Nullity 60
B. Damages 61
1. Pecuniary Penalties 62
2. Damages 64
C. Interim Measures 65

§3. Criminal Enforcement 66
I. Criminal Sanctions for Antitrust Violations 66
II. Other Application of Criminal Law to Relevant Conducts 68
III. Role of Prosecutors 68
IV. Competent Criminal Courts 69

Part II. Application of the Prohibitions 71

Chapter 1. Restrictive Agreements 71

§1. Horizontal Agreements 71
I. Cartels 80
A. Price Fixing 80
B. Market/Client Allocation 90
C. Production/Innovation Limitation 93
D. Group Boycott 95
E. Collusion on Other Objects 95
II. Information Exchange Practices 95
III. Cooperation Agreements 96
A. Research and Development 101
B. Specialisation 101
C. Standardisation 101
D. Joint Production 101
E. Joint Purchasing 102
F. Joint Selling 103

§2. Vertical Agreements 103
I. Distribution 109
A. Exclusive Distributorship 109
B. Exclusive Dealing 109
C. Selective Distribution 111
D. Franchising 112
II. Technology Licencing 113
A. Patent Licencing 113
B. Trademark Licencing 115
C. Know How and Trade Secret Licencing 116

Chapter 2. Dominant Undertakings' Prohibited Practices 117

§1. Exploitative Practices 124
I. Excessive/Unfair Pricing 124
II. Discrimination 125

§2. Exclusionary Practices 126
I. Predation 126
II. Tying 130
III. Rebates 132
IV. Refusal to Deal 133
V. Price Squeeze 135

Chapter 3. Concentrations 137

§1. Horizontal Mergers 141

§2. Vertical Mergers 144

§3. Market/Product Extension Mergers 145

§4. Pure Conglomerate Mergers 145

§5. Joint Ventures 146

Part III. Administrative Procedure 147

Chapter 1. Administrative Investigations Before the Antitrust Authority 147

§1. Initiative 147
I. General Sectors Inquiries 147
II. Ex Officio Investigations 151
III. Complaints 151

§2. Powers 152
I. Requests for Information 152
II. Investigating and Search Powers 155
III. Cooperation with Other State Institutions 158

§3. Right of Defence 158
I. Content and Notification of Opening Decisions 158
II. Proceedings: Hearings, Access to File and Briefs 160
III. Statement of Objections 162
IV. Final Hearing and Decision 162

Chapter 2. Voluntary Notifications and Clearance Decisions & Merger Control 164

§1. Preliminary Filing Obligations 164
I. Criteria and Thresholds 164
II. Turnover Calculation 166
III. Market Share Calculation 166
IV. Other Relevant Notions 167

§2. Structure of Proceedings 167
I. Preliminary Assessment and Full Investigation 167
II. Time Framework 170
III. Right of Defence 170

§3. Clearance and Conditional Clearance 171
I. Conditions and Undertakings 171
A. Content 171
B. Timing 172

§4. Relations with Other Merger Control Authorities 172
I. Other Authorities Within the Local Jurisdiction 172
II. International Coordination 173

Chapter 3. Challenging of the Administrative Decision 175

§1. Competent Courts 175

§2. Time Limits 176

§3. Scope of Judicial Review 176

Selected Bibliography 177

Index 179

Table of Contents

List of Abbreviations

CA	Court of Appeal
CC	Commerce Commission
EDC	Exclusive Dealing Clause
HC	High Court
NZ	New Zealand
s	section
SC	Supreme Court
SSNIP	Small but Significant Non-Transitory Increase in Price
ss	sections
UK	United Kingdom
US	United States

List of Abbreviations

General Introduction

§1. General Background of the Country

1. New Zealand is a small island nation located in the south-western Pacific Ocean. It lies about 1,600 km from Australia, and occupies 269,652 sq km. It is made up of two large islands, known as the North Island and the South Island, and a number of smaller islands, the largest of which is Stewart Island to the south.

2. The Māori name for New Zealand is Aotearoa, and although not designated as the official name of the country, this name is also in common use. For the main islands of New Zealand both English and Māori names were designated in 2013 as alternative official names. The Māori name for the North Island is Te Ika-a-Māui, and the South Island is Te Waipounamu.

3. The Māori people were the first inhabitants of New Zealand, but Māori are now a minority of the population as a result of colonisation and immigration. New Zealand was a colony of Great Britain, and much of the European (or pakeha) population is descended from British migrants. Migrants also came from the Pacific Island nations. However, sources of migration have in recent years become increasingly diverse.

4. The population of New Zealand is increasing, and in 2017, it is approximately 4.8 million people. The 2013 census data on ethnicity showed the composition of the population. Nearly three-quarters of the population (74%) identified themselves as being of European ethnicity, and 14.9% identified themselves as belonging to the Māori ethnic group. Pacific peoples were 7.4%, and 11.8% identified themselves as Asian. 1.2% identified as Middle Eastern, Latin American or African, and 1.7% were in the 'other ethnicity' category. Note that in the census data, people were able to identify with more than one ethnic group, and therefore percentages do not add up to 100.[1]

5. New Zealand has three official languages, English, Te reo Māori and New

1. Statistics New Zealand, Tatauranga Aotearoa, *2013 Census QuickStats about National Highlights: Cultural Diversity*, http://www.stats.govt.nz/Census/2013-census/profile-and-summary-reports/quickstats-about-national-highlights/cultural-diversity.aspx (accessed 7 Aug. 2017).

Zealand Sign Language. English is the most commonly used language. Approximately 21% of Māori are fluent Māori speakers.[2] Of the population as a whole, 3.7% speak Māori.[3]

6. New Zealand's political system is a representative democracy and constitutional monarchy. There are three branches of government, the parliament, the executive and the judiciary.

7. The Head of State is Queen Elizabeth II, the Governor-General is her representative appointed on the advice of the New Zealand government. The Parliament consists of the Governor-General and the elected House of Representatives. The New Zealand House of Representatives is elected every three years under a mixed member proportional system. The Parliament is based on the Westminster model but is unicameral. The doctrine of parliamentary supremacy applies.

8. The executive is the administrative branch of government. It comprises the Governor-General, the Prime Minister and Cabinet, government departments and the public service, local government, state-owned enterprises and various statutory bodies. The judiciary is independent of government.

§2. Economic System

9. New Zealand has a small mixed economy which operates on free market principles. Over the past three decades, the New Zealand economy has undergone a process of deregulation, so that it is now a very open economy and one of the least regulated in the Organisation for Economic Co-operation and Development (OECD).[4] New Zealand's economy is export-driven and historically has had a strong agricultural base. The primary sector contributes just over half of New Zealand's total export earnings.[5] Dairy products, meat and wood products are New Zealand's largest exports. It also has a significant manufacturing industry and services sector, and a growing tourist industry.

---

2. Statistics New Zealand, Tatauranga Aotearoa, *New Zealand Social Indicators: He Kete Tatauranga*, http://www.stats.govt.nz/browse_for_stats/snapshots-of-nz/nz-social-indicators/Home/Culture%20and%20identity/maori-lang-speakers.aspx (accessed 7 Aug. 2017).
3. Statistics New Zealand, Tatauranga Aotearoa, *2013 Census QuickStats about National Highlights: Cultural Diversity*, http://www.stats.govt.nz/Census/2013-census/profile-and-summary-reports/quickstats-about-national-highlights/cultural-diversity.aspx (accessed 25 Mar. 2014).
4. New Zealand Treasury, *New Zealand Economic and Financial Overview 2016: Economic Overview*, https://treasury.govt.nz/publications/economic-overview/new-zealand-economic-and-financial-overview-2016-html#section-3 (accessed 9 Apr. 2019)
5. New Zealand Treasury, *New Zealand Economic and Financial Overview 2016: Economic Overview, Industrial Structure and Principal Economic Sectors: Primary Industries* https://treasury.govt.nz/publications/economic-overview/new-zealand-economic-and-financial-overview-2016-html#section-3 (accessed 9 Apr. 2019).

§3. Legal System

10. The legal system is derived from the British system as New Zealand was settled as a British colony. New Zealand does not have a written constitution, but it has a constitution derived from that history from various documents and from the Treaty of Waitangi of 1840. The Treaty of Waitangi was signed between Māori leaders (chiefs) and the British Crown. The Treaty of Waitangi is regarded as a founding document of New Zealand although its meaning has been a source of dispute over many years, partly as a result of differences between the English and Māori texts. The terms of the Treaty have also frequently been breached by the Crown.

11. After 1840, New Zealand became a Crown colony. British settlement significantly increased, and the New Zealand Constitution Act of 1852 was passed by the British Parliament, setting up self-government for the British settlers in New Zealand. British law was transplanted to New Zealand, and the New Zealand constitution and the system of government is still based on the British system. In the years that followed, New Zealand developed from its status as a colony. In 1907 New Zealand became a dominion and in 1947 New Zealand adopted the Statute of Westminster and accepted full autonomy from Britain. In 1949 New Zealand citizenship came into existence. Voting rights were also gradually extended. Universal suffrage for men over 21 was introduced in 1879 and for women in 1893.

12. New Zealand today is a constitutional monarchy with a system of responsible and representative government and the rule of law. The legal system institutions are the legislature (Parliament), the executive and the judiciary. The legislature comprises the House of Representatives and Governor-General, and it has the power to pass legislation, which is the highest source of law and cannot be declared invalid by any other institution. The executive is the administrative branch of government. The judiciary is independent of government and is responsible for interpreting and applying legislation and the common law. The Supreme Court is the highest court, above, in descending order, the Court of Appeal, High Court and District Court. There are also a number of specialist courts and tribunals, but no specialist court in the area of competition law. The courts generally are run on an adversary system, and the legal profession plays an important role within this system.

§4. Historical Background of Antitrust Law

13. New Zealand's first real antitrust statute was the Commerce Act 1986. Before 1986 there had been various forms of statutory regulation of commerce, but not in the form of an internationally recognisable antitrust law. The Commerce Act 1986 was passed in the context of a radical government of deregulation and privatisation of industry. New Zealand, as a colonial nation, had a strong history of State ownership and control of industry and infrastructure, and the State rather than private enterprise had been the main actor in the development of the modern economy. Post-1984, the then government undertook a radical program in which state-owned industries were first corporatised and then privatised, and industry was deregulated.

Tariffs on imports were also radically reduced or abolished. This resulted in industry mergers and closures in many previously protected industries and greater levels of industry concentration. Industry concentration combined with removal of state ownership and control also opened up greater potential for anti-competitive behaviour in markets.

14. The Commerce Act 1986 was modelled on competition laws in other jurisdictions, particularly the then Australian Trade Practices 1974. It also drew on European law in relation to monopolisation and mergers, using a dominance threshold. The Australian provision used a substantial degree of market power threshold for monopolisation. The New Zealand Commerce Amendment Act 2001 replaced the dominance threshold for monopolisation with a substantial degree of market power threshold, following the Australian model. The Commerce Amendment Act 2001 also changed the threshold for mergers from dominance to a substantially lessening competition test.[6] The Commerce Amendment Act 2001 also inserted a new purpose statement to the Commerce Act, providing that the purpose of the Act 'is to promote competition in markets for the long-term benefit of consumers within New Zealand'.[7]

15. The New Zealand Commerce Act 1986 was originally designed as extremely light-handed regulation. Policy-makers and legislators at the time were strongly influenced by the Chicago School approach to competition law, an approach that was very much in the ascendancy at the time. The New Zealand Commerce Act was also designed to suit a small economy, and was relatively permissive, allowing higher levels of market concentration than in other jurisdictions. Over time the regime proved to be too light-handed and subsequent amendments have been designed to strengthen New Zealand's competition regime. The desirability of harmonisation of New Zealand competition law with that of neighbouring Australia is also a consideration for policy-makers and legislators.

---

6. *See generally* A. Bollard, 'The Role of Antitrust in a Small Open Economy: The Commerce Act in New Zealand' in Round, D.K. (ed.) *The Australian Trade Practices Act 1974: Proscriptions and Prescriptions for a More Competitive Economy* (Kluwer, 1995) 671–694. For a general critical discussion of the reforms generally, *see* Jane Kelsey, *Rolling Back the State: Privatization of Power in Aotearoa/New Zealand* (Bridget Williams, 1993).
7. Commerce Act 1986 s. 1A.

Part I. Structure of Antitrust Law and Its Enforcement

Chapter 1. Sources of Antitrust Law

§1. National Sources

16. The principal source of New Zealand antitrust law is the Commerce Act 1986. The Commerce Act 1986 established a statutory framework for competition law in New Zealand. The Commerce Act establishes the Commerce Commission, the New Zealand competition agency.[8] It contains specific provisions applying to restrictive trade practices, covering agreements between competitors and single firm conduct.[9] Business acquisitions that would have, or would be likely to have, the effect of substantially lessening competition in a market are prohibited.[10] The Act also provides for a regime of clearances and authorisations.[11] Clearances are available for business acquisitions that will not, or would not be likely to have, the effect of substantially lessening competition in a market.[12] The Commerce Commission is empowered to issue such clearances. There is also a regime for authorisation which applies to both restrictive trade practices and business acquisitions. The Commerce Commission may **issue** authorisations for specified restrictive trade practices that will in all the circumstances result, or be likely to result, in a benefit to the public which would outweigh the lessening of competition.[13]

17. The Commerce Act 1986 also contains a regime of regulated goods and services, which is a regime inserted by the Commerce Amendment Act 2008.[14] It provides for the regulation of the price and quality of goods or services in markets where there is little or no competition and little or no likelihood of a substantial increase in competition.[15] It provides for the imposition of three types of regulation on goods or services, and provides for the Commerce Commission to determine

8. *Ibid.* Part 1. *See also* www.comcom.govt.nz (accessed 9 May 2019).
9. *Ibid.*, Part 2.
10. *Ibid.*, Part 3, in particular s. 47.
11. *Ibid.*, Part 5.
12. *Ibid.*, s. 66.
13. *Ibid.*, s. 61.
14. *Ibid.*, Part 4.
15. *Ibid.*, s. 52.

input methodologies applying to the supply of regulated goods or services.[16] There is also provision for industry-specific regulation applying to electricity lines services,[17] gas pipeline services[18] and airports.[19]

18. The Commerce Act provides for enforcement, remedies and appeals under the Act.[20] The Commerce Commission acts as a decision-maker in relation to clearances and authorisations, and these decisions can be appealed to the High Court and potentially upward to the Court of Appeal and Supreme Court. In appeals from Commerce Commission determinations, a Judge and a lay member are required. Lay members are appointed on the basis of their knowledge or experience in industry, commerce, economics, law or accountancy.[21]For contraventions of provisions including the restrictive trade practices provisions, the High Court is the initial decision-maker and High Court decisions may be appealed to higher courts.[22] Available remedies include injunctions, damages, pecuniary penalties and orders for divestiture of assets or shares.[23]

19. The Commerce Act 1986 therefore establishes the statutory framework for competition law. The other major source of law is case law. New Zealand is a common law jurisdiction, and court decisions are an important source of law. The courts interpret and apply the Commerce Act provisions, and decisions have precedent value. In addition, the Commerce Commission is itself a source of law. It issues determinations, and it also produces its own *Guidelines*, which are a form of 'soft' law. Particularly important are the *Mergers and Acquisitions Guidelines*.[24]

§2. International Sources

20. Competition law in New Zealand has always drawn on models from other jurisdictions. The New Zealand Commerce Act was originally modelled on the Australian Trade Practices Act 1974 (now the Competition and Consumer Act 2010). Australian statutory developments and Australian case law are particularly influential in New Zealand courts and in legislative reform. There are also ongoing efforts to harmonise New Zealand business laws with Australia. There are very close trade and economic ties between the two countries; there exists a long-standing Closer Economic Relations (CER) agreement between the two nations which took effect in

16. *Ibid.*, s. 52B.
17. *Ibid.*, Part 4, subpart 9.
18. *Ibid.*, Part 4, subpart 10.
19. *Ibid.*, Part 4, subpart 11.
20. *Ibid.*, Part 6.
21. *Ibid.*, s. 77.
22. *Ibid.*, s. 75.
23. *Ibid.*, s. 85.
24. *See* Commerce Commission New Zealand, *Mergers and Acquisitions Guidelines* (2013) http://www.comcom.govt.nz/business-competition/guidelines-2/mergers-and-acquisitions-guidelines/ (accessed 9 May 2009).

1983.[25] However there are significant differences between the competition law provisions in the two countries, and significant differences in the wider business environments.

21. New Zealand courts also draw on decisions from the United States, Canada, the United Kingdom and Europe, among others.

22. The Commerce Commission is also influenced by the work of competition agencies in other jurisdictions. The Commerce Commission is part of the International Competition Network (ICN).[26] The Commerce Commission also has a number of international agreements with competition agencies in other jurisdictions. These agreements provide for cooperation, including notification, exchange of information, coordination of enforcement and joint educational programmes and publication.[27] The Commerce Commission currently has agreements in place with Australia, Canada and Taiwan.[28]

§3. Secondary Sources

I. Regulations

23. Regulations may be made under the Commerce Act by the Governor-General by Order in Council.[29] There are current regulations covering fees,[30] and regulations relating to the regulation of goods and services using the regulatory regime under Commerce Act 1986 Part 4.

II. Guidelines

24. The Commerce Commission publishes Guidelines to assist businesses to understand how to avoid anti-competitive behaviour and to provide in-depth information about rules and practices for mergers and acquisitions. Current Guidelines

---

25. *See* New Zealand Ministry of Foreign Affairs and Trade, *New Zealand Australia Closer Economic Relations (CER)* https://www.mfat.govt.nz/en/trade/free-trade-agreements/free-trade-agreements-in-force/nz-australia-closer-economic-relations-cer/ (accessed 10 Aug. 2017).
26. *See* the International Competition Network website http://www.internationalcompetitionnetwork.org/ (accessed 10 Aug. 2017).
27. Such agreements are provided for in Commerce Act 1986 ss 99A–99P. *See also* Commerce Commission, *About Us: International Relations*, https://comcom.govt.nz/about-us/working-with-other-agencies (accessed 9 Apr. 2019).
28. Details of agreements can be found at https://comcom.govt.nz/about-us/working-with-other-agencies (accessed 9 Apr. 2019).
29. Commerce Act 1986 s. 108.
30. Commerce Act (Fees) Regulations 1990.

include *Authorisation Guidelines,*[31] *Mergers and Acquisitions Guidelines,*[32] *Competitor Collaboration Guidelines,*[33] *School Uniforms and Supplies-Procurement Guidelines for Schools,*[34] and *How to Recognise and Deter Bid Rigging: Guidelines for Procurers.*[35]

§4. Sources' Relation and Hierarchy

25. The primary source of competition law in New Zealand is the Commerce Act 1986 and associated regulations. Complementary to this is the growing body of case law, which in a common law system also has the status of law. Commerce Commission Guidelines are also a source of 'soft' law in this area.

§5. Role and Authority of Precedents

26. New Zealand is a common law legal system. The doctrine of precedent applies, and the rule of law in one case can be persuasive or binding on courts in subsequent cases. Generally courts are bound by decisions of courts above them in the hierarchy of courts. Decisions of the highest court, the New Zealand Supreme Court, are binding on all courts. Court of Appeal decisions are binding on lower courts, and High Court decisions bind lower courts and the Commerce Commission. Courts will commonly, but are not required, to follow their own previous decisions.

31. Commerce Commission New Zealand, *Authorisation Guidelines* (2013) http://comcom.govt.nz/business-competition/guidelines-2/authorisation-guidelines/ (accessed 10 Aug. 2017).
32. Commerce Commission New Zealand, *Mergers and Acquisitions Guidelines* (2013) http://www.comcom.govt.nz/business-competition/guidelines-2/mergers-and-acquisitions-guidelines/ (accessed 10 Aug. 2017).
33. Commerce Commission New Zealand, Competitor Collaboration Guidelines (January 2018) https://comcom.govt.nz/business/avoiding-anti-competitive-behaviour/what-is-a-cartel
34. Commerce Commission New Zealand, *School Uniforms and Supplies-Procurement Guidelines for Schools (2013)* http://comcom.govt.nz/business-competition/guidelines-2/school-uniforms/ (accessed 10 Aug. 2017).
35. Commerce Commission New Zealand, *How to Recognise and Deter Bid Rigging: Guidelines for Procurers* (March 2018) https://comcom.govt.nz/business/avoiding-anti-competitive-behaviour/how-to-recognise-and-deter-bid-rigging

Chapter 2. Scope of Application

§1. Territorial Reach

27. Section 4 of the Commerce Act sets out the Act's territorial reach, stating the extent of the application of the Act. Section 4 has been the subject of litigation, and the section was amended in 2017.[36] There has been litigation on the question of whether section 4 exhaustively defines the Commerce Act's extraterritorial effect. The New Zealand Supreme Court has held that it does, and that section 4 describes the only circumstances in which the Act applies to conduct outside New Zealand. The Court said it should be regarded as an exhaustive statement of the Act's intended scope in relation to overseas conduct.[37] The Court said that Parliament should not be taken to have legislated with extraterritorial effect without express language or necessary implication.[38]

28. Following the 2017 amendments, a new section 4(1AA) provides that a person engages in conduct in New Zealand if any act or omission forming part of the conduct occurs in New Zealand; and a person (person A) engages in conduct in New Zealand if another person (person B) engages in conduct in New Zealand, and the conduct of person B is deemed (by virtue of section 90) to be the conduct of person A.

29. Section 4(1) provides that the Act 'extends to the engaging in conduct outside New Zealand by any person resident or carrying on business in New Zealand to the extent that such conduct affects a market in New Zealand'.[39] For section 4(1) to apply, the conduct outside New Zealand must be engaged in by a person either resident or carrying on business in New Zealand, and must also affect a market in New Zealand.

30. The Court of Appeal has considered the meaning of 'carrying on business in New Zealand', concluding that it is a question of fact and a number of factors are relevant.[40] It said that the analysis was not confined to whether or not the company maintained a systematic and continuous physical presence in New Zealand, as that would state the test too highly and would not serve the purpose of the Act.[41] The approach required recognition of the practical modes of transacting business, realities of modern commerce including internet communication and globalisation.[42]

---

36. Commerce (Cartels and Other Matters) Amendment Act 2017 s. 5.
37. *Poynter v. Commerce Commission* [2010] NZSC 38, [2010] 3 NZLR 300 (2010), 9 NZBLC 102,293, (2010) 12 TCLR 599 paras [15], [62], [78]–[79].
38. *Poynter v. Commerce Commission* [2010] NZSC 38, [2010] 3 NZLR 300 (2010), 9 NZBLC 102,293, (2010) 12 TCLR 599 paras [38]–[45].
39. Commerce Act 1986 s. 4(1).
40. *Commerce Commission v. Visy Board Pty Ltd* [2012] NZCA 383, para. [29].
41. *Ibid.*, para. [29].
42. *Ibid.*, para. [29].

31. The Court of Appeal has also considered the second limb of section 4(1) which requires that the conduct affects a market in New Zealand. The Court preferred an interpretation that, in this context, 'affects' meant that the conduct should relate to a market in New Zealand, saying that this permitted the use of the section even if the conduct was only directed at a market in New Zealand. However, overseas conduct would only relate to a market in New Zealand to the extent that it impacted or likely impacted competition in the market in New Zealand in which the contravention was alleged to have occurred. This meant that derivative or 'ripple down' effects on a market different from the market in which the contravention occurred would not be covered by the section.[43]

32. Another issue arises where a New Zealand subsidiary of a foreign company engages in unlawful conduct. In these situations the question arises as to the liability of the foreign parent company. There may be an issue as to whether the foreign firm is 'carrying on business in New Zealand' in terms of section 4(1). However liability may also arise by the application of section 90 of the Commerce Act.[44] Section 90 has recently been amended, but the essential principles are the same.[45] Section 90(2) now provides that:

> (2) Conduct by a person (person B) is deemed for the purposes of this Act also to be the conduct of a person other than an individual (person A) if, at the time of the conduct,-
> (a) person B was a director, employee, or agent of person A, acting within the scope of person B's actual or apparent authority; or
> (b) person B was a person who was acting on the direction, or with the consent or agreement (express or implied), of a director, employee, or agent of person A who was acting within the scope of the director's, employee's, or agent's actual or apparent authority.

33. The principles applicable to liability of a foreign firm for the actions of a New Zealand subsidiary under section 90 have been the subject of litigation, and this litigation is likely to remain relevant despite the changes to the section.[46] The Court of Appeal has said that this is a deeming provision which enables conduct engaged in on behalf of a body corporate to be treated as engaged in by the body corporate, and that the use of 'also' means that liability of one party may potentially become the liability of another.[47] The section was an enlarging provision removing the necessity to rely on common law tests, and it was not necessary to demonstrate

43. *Ibid.*, para. [34].
44. Where proceedings are served out of New Zealand without leave, the party served may protest jurisdiction and the High Court will consider jurisdiction in the context of r 6.27 of the High Court Rules, requiring an arguable case that the rule applies. *See* discussion in *Commerce Commission v. Visy Board Pty Ltd* [2012] NZCA 383, paras [15]–[18].
45. Commerce (Cartels and Other Matters) Amendment Bill 2017 s. 20 repealed and replaced s. 90.
46. *See Kuehne + Nagel International AG v. Commerce Commission* [2012] NZCA 221, [2012] 3 NZLR 187, *Commerce Commission v. Visy Board Pty Ltd* [2012] NZCA 383.
47. *Kuehne + Nagel International AG v. Commerce Commission* [2012] NZCA 221, [37].

that the conduct was for the company's benefit.[48] Whether conduct was engaged in on behalf of a body corporate would depend on all of the circumstances of the case and involve an intensely factual evaluation.[49] An analysis in terms of agency concepts was not required.[50]

34. Section 4(2) applies to conduct in trans-Tasman markets covered by section 36A. Section 36A applies to taking advantage of market power in a market in New Zealand, in Australia, or in both New Zealand and Australia. Section 4(2) provides that section 36A extends 'to the engaging in conduct outside New Zealand by any person resident or carrying on business in Australia to the extent that such conduct affects a market, not being a market exclusively for services, in New Zealand'.[51]

35. Sections 47A–47D apply to business acquisitions by overseas persons. These sections were inserted into the Act in 2017.[52] Section 47A provides that the Commerce Commission may apply to the High Court for a declaration if an overseas person acquires, whether directly or indirectly, a controlling interest in a New Zealand body corporate through the acquisition outside New Zealand of the assets of a business or shares.[53] The High Court may make a declaration that it is satisfied that the overseas person has acquired a controlling interest in a New Zealand body corporate through the acquisition outside New Zealand of the assets of a business or shares; and the acquisition of that controlling interest has, or is likely to have, the effect of substantially lessening competition in a market in New Zealand.[54] 'Controlling interest' is defined in section 47A(4), which provides a list of circumstances in which a person would be found to have acquired a controlling interest, and includes control of the composition of the body corporate board, or in a position to exercise more than 20% of the votes, or holding more than 20% of shares.

§2. Special Sectors

36. Part 4 of the Commerce Act provides a regime for regulated goods or services, and there are particular provisions for electricity lines services,[55] gas pipeline services[56] and airport services.[57] There are also regimes for industry-specific regulation outside the Commerce Act.[58]

---

48. *Ibid.*, [37]–[38].
49. *Ibid.*, [39].
50. *Ibid.*, [40].
51. Commerce Act 1986 s. 4(2).
52. Inserted by Commerce (Cartels and Other Matters) Amendment Act 2017 s. 8.
53. Commerce Act 1986 s. 47A(1).
54. *Ibid.*, s. 47A(2).
55. *Ibid.*, Part 4, Subpart 9.
56. *Ibid.*, Part 4, Subpart 10.
57. *Ibid.*, Part 4, Subpart 11.
58. *See* for example the Telecommunications Act 2001.

37. Section 43 of the Commerce Act provides an exception from the restrictive trade practices provisions for matters specifically authorised by statute. There are also specific exceptions in section 44 including specific exceptions applying to international shipping.[59] New provisions relating to international shipping were introduced in 2017, and will come into force in August 2019.[60]

§3. State-Owned Enterprises and Public Utilities

38. The Commerce Act provides an exemption for the activities of the Crown, where those activities are not in trade. Section 5 of the Commerce Act provides that the Act shall bind the Crown in so far as the Crown engages in trade, but the Crown is not liable for pecuniary penalties and cannot be prosecuted for an offence.[61] The 'Crown' is not defined in the Act, but refers to activities of the executive government.

39. The Act applies to Crown-owned corporations engaged in trade.[62] Under the monopolisation provisions, the Crown in respect of the Government of New Zealand is not immune from the Australian provision, and the Australian Crown is not immune from the equivalent New Zealand provision.[63]

40. Section 2(1) defines 'trade' broadly, as meaning 'any trade, business, industry, profession, occupation, activity of commerce, or undertaking relating to the supply or acquisition of goods or services or to the disposition or acquisition of any interest in land'.[64]

§4. Sensible Effect and *De Minimis*

41. New Zealand does not have a general doctrine of sensible effect and *de minimis* in the sense that exists in EU law. However some statutory provisions require that effects be more than trivial, for example the 'substantially lessening of competition' test in the trade practices provisions.[65]

59. Commerce Act 1986 s. 44–44B.
60. Commerce (Cartels and Other Matters) Amendment Act 2017 s. 2(2).
61. Commerce Act 1986 s. 5. These provisions apply to government activity.
62. *Ibid.*, s. 6.
63. *Ibid.*, ss 6A and 6B.
64. *Ibid.*, s. 2(1). *See also Glaxo New Zealand Ltd v. Attorney-General* [1991] 3 NZLR 129.
65. *See* for example Commerce Act 1986 s. 27. *See also* s. 2(5) requirement that a purpose or reason be a substantial purpose or reason.

Chapter 3. Overview of Substantive Provisions

§1. Restrictive Agreements

42. Restrictive agreements are covered in Part 2 of the Commerce Act, in sections 27–34 and 37–42.

43. The broadest prohibition on restrictive agreements is contained in section 27, which provides that:[66]

> No person shall enter into a contract or arrangement, or arrive at an understanding, containing a provision that has the purpose, or has or is likely to have the effect, of substantially lessening competition in a market.

44. Giving effect to such a provision is also prohibited,[67] and no provision to which the section applies is enforceable.[68] Covenants that have the purpose, or have or are likely to have the effect, of substantially lessening competition in a market are also prohibited.[69]

45. These provisions are very broad, they cover horizontal and vertical agreements, there is no requirement that the parties to the agreement are in competition with each other and the effect may take place in any market, not necessarily the market in which the parties to the agreement compete. However liability is not per se, it requires a rule of reason analysis with evidence of purpose, effect or likely effect of substantially lessening competition in a market.

46. The Commerce Act 1986 originally also contained a specific per se provision prohibiting certain exclusionary provisions in agreements between competitors.[70] However this provision was progressively narrowed by statutory amendments to the point that cases were no longer being brought under the section, and, with effect from 15 August 2017, the provision was repealed.[71]

47. The New Zealand Commerce Act has also had a longstanding per se prohibition on horizontal price-fixing agreements. These provisions have recently been very substantially amended as part of a process of cartel law reform, and from 15

66. Commerce Act 1986 s. 27(1).
67. *Ibid.*, s. 27(2).
68. *Ibid.*, s. 27(4).
69. *Ibid.*, s. 28.
70. *Ibid.*, s. 29 (now repealed).
71. Commerce (Cartels and Other Matters) Amendment Act 2017 s. 6.

August 2017 a new price-fixing regime has applied.[72] The new cartel provisions prohibit cartel agreements[73] and provide that no cartel provision is enforceable.[74] Section 30 now provides that:

> No person may –
>
> (a) enter into a contract or arrangement, or arrive at an understanding, that contains a cartel provision; or
> (b) give effect to a cartel provision.

48. Section 30A provides a definition of 'cartel provision' and related terms. It defines a cartel provision as follows:[75]

> A cartel provision is a provision, contained in a contract, arrangement, or understanding, that has the purpose, effect, or likely effect of 1 or more of the following in relation to the supply or acquisition of goods or services in New Zealand:
>
> (a) price fixing:
> (b) restricting output:
> (c) market allocating.

The section then defines each of the terms 'price fixing', 'restricting output' and 'market allocating'.[76]

49. There are exceptions to the cartel prohibition. Where a cartel provision in an agreement is covered by one of these exceptions, the effect is that the cartel prohibitions do not apply, but it is still possible for the agreement to be covered by other provisions, particularly the broad prohibition on anti-competitive agreements in section 27.

50. Section 31 provides an exception for 'collaborative activity' if, at the time the agreement was entered into or arrived at, or at the time of giving effect to the cartel provision, the parties were involved in a collaborative activity and the cartel provision was reasonably necessary for the purpose of the collaborative activity.[77] The term 'collaborative activity' is defined as follows:[78]

---

72. *Ibid.*, s. 7 repealed the former ss 30–34 and replaced with new ss 30–33 under the heading 'Cartel provisions'.
73. Commerce Act 1986 s. 30.
74. *Ibid.*, s. 30C(1).
75. *Ibid.*, s. 30A(1).
76. *Ibid.*, s. 30A(2)–30A(4).
77. *Ibid.*, s. 31.
78. Commerce Act 1986 s. 31(4).

In this Act, collaborative activity means an enterprise, venture, or other activity, in trade, that –

(a) is carried on in co-operation by 2 or more persons; and
(b) is not carried on for the dominant purpose of lessening competition between any 2 or more of the parties.

51. There are additional exceptions for vertical supply contracts and for joint buying and promotion agreements. The exception for vertical supply contracts applies to cartel provisions in contracts between supplier and customer that do not have the dominant purpose of lessening competition between any two or more of the parties.[79] The exception for joint buying and promotion agreements applies to provisions relating to price for collectively acquired goods, to joint advertising of price for resupply, to collective negotiation of price followed by individual purchasing or to an agreement that an intermediary take title and resell or resupply to a party to the agreement.[80]

52. The cartel provisions in the Commerce Act 1986 were originally designed as part of a larger reform that would have criminalised cartel conduct.[81] The cartel bill as initially introduced included criminal sanctions for cartel conduct. Then on 8 December 2015 the Minister of Commerce and Consumer Affairs announced that criminalisation of cartel conduct would not proceed and criminal sanctions for cartel behaviour would be removed from the bill.[82] The bill was finally passed in August 2017 without the criminal provisions, and New Zealand does not therefore have law imposing criminal sanctions on cartel conduct. However, the New Zealand Parliament has recently passed legislation that introduces criminal sanctions for cartel conduct. The Commerce (Criminalisation of Cartels) Amendment Act was passed in 2019, introducing criminal sanctions to come into force two years from date of assent, on 8 April 2021.[83]

---

79. Commerce Act 1986 s. 32.
80. *Ibid.*, s. 33.
81. *See* Ministry of Economic Development *Cartel Criminalisation: Discussion Document* (January 2010) https://www.mbie.govt.nz/business-and-employment/business/competition-regulation-and-policy/reviews-of-the-commerce-act-1986/cartels-and-collaborative-activities-2017/submissions-on-the-cartel-criminalisation-discussion-document-2010/ (accessed 9 May 2019) *See also* David King, *Criminalisation of Cartel Behaviour*, (Ministry of Economic Development Occasional Paper 10/01) (January 2010).
82. Paul Goldsmith, *Amendments to Cartels Bill*, (press release) (8 Dec. 2015). *See also* Paul Goldsmith, Minister of Commerce and Consumer Affairs, *Removal of the Criminal Offence for Cartels from the Commerce (Cartels and Other Matters) Amendment Bill* (Cabinet Committee Paper) Available from www.mbie.govt.nz/business-and-employment/business/competition-regulation-and-policy/reviews-of-the-commerce-act-1986/cartels-and-collaborative-activities-2017/how-the-cartel-reform-came-to-be/ (accessed 9 May 2019), and Cabinet Economic Growth and Infrastructure Committee, *Minute of Decision*, *www.mbie.govt.nz/business-and-employment/business/competition-regulation-and-policy/reviews-of-the-commerce-act-1986/cartels-and-collaborative-activities-2017/how-the-cartel-reform-came-to-be/* (accessed 9 Apr. 2019).
83. Commerce (Criminalisation of Cartels) Amendment Act 2019.

53. Resale price maintenance is also prohibited in the Commerce Act, and is per se unlawful, meaning that it is prohibited without a need to establish a purpose, effect or likely effect of substantially lessening competition in a market.[84]

54. Authorisation is available for some restrictive trade practices, and is granted on application by the Commerce Commission.[85] It is not available for cartel provisions. The test for authorisation of restrictive trade practices is a public benefit test. The Commission will grant an authorisation if the practice 'will in all the circumstances result, or be likely to result, in a benefit to the public which would outweigh the lessening in competition that would result, or would be likely to result'.[86]

55. The 2017 amendments added a new regime of clearances relating to cartel provisions.[87] Under this new regime, the Commerce Commission is required to give a clearance for a proposed contract, arrangement or understanding if the parties are involved in a collaborative activity; the cartel provision is reasonably necessary for the purpose of the collaborative activity, and it will not have the effect or likely effect of substantially lessening competition in a market.[88] The effect of a clearance is that the parties do not contravene section 27 or section 30 and the provision may be enforced.[89]

§2. Dominant Undertakings

56. The New Zealand Commerce Act in its current form does not use the terminology of 'dominance' or of 'undertaking'. The equivalent restrictive trade practices concept applying to single firm conduct is 'taking advantage of market power'. This is the New Zealand monopolisation law. The Commerce Act provision, and the merger provision, both formerly used the term 'dominant' but now operates a 'substantially lessening competition' test.[90] The New Zealand provisions are currently under review and likely to be amended.[91]57 Section 36 of the Commerce Act 1986 prohibits the taking advantage of market power. Section 36 sets out three requirements that must be satisfied for a firm to have contravened. Section 36(2) provides that:[92]

> A person that has a substantial degree of power in a market must not take advantage of that power for the purpose of–

84. Commerce Act 1986 ss 37–42.
85. *Ibid.*, s. 58.
86. *Ibid.*, s. 61(6).
87. *Ibid.*, ss 65A–65D.
88. *Ibid.*, s. 65A(2).
89. *Ibid.*, s. 65B.
90. The Commerce Amendment Act 2001 s. 9(1) amended s. 36, and s. 11 amended the merger threshold in s. 47.
91. Ministry of Business, Innovation and Employment, *Review of Section 36 the Commerce Act 1986 and Other Matters*, https://www.mbie.govt.nz/have-your-say/review-of-section-36-of-the-commerce-act-and-other-matters/ (accessed 9 May 2019).
92. Commerce Act 1986 s. 36(2).

(a) restricting the entry of a person into that or any other market; or
(b) preventing or deterring a person from engaging in competitive conduct in that or any other market; or
(c) eliminating a person from that or any other market.

58. A reference to a person includes an interconnected body corporate.[93] Mere enforcement of a statutory intellectual property right does not constitute taking advantage of market power.[94] Section 36A is a similar provision to section 36; it prohibits taking advantage of market power in trans-Tasman (New Zealand and Australia) markets.[95]

59. New Zealand courts have emphasised that it is not unlawful simply to have market power; monopolies are not unlawful in themselves. It is also not unlawful to have an anti-competitive purpose. Firms with market power have a right to compete vigorously. It is only unlawful if a firm with substantial market power takes advantage of its substantial market power for a proscribed purpose.[96]

Authorisation is available for most restrictive trade practices, but is not available for conduct constituting taking advantage of market power under sections 36 and 36A. This conduct is not authorisable.[97]

§3. Business Acquisitions (Concentrations)

60. Part 3 of the Commerce Act 1986 deals with business acquisitions. Section 47(1) of the Act provides that a person must not acquire assets of a business or shares if the acquisition would have, or would be likely to have, the effect of substantially lessening competition in a market.[98] 'Person' includes interconnected or associated persons, including bodies corporate.[99] A person is 'associated if 'that person is able, whether directly or indirectly, to exert a substantial degree of influence over the activities of the other'.[100] A 'substantial degree of influence' in this context is not satisfied by reason only of the fact that they are in the same market or one supplies to the other.[101]

---

93. *Ibid.*, s. 36(5).
94. *Ibid.*, s. 36(3).
95. *Ibid.*, s. 36A.
96. *See* for example *Telecom Corporation of New Zealand Ltd v. Clear Communications Ltd* [1995] 1 NZLR 385 (PC), *Carter Holt Harvey Building Products Ltd v Commerce Commission* [2006] 1 NZLR 145 (PC), *Commerce Commission v. Telecom Corporation of New Zealand* [2010] NZSC 111, [2011] 1 NZLR 577.
97. Commerce Act 1986 ss 36–36A and s. 58.
98. *Ibid.*, s. 47(1).
99. *Ibid.*, s. 47(2).
100. *Ibid.*, s. 47(3).
101. *Ibid.*, s. 47(4).

61. Parties to a proposed merger or acquisition may apply to the Commerce Commission for a clearance or authorisation.[102] Clearances are available for business acquisitions that will not, or would not be likely to have, the effect of substantially lessening competition in a market.[103] Authorisations are available for business acquisitions that will result, or will be likely to result, in such a benefit to the public that they should be permitted.[104] The effect of a clearance or authorisation is that the prohibition in section 47 or section 47A will not apply.[105] Decisions of the Commission on clearances and authorisations may be appealed to the High Court and potentially upward to the Court of Appeal and Supreme Court.

62. The Commerce Commission has issued *Mergers and Acquisitions Guidelines* to explain how it assesses whether a merger or acquisition would be likely to substantially lessen competition in a market and the process for considering clearance applications.[106] The *Guidelines* set out the counterfactual test for substantially lessening competition. The test is a comparison of the likely state of competition if the merger proceeds with the likely state of competition or if the merger does not proceed. Both scenarios are forward-looking.[107]

63. In 2017 new sections 47A–47D were inserted into the Act.[108] These sections provide for the High Court to make a declaration if an overseas person acquires directly or indirectly a controlling interest in a New Zealand body corporate through acquiring assets or shares outside New Zealand, and the acquisition of the controlling interest has the effect or likely effect of substantially lessening competition in a market in New Zealand.[109] 'Controlling interest' in this context is defined as the overseas person:[110]

(a) controls the composition of the board of the body corporate; or
(b) is in a position to exercise, or control the exercise of, more than 20% of the maximum number of votes that can be exercised at a meeting of the body corporate; or
(c) holds more than 20% of the issued shares of the body corporate, other than shares that carry no right to participate beyond an entitlement to a specified amount in a distribution of either profits or capital; or

102. *Ibid.*, Part 5.
103. *Ibid.*, ss 66 and 67(3).
104. *Ibid.*, s. 67(3).
105. *Ibid.*, s. 69.
106. *See* Commerce Commission New Zealand, *Mergers and Acquisitions Guidelines* (2013) http://www.comcom.govt.nz/business-competition/guidelines-2/mergers-and-acquisitions-guidelines/ (accessed 9 May 2019).
107. *Ibid.*, 16–20.
108. Commerce (Cartels and other Matters) Amendment Act 2017 s. 11.
109. Commerce Act 1986 s. 47A(1)–(2).
110. *Ibid.*, s. 47A(5).

(d) is entitled to receive more than 20% of every dividend paid on shares issued by the body corporate, other than shares that carry no right to participate beyond an entitlement to a specified amount in a distribution of either profits or capital; or
(e) is the holding company … of the body corporate; or
(f) holds assets in circumstances where the holding of those assets results in the overseas person having effective control of the body corporate.

64. 'Overseas person' is defined as neither resident nor carrying on business in New Zealand.[111] The High Court may make orders including the requiring of disposal of shares or assets or that a New Zealand body corporate cease carrying on business in New Zealand.[112]

§4. Other Prohibitions

65. As previously noted, the New Zealand Commerce Act 1986 also contains a regime prohibiting resale price maintenance. Resale price maintenance is per se unlawful, meaning that it is prohibited without a need to establish a purpose, effect or likely effect of substantially lessening competition in a market.[113] The prohibition applies to resale price maintenance by suppliers[114] and resale price maintenance by others.[115] Recommended prices are permitted so long as they are not enforced.[116] Resale price maintenance may be authorised, authorisation is granted on application by the Commerce Commission.[117] The test for authorisation is a public benefit test. The Commission will grant an authorisation if the practice 'will in all the circumstances result, or be likely to result, in a benefit to the public which would outweigh the lessening in competition that would result, or would be likely to result'.[118]

§5. Tests of Illegality

I. Per Se Prohibitions and Naked Restraints

66. The Commerce Act 1986 provides that some conduct is per se unlawful and not subject to a rule of reason-style analysis.

67. Horizontal price-fixing has been prohibited per se since the Commerce Act was passed in 1986.

111. *Ibid.*, s. 47A(5).
112. *Ibid.*, s. 47B.
113. *Ibid.*, ss 37–42.
114. *Ibid.*, s. 37.
115. *Ibid.*, s. 38.
116. *Ibid.*, s. 39.
117. *Ibid.*, s. 58.
118. *Ibid.*, s. 61(6).

68. In 2017 the horizontal price-fixing regime was replaced with the new cartel provisions.[119] Section 30 now prohibits entering into a contract or arrangement, or arriving at an understanding, that contains a cartel provision. It also prohibits giving effect to a cartel provision.[120] A cartel provision is a provision that has the purpose, effect, or likely effect of one or more of price fixing, restricting output or market allocating.[121] Cartel provisions are prohibited without regard to purpose, effect, or likely effect of substantially lessening competition in a market. However, there are exceptions for collaborative activity as defined,[122] vertical supply contracts[123] and joint buying and promotion agreements.[124]

69. Resale price maintenance is also prohibited per se. It is prohibited irrespective of whether it has the purpose, effect or likely effect of substantially lessening competition in a market.[125] However, resale price maintenance is subject to authorisation, which is granted on application by the Commerce Commission using a public benefit test.[126]

II. Balancing Tests

70. The balancing test, or rule of reason, is also present in analysis under the Commerce Act 1986. The Commerce Act uses a substantially lessening competition test in relation to restrictive agreements that are not covered by the per se provisions, and in merger analysis.

71. For restrictive agreements, the court is required to determine whether the agreement contains a provision that has the purpose, or has or is likely to have the effect, of substantially lessening competition in a market.[127] This analysis requires a market definition exercise and an assessment of the elements of purpose, likely effect and effect and of substantially lessening of competition. The substantial lessening of competition element is assessed using a counterfactual with and without test, which involves a comparison of the probable nature and extent of competition that would exist with and without the conduct.[128]

72. A more limited inquiry is involved for cartel provisions, which are agreements between parties in competition with each other, and are prohibited per se.[129]

---

119. *Ibid.*, ss 30–33.
120. *Ibid.*, s. 30.
121. *Ibid.*, s. 30A.
122. *Ibid.*, s. 31.
123. *Ibid.*, s. 32.
124. *Ibid.*, s. 33.
125. *Ibid.*, ss 37–42.
126. *Ibid.*, ss 58 and 61.
127. *Ibid.*, s. 27.
128. *See Auckland Regional Authority v. Mutual Rental Cars (Auckland Airport) Ltd* [1987] 2 NZLR 647, 674, referring to *Dandy Power Equipment Pty Ltd v. Mercury Marine Pty Ltd* (1982) 44 ALR 173, 191–192.
129. Commerce Act 1986 s. 30.

In such cases, market definition is only required in order to assess whether the parties are in competition. However, the collaborative activity exception to the cartel prohibition does require a limited market assessment as it requires a purpose of lessening competition. Section 31 provides an exception for 'collaborative activity' if at the time the agreement was entered into or arrived at, or at the time of giving effect to the cartel provision the parties were involved in a collaborative activity and the cartel provision was reasonably necessary for the purpose of the collaborative activity.[130] The definition of 'collaborative activity' provides that collaborative activity means an enterprise, venture or other activity, in trade, that is carried on in cooperation by two or more persons, and is not carried on for the dominant purpose of lessening competition between any two or more of the parties. [131]

73. There is a clearance provision for mergers and acquisitions, and this also involves a rule of reason-type substantially lessening of competition test. Clearances are available for business acquisitions that will not, or would not be likely to have, the effect of substantially lessening competition in a market.[132] There is also a new regime making provision for clearances for cartel provisions, and this regime also employs a substantially lessening competition test.[133] Under this new regime, the Commerce Commission is required to give a clearance for a proposed contract, arrangement or understanding if the parties are involved in a collaborative activity; the cartel provision is reasonably necessary for the purpose of the collaborative activity, and it will not have the effect or likely effect of substantially lessening competition in a market.[134]

74. Authorisation of both restrictive trade practices and business acquisitions also involves a balancing exercise. For authorisation, this requires an application of a public benefit test. Authorisation is available for some restrictive trade practices, and it is granted by the Commerce Commission.[135] It is not available for cartel provisions or for taking advantage of substantial market power under section 36. The test for authorisation of restrictive trade practices is a public benefit test. The Commission will grant an authorisation if the practice 'will in all the circumstances result, or be likely to result, in a benefit to the public which would outweigh the lessening in competition that would result, or would be likely to result'.[136] It therefore involves weighing the harm to competition against the resulting public benefit. A similar exercise is required for authorisation of business acquisitions. Authorisations are available for business acquisitions that will result, or will be likely to result, in such a benefit to the public that they should be permitted.[137]

---

130. *Ibid.*, s. 31.
131. *Ibid.*, s. 31(4).
132. *Ibid.*, ss 66 and 67(3).
133. *Ibid.*, ss 65A–65D. These provisions came into force on 15 August 2017.
134. *Ibid.*, s. 65A(2).
135. *Ibid.*, s. 58.
136. *Ibid.*, s. 61(6).
137. *Ibid.*, s. 67(3).

III. Merger Tests

75. Mergers and acquisitions are prohibited if they would have, or would be likely to have, the effect of substantially lessening competition in a market.[138] Parties to a proposed merger or acquisition may apply to the Commerce Commission for a clearance or authorisation.[139] Clearances are available for business acquisitions that will not have, or would not be likely to have, the effect of substantially lessening competition in a market.[140] Authorisations are available for business acquisitions that will result, or will be likely to result, in such a benefit to the public that they should be permitted.[141]

76. The Commerce Commission's *Mergers and Acquisitions Guidelines* are a guide to the approach of the Commission in assessing whether a merger or acquisition would be likely to substantially lessen competition in a market and the process for considering clearance applications. [142]

The *Guidelines* set out the counterfactual test for substantially lessening competition. The test is a comparison of the likely state of competition if the merger proceeds, with the likely state of competition if the merger does not proceed. Both scenarios are forward-looking.[143] If the competition would be substantially lessened with the merger when compared to any of the likely states of competition without the merger, then the merger will have the likely effect of substantially lessening competition.[144] The Commission makes a pragmatic and commercial assessment of what is likely to occur, taking account of factors such as market growth and technological changes.[145] The decision of the Commission may be appealed to the High Court and thence to the Court of Appeal and Supreme Court.[146]

---

138. *Ibid.*, s. 47(1).
139. *Ibid.*, Part 5.
140. *Ibid.*, ss 66 and 67(3).
141. *Ibid.*, s. 67(3).
142. *See* Commerce Commission New Zealand, *Mergers and Acquisitions Guidelines* (2013) http://www.comcom.govt.nz/business-competition/guidelines-2/mergers-and-acquisitions-guidelines/ (accessed 9 May 2019).
143. *Ibid.*, 16–20.
144. *Ibid.*, 18.
145. *Ibid.*, 19.
146. Commerce Act 1986 s. 75.

Chapter 4. Overview of Main Notions

§1. Undertaking

77. The term 'undertaking' is not used in New Zealand competition law in the sense that it is used in European law.[147] The restrictive trade practices provisions of the Commerce Act 1986 generally prohibit a 'person' from engaging in prohibited conduct. The definition of 'person' provides that the term 'includes a local authority, and any association of persons whether incorporated or not'.[148] The definition therefore covers both individuals and body corporates, and more broadly any association of persons. In some circumstances interconnected bodies corporates are also caught by restrictive trade practices provisions.[149]

78. The merger provisions also refer to a 'person'. Section 47(1) provides that:[150]

> A person must not acquire assets of a business or shares if the acquisition would have, or would be likely to have, the effect of substantially lessening competition in a market.

79. Additional provisions in section 47 define 'person' in this context. They provide:[151]

> (2) For the purposes of this section, a reference to a person includes 2 or more persons that are interconnected or associated.
> (3) For the purposes of this section, a person is associated with another person if that person is able, whether directly or indirectly, to exert a substantial degree of influence over the activities of the other.
> (4) A person is not able to exert a substantial degree of influence over the activities of another person for the purposes of subsection (3) by reason only of the fact that –
> (a) those persons are in competition in the same market; or
> (b) one of them supplies goods or services to the other.

80. In the merger context, 'person' therefore has an extended meaning including not only individuals and associations in various forms, but also interconnected and associated individuals, associations and body corporates.

---

147. Note however that the term 'undertaking' is used in a different sense in the enforcement context. *See* Commerce Act 1986 ss 74AA-74C.
148. *Ibid.*, s. 2(1). *See also* s. 2(7).
149. *See* for example Commerce Act 1986 s. 30B, s. 36(4).
150. Commerce Act 1986 s. 47(1).
151. *Ibid.*, s. 47(2)–(4).

§2. RELEVANT MARKET

81. The concept of a 'market' is central to many of the provisions of the Commerce Act 1986. A market definition exercise is required for all of the restrictive trade practices prohibitions on conduct that has the purpose, effect or likely effect of substantially lessening competition in a market.[152] Market definition is also required in the monopolisation provision, in which the first element involves substantial power in a market and the third element refers to anti-competitive purpose in that or any other market.[153]A more limited market definition is required where provisions apply to parties in competition with each other.[154] Market definition is also important in merger analysis. Mergers are prohibited if they have the effect or likely effect of substantially lessening competition in a market.[155]

82. 'Market' is defined in section 3(1A) of the Commerce Act, which provides that:

> Every reference in this Act … to the term market is a reference to a market in New Zealand for goods or services as well as other goods or services that, as a matter of fact and commercial common sense, are substitutable for them.

83. The definition therefore gives weight to both commercial common sense and to substitutability. New Zealand court have drawn heavily on Australian case law on market, particularly the decision of the Trade Practices Tribunal in the *QCMA* case.[156] In *QCMA* the Tribunal said that 'the identification of markets must be the essential first step in assessment of present competition and likely competitive effects'.[157] It referred to 'the identification of rivalrous relationship between sellers', and said that the concept of a market was basically a very simple idea.[158] The Tribunal said that 'a market is the field of actual and potential transactions between buyers and sellers amongst whom there can be strong substitution, at least in the long run, if given a sufficient price incentive'.[159] The Tribunal then set out its approach to defining a market:

> [I]n determining the outer boundaries of the market we ask a quite simple but fundamental question: if the firm were to 'give less and charge more' would there be, to put the matter colloquially, much of a reaction? And if so, from

152. *Ibid.*, ss 27 and 28.
153. *Ibid.*, ss 36 and 36A.
154. *Ibid.*, ss 30 and 30A.
155. *Ibid.*, s. 47(1).
156. *Re Queensland & Co-Operative Milling Associates Ltd* – Proposed Merger; *Re Defiance* – Proposed Mergers 1 and 2 (1976) 8 ALR 481, 516–518.
157. *Ibid.*, 516.
158. *Ibid.*, 516–517.
159. *Ibid.*, 517.

whom? In the language of economics the question is this: From which products and which activities could we expect a relatively high demand or supply response to price change, ie a relatively high cross-elasticity of demand or cross-elasticity of supply?

The Tribunal's approach to markets and competition was routinely followed by New Zealand courts in the early days of the Commerce Act,[160] is a continuing influence on case law,[161] and has influenced the Commerce Commission in its *Mergers and Acquisitions Guidelines*.[162] The New Zealand Court of Appeal has said that market is 'ordinarily regarded as a multi-dimensional concept with dimensions of product, functional level, space and time'.[163] In its *Mergers and Acquisitions Guidelines,* the Commerce Commission refers to five dimensions, product, geographic, supply chain level, customer and time.[164] In defining the dimensions of a market, the Commerce Commission uses the hypothetical monopolist test as a tool, asking whether a hypothetical sole supplier would profitably increase prices by at least a small but significant amount, a small but significant non-transitory increase in prices (or SSNIP). The smallest set of products or locations for which the SSNIP can be profitably sustained is the relevant product or geographic market. [165] The Commission sets out its approach to each dimension in the *Mergers and Acquisitions Guidelines*,[166] which reflect the statutory definition and the approach of case law.

§3. Market Power/Dominant Position

84. Market power is the power to raise price and exclude entry, and is the antithesis of competition.[167] Market power is a central concept in the monopolisation provisions. The New Zealand Commerce Act used a dominance standard for both monopolisation and mergers until 2001, but the current provisions do not use the term 'dominant position'.

85. Section 36(2) provides that:[168]

160. *See* for example *Auckland Regional Authority v. Mutual Rental Cars (Auckland Airport) Ltd* [1987] 2 NZLR 647, 670, *Telecom v. Commerce Commission* (1991) 4 TCLR 473, 497–500.
161. *See* for example *Brambles NZ Ltd v. Commerce Commission* (2003) 10 TCLR 868, 892.
162. Commerce Commission New Zealand, *Mergers and Acquisitions Guidelines* (2013) http://www.comcom.govt.nz/business-competition/guidelines-2/mergers-and-acquisitions-guidelines/ 23–29 (accessed 9 May 2019).
163. *Tru Tone Ltd v. Festival Records Marketing Ltd* [1988] 2 NZLR 352, 359.
164. Commerce Commission New Zealand, *Mergers and Acquisitions Guidelines* (2013) http://www.comcom.govt.nz/business-competition/guidelines-2/mergers-and-acquisitions-guidelines/ 23 (accessed 9 May 2019).
165. *Ibid.*, 24.
166. *Ibid.*, 23–29.
167. *Re Queensland & Co-Operative Milling Associates Ltd* – Proposed Merger; *Re Defiance* – Proposed Mergers 1 and 2 (1976) 8 ALR 481, 515.
168. Commerce Act 1986 s. 36(2).

> A person that has a substantial degree of power in a market must not take advantage of that power for the purpose of–
>
> (a) restricting the entry of a person into that or any other market; or
> (b) preventing or deterring a person from engaging in competitive conduct in that or any other market; or
> (c) eliminating a person from that or any other market.

86. Section 36A is a similar provision to section 36, it prohibits the taking advantage of market power in trans-Tasman (New Zealand and Australia) markets.[169]

87. The first element of section 36 analysis is substantial degree of market power. This requires market definition, and an assessment of market power. The assessment of market power involves an assessment of the extent to which the firm faces competitive constraints, and a firm is regarded as having substantial market power if it can profitably raise its prices above competitive levels for a sustained period.[170] A large market share may be evidence of market power, as may vertical integration, but assessment of constraints is the focus. Barriers to entry are an essential element as the threat of new entry is a powerful constraint.[171] Constraints may be from existing or potential competitors, and any countervailing power, for example from buyers or sellers, is relevant. The New Zealand courts' approach to market power can be seen in the words of the New Zealand Supreme Court, which has said that:[172]

> A firm has market power when it is not constrained in the way in which it would be constrained in a competitive market. Any firm that is substantially unconstrained by competitive pressure has substantial market power. Market power gives some advantage if it makes it easier – that is, materially facilitates – the conduct in issue. The question whether dominance or substantial market power exists implies a comparison between the position of the firm in the actual market and a firm in the same general circumstances but otherwise in a workably competitive market. The contrast inherent in the concepts of dominance or substantial degree of market power is the contrast between the actual market and a hypothetically competitive market.

Market power as the antithesis of competition is also relevant to the assessment of competition, which arises in provisions employing a substantial lessening of competition test, particularly section 27 and the merger provision in section 47.

---

169. *Ibid.*, s. 36A.
170. This is similar to the approach taken in *Queensland Wire Industries Pty Ltd v. The Broken Hill Proprietary Co. Ltd* (1989) 83 ALR 577, 583.
171. *Queensland Wire Industries Pty Ltd v. The Broken Hill Proprietary Co. Ltd* (1989) 83 ALR 577, 583.
172. *Commerce Commission v. Telecom Corporation of New Zealand Ltd* [2011] 1 NZLR 577, 601.

§4. Agreements and Concerted Practices

88. The New Zealand competition law provisions applying to agreements are based on the concept encompassed by the phrase 'contract, arrangement or understanding'. Section 27 is the broadest provision, and it prohibits entering into a contract or arrangement, or arriving at an understanding, containing a provision that has the purpose, or has or is likely to have the effect, of substantially lessening competition in a market.[173] The new cartel provisions also refer to 'contract, arrangement or understanding'. Entering into or giving effect to a cartel provision is prohibited, subject to defences.[174] A cartel provision is defined as a provision, contained in a contract, arrangement or understanding, that has the purpose, effect or likely effect of one or more of price fixing, restricting output or market allocating.[175] The concepts 'contract', 'arrangement' and 'understanding' are therefore fundamental to this part of New Zealand competition law.

I. Contracts

89. The term 'contract' has not created difficulty in the courts; it is understood to have the same meaning as in the law of contract. The meaning of 'contract' in the Commerce Act is somewhat extended by section 2(6)(a), which provides that it includes a reference to 'a lease of, or a licence in respect of, any land or building or part of a building'.[176]

II. Arrangements and Understandings

90. The Act refers to arrangements and understandings. Generally understandings may be less formal than arrangements, and arrangements may arise from negotiations while understandings may arise from observed conduct. However, courts do not generally make clear distinctions between the two concepts.[177] Section 27 refers to entering into an arrangement and arriving at an understanding.[178] Section 2(1) provides that 'arrive at' in relation to an understanding, includes reach, and enter into.[179]

91. An arrangement or understanding is something less than a contract. The term is not defined in the Commerce Act. New Zealand courts initially referred to the *Re*

173. Commerce Act 1986 s. 27.
174. *Ibid.*, s. 30.
175. *Ibid.*, s. 30A.
176. *Ibid.*, s. 2(6)(a).
177. *Auckland Regional Authority v. Mutual Rental Cars (Auckland Airport) Ltd* [1987] 2 NZLR 647, 661–622.
178. Commerce Act 1986 s. 27.
179. *Ibid.*, s. 2(1).

British Basic Slag case[180], and focused on the concepts of mutual communication and obligation.[181] Then, in 2003, the Court of Appeal considered the meaning of 'arrangement', and said that:[182]

> We do not consider it appropriate to be tied in any determinative way to the concepts of mutuality, obligation and duty. While the concept of moral obligation is helpful in that it will often reflect the effect of an arrangement or understanding under section 27, the flexible purpose of the section is such that it is best to focus the ultimate inquiry on the concepts of consensus and expectation. A finding that there was a consensus giving rise to an expectation that the parties would act in a certain way necessarily involves communication among the parties of the assumption of a moral obligation.

92. The Court of Appeal therefore preferred to focus on consensus and expectation. The Court said that parties' minds must have met and they must have agreed upon the subject matter. The consensus must also engender an expectation that at least one person will act or refrain from acting in the manner the consensus envisages.[183] The Court went on to state a test saying that the question whether there was an arrangement or understanding was:[184]

> whether that person was part of a consensus giving rise to an expectation that some proscribed action or inaction take place. If they were, they will have entered into an arrangement. If they were not, they will not have entered into any arrangement …

93. The courts have also considered the question of proof of the existence of an arrangement or understanding. The High Court has referred to the test in *R v. Associated Northern Collieries,*[185] which referred to 'such a concurrence of time, character, direction and result as naturally to lead to the inference that these separate acts were the outcome of pre-concert … '

94. The Court of Appeal also considered proof in the *Giltrap City* case,[186] and said that it was appropriate to take the same approach to proof of arrangements and understandings as that taken with contracts. The Court said that:[187]

---

180. *Re British Basic Slag Ltd's Agreements* [1963] 2 All ER 807, 819, referred to in *Auckland Regional Authority v. Mutual Rental Cars (Auckland Airport) Ltd* [1987] 2 NZLR 647, 662.
181. *See Commerce Commission v. Caltex New Zealand Ltd* (1999) 9 TCLR 305, 314–5.
182. *Giltrap City Ltd v. Commerce Commission* [2004] 1 NZLR 608, 613 (CA).
183. *Ibid.*
184. *Giltrap City Ltd v. Commerce Commission* [2004] 1 NZLR 608, 614 (CA).
185. *R v. Associated Northern Collieries* (1911) 14 CLR 387, 400 (HCA), referred to in *Commerce Commission v. Caltex New Zealand Ltd* (1999) 9 TCLR 305, 314.
186. *Giltrap City Ltd v. Commerce Commission* [2004] 1 NZLR 608 (CA).
187. *Giltrap City Ltd v. Commerce Commission* [2004] 1 NZLR 608, 615 (CA).

> The existence of the necessary consensus is therefore to be judged by reference to what reasonable people would infer from the conduct of the person whose participation in the consensus is in issue. [T]he consensus must of course be such that it engenders an expectation in the minds of the participants that at least one person will act in a proscribed manner.

§5. Restriction of Competition

95. There are provisions in the Commerce Act where rule of reason-type analysis is required, and the Commerce Commission or the courts are required to assess the impact of particular conduct on completion. The Commerce Act language establishes a test of substantially lessening of competition.

I. Purpose and Likely Effect

96. Under section 27, the requirement is to establish that a provision has the purpose, effect or likely effect of substantially lessening competition. The substantial lessening of competition purpose may be one of a number of purposes so long as it is a substantial purpose.[188] The purpose may be unilateral, that is, it may be the purpose of only one of the parties to the agreement.[189] The test for purpose is generally objective, but there is scope for subjective evidence.[190] The courts have also considered the meaning of 'likely effect', which has been described as 'a real and substantial risk that the stated consequence will happen',[191] and a 'real chance'.[192] The courts have also considered whether a provision may have the purpose of substantially lessening of competition in the absence of effect or likely effect, with some differences of opinion.[193]

II. Substantial Lessening of Competition

97. The final element in section 27 is 'substantial lessening of competition'. Section 2(1A) provides that 'substantial' means 'real or of substance'.[194] 'Lessening of competition' includes 'hindering or preventing of competition'.[195] The substantial

---

188. Commerce Act 1986 s. 2(5).
189. *Port Nelson Ltd v. Commerce Commission* (1996) 5 NZBLC 104,142 (CA), 104,151.
190. *Commerce Commission v. Port Nelson Ltd* (1995) 5 NZBLC 103,764, pp 103, 777. *See also ANZCO Foods Waitara Ltd v. AFFCO NZ Ltd* [2006] 3 NZLR 351.
191. *Port Nelson Ltd v. Commerce Commission* (1996) 5 NZBLC 104,142 (CA), 104,150.
192. *Commerce Commission v. Woolworths Ltd* (2008) 12 TCLR 194, 209 (CA).
193. *See ANZCO Foods Waitara Ltd v. AFFCO NZ Ltd* [2006] 3 NZLR 351.
194. Commerce Act 1986 s. 2(1A).
195. *Ibid.*, s. 3(2).

lessening of competition element is assessed using a counterfactual with and without test, which involves a comparison of the probable nature and extent of competition that would exist with and without the conduct.[196] The focus is on future competition in the market with and without the conduct, and courts consider the net effect on competition.[197] The issue is the effect on competition, not on individual competitors.[198] Competition in the Commerce Act means 'workable or effective competition'.[199] The substantial lessening of competition assessment also requires a market definition exercise.

98. Cartel provisions also prohibit conduct that restricts competition. The new cartel provisions prohibit cartel agreements without a substantially lessening of competition test.[200] These are subject to specific exceptions.[201]

99. Merger law also has a requirement for a rule of reason style analysis of the impact on competition. Mergers and acquisitions are prohibited if they would have, or would be likely to have, the effect of substantially lessening competition in a market.[202]

§6. Monopolisation and Abuse of Dominance

100. Section 36 of the Commerce Act 1986 prohibits the taking advantage of market power. Section 36 sets out three requirements that must be satisfied for a firm to have contravened. Section 36(2) provides that:[203]

> A person that has a substantial degree of power in a market must not take advantage of that power for the purpose of–
>
> (a) restricting the entry of a person into that or any other market; or
> (b) preventing or deterring a person from engaging in competitive conduct in that or any other market; or
> (c) eliminating a person from that or any other market.

101. A reference to a person includes an interconnected body corporate.[204] Mere enforcement of a statutory intellectual property right does not constitute taking

196. *See Auckland Regional Authority v. Mutual Rental Cars (Auckland Airport) Ltd* [1987] 2 NZLR 647, 674, referring to *Dandy Power Equipment Pty Ltd v. Mercury Marine Pty Ltd* (1982) 44 ALR 173, 191–192.
197. *ANZCO Foods Waitara Ltd v. AFFCO NZ Ltd* [2006] 3 NZLR 351, 404–405.
198. *ANZCO Foods Waitara Ltd v. AFFCO NZ Ltd* [2006] 3 NZLR 351, 405.
199. Commerce Act 1986 s. 3(1).
200. *Ibid.*, s. 30.
201. *Ibid.*, ss 31–33.
202. *Ibid.*, s. 47(1).
203. *Ibid.*, s. 36(2).
204. *Ibid.*, s. 36(4).

advantage of market power.[205] Section 36A is a similar provision to section 36, but its focus is on prohibiting taking advantage of market power in trans-Tasman (New Zealand and Australia) markets.[206]

102. Section 36 has proved to be a controversial provision. The courts have interpreted it in a manner that has made it extremely difficult to bring a successful action for contravention of the section. Similar issues have arisen in Australia. Both countries are reviewing their statutory provisions and considering possible reform. In New Zealand, the Ministry of Business, Innovation and Employment is undertaking a review of section 36, among other issues.[207]

103. The three elements for an action under section 36 are:

(1) a substantial degree of market power;
(2) taking advantage of that power; and
(3) anti-competitive purpose.

I. Market Power

104. The first element, substantial degree of market power, requires market definition, and an assessment of market power. The assessment of market power involves an assessment of the extent to which the firm faces competitive constraints, and a firm is regarded as having substantial market power if it can profitably raise its prices above competitive levels for a sustained period.[208] A large market share may be evidence of market power, as may vertical integration, but assessment of constraints is the focus. Barriers to entry are an essential element.[209] Constraints may be from existing or potential competitors, and any countervailing power, for example from buyers or sellers, is relevant. The New Zealand courts' approach to market power can be seen in the words of the New Zealand Supreme Court, which has said that:[210]

> A firm has market power when it is not constrained in the way in which it would be constrained in a competitive market. Any firm that is substantially unconstrained by competitive pressure has substantial market power. Market power gives some advantage if it makes it easier – that is, materially facilitates – the conduct in issue. The question whether dominance or substantial market

205. *Ibid.*, s. 36(3).
206. *Ibid.*, s. 36A.
207. Ministry of Business, Innovation and Employment, *Review of Section 36 the Commerce Act 1986 and Other Matters*, https://www.mbie.govt.nz/have-your-say/review-of-section-36-of-the-commerce-act-and-other-matters/ (accessed 9 May 2019).
208. This is similar to the approach taken in *Queensland Wire Industries Pty Ltd v. The Broken Hill Proprietary Co. Ltd* (1989) 83 ALR 577, 583.
209. *Queensland Wire Industries Pty Ltd v. The Broken Hill Proprietary Co. Ltd* (1989) 83 ALR 577, 583.
210. *Commerce Commission v. Telecom Corporation of New Zealand Ltd* [2011] 1 NZLR 577, 601.

power exists implies a comparison between the position of the firm in the actual market and a firm in the same general circumstances but otherwise in a workably competitive market. The contrast inherent in the concepts of dominance or substantial degree of market power is the contrast between the actual market and a hypothetically competitive market. That same contrast is inherent in the inquiry into whether market power has been 'used' within the meaning of s 36.

II. Taking Advantage

105. The second element, taking advantage of that market power, has proved the most controversial. It is not unlawful simply to have market power, monopolies are not unlawful in themselves. It is also not unlawful to have an anti-competitive purpose. Firms with market power have a right to compete vigorously. It is only unlawful if a firm with substantial market power takes advantage of its substantial market power for a proscribed purpose. The 'take advantage' element constitutes a bridge between the market power and the purpose. This element has proved the most difficult element in section 36.

106. As originally enacted, the section referred to 'use' of a dominant position, and an amendment in 2001 changed this to taking advantage of market power. The courts have taken a restrictive approach to the test for take advantage, requiring a counterfactual test which compares the conduct of the firm with market power with the conduct of a firm in a hypothetical competitive market.[211] The shift from 'use' to 'take advantage' was intended to mean that New Zealand courts would adopt a more flexible approach to the test, as in Australia.[212] However the New Zealand judicial approach has remained largely unchanged, and the New Zealand Supreme Court has emphasised the need for predictability, which would not be assisted by having a range of possible tests.[213] The Supreme Court has said that:[214]

> The essential point is that if the dominant firm would, as a matter of commercial judgment, have acted in the same way in a hypothetically competitive market, it cannot logically be said that its dominance has given it the advantage that is implied in the concepts of using or taking advantage of dominance or a substantial degree of market power. Conversely, if the dominant firm would not have acted in the same way in a hypothetically competitive market, it can logically be said that its dominance did give it the necessary advantage. This is

211. This was the approach taken in *Telecom Corporation of New Zealand Ltd v. Clear Communications Ltd* [1995] 1 NZLR 385 (PC); (1992) 5 TCLR 166 (HC); (1993) 5 TCLR 413 (CA).
212. *Report of the Commerce Select Committee on the Commerce Amendment Bill* (2001) 13–14. The expressed intention was to adopt what was regarded as the more flexible approach in *Queensland Wire Industries Pty Ltd v. The Broken Hill Proprietary Co. Ltd* (1989) 83 ALR 577.
213. *Commerce Commission v. Telecom Corporation of New Zealand Ltd* [2011] 1 NZLR 577, 600.
214. *Ibid.*

because it can then be reasonably concluded that it was its dominance or substantial degree of market power that caused, enabled or facilitated its acting as it did in the actual market.

107. The Supreme Court has therefore firmly continued to require the application of the counterfactual test, with the result that it is rare to see successful actions under section 36. This is the background to the current review of the section, in which a number of options are under discussion, including removing the taking advantage element, and the use of an effect test of substantially lessening competition.[215]

III. Purpose

108. The third element of section 36 is the requirement of an anticompetitive purpose. The section requires that the defendant have a purpose of restricting the entry of a person into, preventing or deterring a person from engaging in competitive conduct in, or eliminating a person, from that or any other market. Section 36B provides that purpose may be inferred from conduct or from any other relevant circumstances. Purpose can be distinguished from intention. 'Purpose' implies object or aim.[216] The anti-competitive purpose can be one of a number of purposes so long as it is a substantial purpose.[217] The test for purpose is not clearly established, but the Court of Appeal has taken the view that purpose may be established or negatived using subjective or objective analysis.[218] It is, of course, not unlawful simply to have an anti-competitive purpose. The other elements of sections 36 are also required.

109. Each of the prohibited purposes listed in section 36 refer to 'that or any other market'. That is, the purposes of restricting entry, preventing or deterring the engaging in competitive conduct or eliminating a person may be in that or any other market. This means that the defendant may have market power in one market and the purpose of affecting competition in another market. There is also no requirement that the plaintiff be a person harmed by the conduct.

---

215. *See* Ministry of Business, Innovation and Employment, *Targeted Review of the Commerce Act 1986*, https://www.mbie.govt.nz/business-and-employment/business/competition-regulation-and-policy/reviews-of-the-commerce-act-1986/targeted-review-of-the-commerce-act-2015/ (accessed 9 May 2019), Ministry of Ministry of Business, Innovation and Employment, *Discussion Paper: Review of Section 36 of the Commerce Act and Other Matters* (January 2019) https://www.mbie.govt.nz/have-your-say/review-of-section-36-of-the-commerce-act-and-other-matters/ (accessed 9 May 2019).
216. *Union Shipping NZ Ltd v. Port Nelson Ltd* [1990] 2 NZLR 662, 707.
217. Commerce Act 1986 s. 2(5)(b).
218. *Port Nelson Ltd v. Commerce Commission* [1996] 3 NZLR 554, 564.

110. Authorisation is available for most restrictive trade practices, but is not available for conduct constituting taking advantage of market power under section 36 and section 36A. This conduct is not authorisable.[219]

§7. CONCENTRATIONS

111. The New Zealand Commerce Act 1986 does not refer expressly to the term 'concentrations'. Mergers are governed by the Commerce Act provisions relating to business acquisitions. Part 3 of the Commerce Act 1986 deals with business acquisitions. Section 47(1) of the Act provides that a person must not acquire assets of a business or shares if the acquisition would have, or would be likely to have, the effect of substantially lessening competition in a market.[220] 'Person' includes interconnected or associated persons, including bodies corporate.[221] A person is 'associated if 'that person is able, whether directly or indirectly, to exert a substantial degree of influence over the activities of the other'.[222] A 'substantial degree of influence' in this context is not satisfied by reason only of the fact that they are in the same market or one supplies to the other.[223]

112. Parties to a proposed merger or acquisition may apply to the Commerce Commission for a clearance or authorisation.[224] Clearances are available for business acquisitions that will not, or would not be likely to have, the effect of substantially lessening competition in a market.[225] Authorisations are available for business acquisitions that will result, or will be likely to result, in such a benefit to the public that they should be permitted.[226] The effect of a clearance or authorisation is that the prohibitions in section 47 or section 47A will not apply.[227] Decisions of the Commission on clearances and authorisations may be appealed to the High Court and potentially upward to the Court of Appeal and Supreme Court.

113. The Commerce Commission has issued *Mergers and Acquisitions Guidelines* to explain how it assesses whether a merger or acquisition would be likely to substantially lessen competition in a market and the process for considering clearance applications. [228] The *Guidelines* discuss market share and concentration measures.[229] The Commerce Commission uses market share and concentration indicators to identify mergers which are less likely to raise competition concerns.

219. Commerce Act 1986 ss 36–36A and s. 58.
220. *Ibid.*, s. 47(1).
221. *Ibid.*, s. 47(2).
222. *Ibid.*, s. 47(3).
223. *Ibid.*, s. 47(4).
224. *Ibid.*, Part 5.
225. *Ibid.*, ss 66 and 67(3).
226. *Ibid.*, s. 67(3).
227. *Ibid.*, s. 69.
228. *See* Commerce Commission New Zealand, *Mergers and Acquisitions Guidelines* (2013) http://www.comcom.govt.nz/business-competition/guidelines-2/mergers-and-acquisitions-guidelines/ (accessed 10 Aug. 2017).
229. *Ibid.*, 30–31.

The *Guidelines* are clear that this is to provide an initial guide, but is not a substitute for full competition analysis.[230] The Commission's stated view is that a merger is unlikely to require a clearance where, post-merger, the three largest firms in the market have a combined market share of less than 70%, and the merged firm's combined market share is less than 40%, and/or where the three largest firms in the market have a combined market share of 70% or more, and the merged firm's combined market share is less than 20%.[231] However these indicators are not conclusive and do not substitute for a full analysis.

§8. Joint Ventures

114. The term 'joint venture' no longer appears in the New Zealand Commerce Act. Section 31 of the Act previously provided a joint venture exception to price fixing. However from 15 August 2017 this was replaced with an exception to the cartel provisions for 'collaborative activity'. [232]

115. The new cartel provisions prohibit cartel agreements,[233] and provide that no cartel provision is enforceable.[234] Section 30 provides that:

> No person may –
>
> (a) enter into a contract or arrangement, or arrive at an understanding, that contains a cartel provision; or
> (b) give effect to a cartel provision.

116. Section 30A provides a definition of 'cartel provision' and related terms. It defines a cartel provision as follows:[235]

> A cartel provision is a provision, contained in a contract, arrangement, or understanding, that has the purpose, effect, or likely effect of 1 or more of the following in relation to the supply or acquisition of goods or services in New Zealand:
>
> (a) price fixing:
> (b) restricting output:
> (c) market allocating.

---

230. *Ibid.*, 30.
231. *Ibid.*
232. Commerce (Cartels and Other Matters) Amendment Act 2017 s. 7 repealed the former ss 30–34 and replaced with new ss 30–33 under the heading 'Cartel provisions'. Section 31 provides an exception for collaborative activity.
233. Commerce Act 1986 s. 30.
234. *Ibid.*, s. 30C(1).
235. *Ibid.*, s. 30A(1).

117. The section then defines each of the terms 'price fixing', 'restricting output' and 'market allocating'.[236]

118. There is an exception to the cartel prohibition for collaborative activity. Where the exception for collaborative activity applies, the effect is that the cartel prohibitions do not apply, but it is still possible for the agreement to be covered by other provisions, particularly the broad prohibition on anti-competitive agreements in section 27. Section 31 provides the exception for 'collaborative activity'. The exception applies if, at the time the agreement was entered into or arrived at, or at the time of giving effect to the cartel provision, the parties were involved in a collaborative activity and the cartel provision was reasonably necessary for the purpose of the collaborative activity.[237] The term 'collaborative activity' is defined:[238]

> In this Act, collaborative activity means an enterprise, venture, or other activity, in trade, that –
>
> (a) is carried on in co-operation by 2 or more persons; and
> (b) is not carried on for the dominant purpose of lessening competition between any 2 or more of the parties.

119. This definition of collaborative activity requires two main elements. The first is carrying on an enterprise, venture or other activity in trade, in cooperation. One commentator has suggested that this could apply to 'consortia, partnerships, strategic alliances, syndicated lending arrangements, lender work-out arrangements for insolvent borrowers, litigation settlement agreements, franchisors and franchisees under a franchise agreement and other kinds of collaborative activity between competitors'.[239] It has also been suggested that it would extend to such activities as 'arrangements for cost sharing and capacity allocation on shared infrastructure, joint buying (buyers clubs), research and development joint ventures, and committees for establishing technology standards'.[240]

120. The Commerce Commission has produced *Competitor Collaboration Guidelines* providing guidance on its approach to the new legislation.[241] The *Competitor Collaboration Guidelines* make clear that the collaborative activity exception is focused on the substance rather than the form of the parties' cooperation. The

236. *Ibid.*, s. 30A(2)–30A(4).
237. *Ibid.*, s. 31.
238. *Ibid.*, s. 31(4).
239. Caron Beaton-Wells 'The Harper Review: Qualified Hope for Australian Competition law' (2015) 48:4 *Australian Economic Review* 417, 424.
240. John Land and Aaron Schiff, 'Analysing Collaborative Activities' [2014] *New Zealand Law Journal* 230, 230, *See also* John Land, 'Joint Ventures and the Collaborative Activity Exemption' [2014] *New Zealand Law Journal* 190.
241. Commerce Commission New Zealand, *Competitor Collaboration Guidelines* (January 2018) http://www.comcom.govt.nz/business-competition/guidelines-2/competitor-collaboration-guidelines/ (accessed 1 Mar. 2018).

Commission's approach is to ask 'does this look like a cartel?', and this is the lens through which the Commission views the definition of collaborative activity.[242] The first part of the definition requires an enterprise, venture or other activity, in trade, that is carried on in cooperation by 2 or more persons. The Commission interpretation of this is that the parties must be 'combining their businesses, assets or operations in some way in a commercial activity, or otherwise operating a commercial activity jointly'.[243] By 'commercial activity' the Commission means cooperation in relation to buying and selling goods or services or acquisition of land. The cooperation must constitute more than simply agreeing on how to run their separate businesses and will likely involve some continuity or repetition.[244] The *Competitor Collaboration Guidelines* also state that 'the parties should be able to identify and to explain how they intend to combine their businesses, assets or operations in a commercial activity, or otherwise operate in a commercial activity jointly'.[245] A simple agreement between competitors without the carrying on in cooperation element will not therefore be sufficient on the Commerce Commission's interpretation.

121. The second element of the collaborative activity definition requires that the activity is not carried on for the dominant purpose of lessening competition between any 2 or more of the parties. The purpose referred to in 4(b) above may be inferred from the conduct of any relevant person or from any other relevant circumstance.[246] The requirement here is that it should not be for the dominant purpose of lessening competition. Any effect or likely effect of lessening competition is not a consideration. There is therefore no requirement that a defendant show that the collaborative activity will not have the effect or likely effect of lessening competition. Purpose is the only relevant consideration in applying this aspect of the exemption. In relation to determining purpose, the Commerce Commission *Competitor Collaboration Guidelines* refer to dominant purpose as the 'prevailing objective' of the

242. Commerce Commission New Zealand, *Competitor Collaboration Guidelines* (January 2018) 29, at [97], http://www.comcom.govt.nz/business-competition/guidelines-2/competitor-collaboration-guidelines/ (accessed 1 Mar. 2018).
243. Commerce Commission New Zealand, *Competitor Collaboration Guidelines* (January 2018) 30, at [102]. http://www.comcom.govt.nz/business-competition/guidelines-2/competitor-collaboration-guidelines/ (accessed 1 Mar. 2018).
244. Commerce Commission New Zealand, *Competitor Collaboration Guidelines* (January 2018) 30–31, at [102]–[107], http://www.comcom.govt.nz/business-competition/guidelines-2/competitor-collaboration-guidelines/ (accessed 1 Mar. 2018). The Commission referred here to *Commerce Commission v. Visy Board Pty Ltd* [2012] NZCA 383, at [28].
245. Commerce Commission New Zealand, *Competitor Collaboration Guidelines* (January 2018) 31, at [107], http://www.comcom.govt.nz/business-competition/guidelines-2/competitor-collaboration-guidelines/ (accessed 1 Mar. 2018).
246. Commerce Act 1986 s. 31(5).

collaborative activity.[247] The Commerce Commission takes the view that there is no bright line determining when an aim or objective is the dominant purpose.[248] The test is primarily objective.[249]

122. Under section 31, the parties must not only establish a collaborative activity, but must also show that the cartel provision is reasonably necessary for the purpose of the collaborative activity.[250] The test is objective, and the provision requires that it be assessed at the time of entering into or giving effect to the contract, arrangement or understanding.[251] The Commerce Commission in its *Competitor Collaboration Guidelines* notes that 'reasonably necessary' does not require that the cartel provision be essential, and a 'but for' test will not apply.[252] A determination of 'reasonably necessary' will require consideration of why the parties have included the cartel provision, consideration of the scope of the provision and an assessment of other available options.[253]

123. Where a cartel provision constitutes a restraint of trade, the cartel prohibition does not apply if the parties were involved in a collaborative activity that has ended, the provision was reasonably necessary for the purpose of the collaborative activity and the agreement did not end because lessening of competition between any two or more parties became its dominant purpose.[254]

124. The 2017 amendments added a new regime of clearances relating to cartel provisions.[255] Under this new regime, the Commerce Commission is required to give a clearance for a proposed contract, arrangement or understanding if the parties are involved in a collaborative activity, the cartel provision is reasonably necessary for the purpose of the collaborative activity, and it will not have the effect or

247. Commerce Commission New Zealand, *Competitor Collaboration Guidelines* (January 2018) 32, at [109]–[110], http://www.comcom.govt.nz/business-competition/guidelines-2/competitor-collabo ration-guidelines/ (accessed 1 Mar. 2018).
248. Commerce Commission New Zealand, *Competitor Collaboration Guidelines* (January 2018) 32, at [115], http://www.comcom.govt.nz/business-competition/guidelines-2/competitor-collaboration-guidelines/ (accessed 1 Mar. 2018).
249. Commerce Commission New Zealand, *Competitor Collaboration Guidelines* (January 2018) 32–33, at [113]–[114], [118]–[119]. http://www.comcom.govt.nz/business-competition/guidelines-2/competitor-collaboration-guidelines/ (accessed 1 Mar. 2018).
250. Commerce Act 1986 s. 31(1)(b).
251. Commerce Act 1986 s. 31(1), Commerce Commission New Zealand, *Competitor Collaboration Guidelines* (January 2018) 34, at [121], referring to *Mana v. Fleming* [2007] NZCA 324. http://www.comcom.govt.nz/business-competition/guidelines-2/competitor-collaboration-guidelines/ (accessed 1 Mar. 2018).
252. Commerce Commission New Zealand, *Competitor Collaboration Guidelines* (January 2018) 34, at [124]. http://www.comcom.govt.nz/business-competition/guidelines-2/competitor-collaboration-guidelines/ (accessed 1 Mar. 2018).
253. Commerce Commission New Zealand, *Competitor Collaboration Guidelines* (January 2018) 35, at [128]–[131] http://www.comcom.govt.nz/business-competition/guidelines-2/competitor-collabo ration-guidelines/ (accessed 1 Mar. 2018).
254. Commerce Act 1986 s. 31(3). *See also* Commerce Commission New Zealand, *Competitor Collaboration Guidelines* (January 2018) 36, at [134]–[135], http://www.comcom.govt.nz/business-competition/guidelines-2/competitor-collaboration-guidelines/ (accessed 1 Mar. 2018).
255. Commerce Act 1986 ss 65A–65D.

likely effect of substantially lessening competition in a market.[256] The effect of a clearance is that the parties do not contravene section 27 or section 30 and the provision may be enforced.[257] Authorisations are not available for cartel provisions.

125. Joint ventures are also subject to the business acquisitions provisions in section 47. Section 47(1) of the Act provides that a person must not acquire assets of a business or shares if the acquisition would have, or would be likely to have, the effect of substantially lessening competition in a market.[258] Parties to a proposed joint venture that potentially contravenes section 47 may apply to the Commerce Commission for a clearance or authorisation, as discussed earlier.[259] Clearances are available for business acquisitions that will not, or would not be likely to have, the effect of substantially lessening competition in a market.[260] Authorisations are available for business acquisitions that will result, or will be likely to result, in such a benefit to the public that they should be permitted.[261] The effect of a clearance or authorisation is that the prohibition in section 47 or section 47A will not apply.[262] Decisions of the Commission on clearances and authorisations may be appealed to the High Court and potentially upward to the Court of Appeal and Supreme Court.

256. *Ibid.*, s. 65A(2).
257. *Ibid.*, s. 65B.
258. *Ibid.*, s. 47(1).
259. *Ibid.*, Part 5.
260. *Ibid.*, ss 66 and 67(3).
261. *Ibid.*, s. 67(3).
262. *Ibid.*, s. 69.

Chapter 5. Consequences of Violations and Enforcement Institutions

§1. Administrative Enforcement

I. Antitrust Authorities

126. The New Zealand Commerce Commission is the regulatory agency responsible for competition law. The Commerce Commission is established under the Commerce Act 1986.[263] The Commission is a Crown entity,[264] and is required to act independently in performing its statutory functions and duties and exercising its statutory powers.[265]

127. The Commission enforces the Commerce Act, and also enforces consumer protection legislation, particularly the Fair Trading Act 1986 and the Credit Contracts and Consumer Finance Act 2003. It also has a role in industry specific regulation in relation to the telecommunications, electricity, gas pipelines, dairy and airport sectors.[266]

128. In competition law, the Commerce Commission acts as a decision-maker in relation to clearances and authorisations of mergers and restrictive trade practices as provided in the Commerce Act. It also conducts investigations and brings court proceedings where it believes the statutory provisions have been contravened. It will also be involved as a party to court proceedings where its decisions are appealed.

A. Formation, Composition

129. The Commerce Commission was established under the Commerce Act 1986 and is an independent Crown entity.[267] The Commerce Act also provides for the composition of the Commission. The Commission is required to have no less than four, and no more than six, members appointed by the Governor-General in accordance with the Act, and may also have associate members.[268] Members include a chairperson and deputy chairperson.[269] Members are required to be qualified, having regard to the functions of the Commission, by virtue of their knowledge of or

263. *Ibid.*, s. 8.
264. *Ibid.*, s. 8A.
265. *Ibid.*, s. 8(2). *See also* Commerce Commission New Zealand, *About Us*, http://www.comcom.govt.nz/the-commission/about-us/ (accessed 31 Aug. 2017).
266. Commerce Act 1986 Part 4, Dairy Industry Restructuring Act 2001, Telecommunications Act 2001.
267. Commerce Act 1986 ss 8–8A.
268. *Ibid.*, s. 9(1).
269. *Ibid.*, s. 12.

experience in industry, commerce, economics, law, accountancy, public administration or consumer affairs.[270] At least three of the members must be lawyers.[271] One of the members must be appointed as Telecommunications Commissioner under the Telecommunications Act 2001.[272] Associate members may be appointed only in relation to specified matters or classes of matters, and for periods not exceeding five years.[273] Members of the Commission may only be removed from office for just cause.[274]

130. The Commission is an independent agency, but it is required to have regard to the economic policies of the Government as transmitted in writing from time to time to the Commission by the responsible Minister.[275]

B. Investigating Powers

131. The powers of the Commerce Commission are set out in the Commerce Act 1986.

132. Where the Commission considers it necessary or desirable for the purposes of carrying out its functions and exercising its powers under the Act, the Commission may, by a notice in writing, require a person to provide information, produce documents or appear before the Commission to give evidence.[276] In this provision the powers of the Commission include the power to investigate whether an exception or exemption from the Act applies to a person or their conduct.[277] The Commerce Commission also has the ability to seek an opinion from the High Court by stating a case for the opinion of the Court on any question of law arising before the Commission.[278]

133. The Commission has powers to receive and take evidence, including evidence that may not be admissible in a court of law.[279] It can require and take the giving of evidence on oath.[280] The Commission also has the power to prohibit disclosure of information, documents or evidence.[281]

---

270. *Ibid.*, s. 9(4).
271. *Ibid.*, s. 9(2).
272. *Ibid.*, s. 9(3).
273. *Ibid.*, s. 11.
274. *Ibid.*, s. 12(2) and s. 13, Crown Entities Act 2004 s. 39.
275. *Ibid.*, s. 26. *See also* s. 2 definition of 'Minister'.
276. *Ibid.*, s. 98.
277. *Ibid.*, s. 98(2).
278. *Ibid.*, s. 100A.
279. *Ibid.*, s. (1).
280. *Ibid.*, s. 99(2)–(3).
281. *Ibid.*, s. 100.

134. The Commission may also receive information and documents on behalf of the Australian Competition and Consumer Commission,[282] and there are also provisions applying to overseas regulators generally.[283]

135. The Commission encourages individuals and businesses to provide assistance with its investigations. If an individual or business has been involved in conduct that may contravene the Commerce Act, and comes forward to the Commission, the Commission may, after consideration of the relevant circumstances, agree to a lower level of enforcement action. The Commerce Commission *Cooperation Policy* applies to conduct other than cartel conduct that contravenes the Commerce Act. The *Cooperation Policy* provides a guide to the cooperation conditions. [284] The Commerce Commission also has a *Cartel Leniency Policy*. The *Cartel Leniency Policy* states that the Commission will grant conditional immunity to the first participant in a cartel to apply to the Commission and to meet the prescribed conditions. For parties that do not qualify for conditional immunity, the Commission may also exercise its discretion by taking a lower level of enforcement action, or no action at all, in exchange for information and full cooperation.[285]

136. The Commerce Commission has published *Enforcement Response Guidelines*[286] to outline the approach of the Commission to choosing enforcement options. It has also published *Enforcement Criteria*.[287] In general, the Commerce Commission applies its enforcement criteria, which focus on the extent of the harm or detriment, the seriousness of the conduct and the public interest.[288]

137. The Commission also has powers to search. Section 98A sets out the search powers, providing that the Commission may authorise an employee, under a search warrant, to search a place named in the warrant.[289] Search warrants are granted by issuing officers where there are reasonable grounds to believe that it is necessary for the purpose of ascertaining whether or not a person has engaged or is engaging in conduct that contravenes the Act.[290] The power also extends to searches by the

282. *Ibid.*, s. 99A.
283. *Ibid.*, ss 99B-99P.
284. Commerce Commission New Zealand, *Cooperation Policy*, https://comcom.govt.nz/about-us/our-policies-and-guidelines/leniency-and-cooperation/cooperation-policy (accessed 9 May 2019).
285. Commerce Commission New Zealand, *Cartel Leniency Policy and Guidelines* (June 2018) https://comcom.govt.nz/about-us/our-policies-and-guidelines/leniency-and-cooperation/cartel-leniency-policy-and-guidelines (accessed 9 May 2019).
286. Commerce Commission New Zealand, *Enforcement Response Guidelines* (October 2013), http://www.comcom.govt.nz/the-commission/commission-policies/enforcement-response-guidelines/ (accessed 9 May 2019).
287. Commerce Commission New Zealand, *Enforcement Criteria*, http://www.comcom.govt.nz/the-commission/commission-policies/enforcement-criteria/ (accessed 9 May 2019).
288. Commerce Commission New Zealand, *Enforcement Criteria*, 1–3, http://www.comcom.govt.nz/the-commission/commission-policies/enforcement-criteria/ (accessed 2 Oct. 2017). *See also* Commerce Commission New Zealand, *Enforcement Response Guidelines* (October 2013), 4–5, http://www.comcom.govt.nz/the-commission/commission-policies/enforcement-response-guidelines/ (accessed 2 Oct. 2017).
289. Commerce Act 1986 s. 98A(1).
290. *Ibid.*, s. 98A(2).

Commission in cooperation with an overseas regulator that is investigating conduct contravening its own competition law provisions.[291]

138. In 2015 the New Zealand Ministry of Business, Innovation and Employment commenced a *Targeted Review of the Commerce Act 1986.*[292] As part of the *Review* the Ministry considered whether the Commerce Commission should be given powers and resources to undertake market studies. There was concern that there was an institutional gap in New Zealand's competition regime regarding the ability to promote competition, and that a market studies power could fill this gap.[293] On 27 June 2017, the Government announced proposed amendments to the Commerce Act 1986 providing the Commission with a market studies power.[294] On 28 March 2018 the Government introduced a new Commerce Amendment Bill that provided for a competition studies (market studies) power. In October 2018 and Commerce Amendment Act 2018 came into force, empowering the Commerce Commission to undertake studies into the competitive conditions relating to goods or services in a particular sector if it is in the public interest.[295] The Commission may commence a study on its own initiative or at the direction of the Minister.[296]

C. Adjudicating Powers (Ascertaining and Sanctioning)

139. The Commerce Commission has an adjudication role in relation to clearances and authorisations of restrictive trade practices and mergers.

140. Clearances have not generally been available for restrictive trade practices, under the Commerce Act provisions. However, the 2017 amendments to the Commerce Act added a new regime of clearances for cartel provisions. These new provisions involve the Commerce Commission taking an adjudicatory role.[297] Under the new regime, the Commerce Commission is required to give a clearance for a proposed contract, arrangement or understanding if the parties are involved in a collaborative activity, the cartel provision is reasonably necessary for the purpose of

291. *Ibid.*, s. 98A(5).
292. *See* New Zealand Ministry of Business, Innovation and Employment, *Targeted Review of the Commerce Act 1986*, /business/competition-regulation-and-policy/reviews-of-the-commerce-act-1986/targeted-review-of-the-commerce-act-2015/ (accessed 9 May 2019).
293. Cabinet paper: *Targeted Review of the Commerce Act: Initiation and Financing of Market Studies* https://www.mbie.govt.nz/business-and-employment/business/competition-regulation-and-policy/reviews-of-the-commerce-act-1986/targeted-review-of-the-commerce-act-2015/ (accessed 9 May 2019).
294. Jacqui Dean, *Changes to Commerce Act will Enhance Competition: Press Release* 27 June 2017, https://www.beehive.govt.nz/release/changes-commerce-act-will-enhance-competition (accessed 9 May 2019).
295. Commerce Act 1986 s 50.
296. *Ibid.*, s 51
297. *Ibid.*, ss 65A–65D.

the collaborative activity, and it will not have the effect or likely effect of substantially lessening competition in a market.[298] The effect of a clearance is that the parties do not contravene section 27 or section 30 and the cartel provision may be enforced.[299] Procedures for applications for clearances are generally the same as for authorisations, and are set out in section 60 of the Commerce Act.[300] Clearances must be given by written notice to the applicant.[301]

141. The Commerce Commission's adjudication role also extends to authorisations for restrictive trade practices. Some, but not all, restrictive trade practices are authorisable, and authorisation is granted by the Commerce Commission.[302] Authorisation is not available for cartel provisions or for conduct that constitutes taking advantage of market power under section 36. The test for authorisation of restrictive trade practices is a public benefit test. The Commission will grant an authorisation if the practice 'will in all the circumstances result, or be likely to result, in a benefit to the public which would outweigh the lessening in competition that would result, or would be likely to result'.[303] Determinations are required to be made in writing and to provide reasons for the determination.[304] Before making its determination, the Commission is required to issue a draft determination and if requested is required to hold a conference.[305]The Commission may grant an authorisation after the contravening conduct has commenced, but the conduct will still constitute a contravention up until the time of authorisation.[306] The effect of an authorisation is generally that nothing in the relevant sections prevents the applicant from engaging in the conduct to which the authorisation relates.[307] The Commission may revoke or amend an authorisation if it was granted on false or misleading information, if there has been a material change in circumstances, or if a condition has not been complied with.[308]

142. The Commerce Commission is also empowered to adjudicate on applications for clearances and authorisations of mergers, referred to as business acquisitions in the Commerce Act 1986. Section 47(1) provides that a person must not acquire assets of a business or shares if the acquisition would have, or would be likely to have, the effect of substantially lessening competition in a market.[309] Parties to a proposed merger or acquisition may apply to the Commerce Commission for a clearance or authorisation. Application needs to be made before the acquisition takes place.

298. *Ibid.*, s. 65A(2).
299. *Ibid.*, s. 65B.
300. *Ibid.*, ss 60 and 65C.
301. *Ibid.*, s. 65C(2).
302. *Ibid.*,s 58.
303. *Ibid.*, s. 61(6)–(8).
304. *Ibid.*, s. 61(1)–(4).
305. *Ibid.*, ss 62 and 64.
306. *Ibid.*, ss 59A and 59B.
307. *Ibid.*, s. 58A.
308. *Ibid.*, s. 65.
309. *Ibid.*, s. 47(1).

143. Section 66 empowers the Commission to give clearances,[310] and section 67 empowers the Commission to grant authorisations.[311] Clearances are given for business acquisitions that will not, or will not be likely to have, the effect of substantially lessening competition in a market.[312] Authorisations are granted for business acquisitions that will result, or will be likely to result, in such a benefit to the public that they should be permitted.[313] The Commission may consult with any person the Commission regards is able to assist in making the determination.[314] The Commission may also hold a conference before making a determination.[315] In giving a clearance or granting an authorisation, the Commission may accept a written undertaking to dispose of assets or shares.[316]

144. The effect of a clearance or authorisation is that the prohibition in section 47 or section 47A will not apply.[317] Clearances and authorisations are required to be in writing,[318] and generally expire 12 months after the date on which they are granted by the Commission.[319] Decisions of the Commission on clearances and authorisations may be appealed to the High Court and potentially upward to the Court of Appeal and Supreme Court. The Commerce Commission has issued *Mergers and Acquisitions Guidelines* to explain how it assesses whether a merger or acquisition would be likely to substantially lessen competition in a market and the process for considering clearance applications. [320]

145. The Commerce Commission also has the ability to accept an undertaking in connection with any matter relating to the enforcement of the Commerce Act.[321] These undertakings are enforceable by the High Court.[322]

D. Other Institutional Tasks (Consultancy to Parliament/Government)

146. In addition to its other statutory functions, the Commerce Commission has a statutory obligation in relation to dissemination of information. The Commission is required to make available or cooperate in making available information with

310. *Ibid.*, s. 66.
311. *Ibid.*, s. 67.
312. *Ibid.*, ss 66 and 67(3).
313. *Ibid.*, s. 67(3).
314. *Ibid.*, s. 68(5).
315. *Ibid.*, s. 69B.
316. *Ibid.*, s. 69A.
317. *Ibid.*, s. 69.
318. *Ibid.*, s. 66(3) and s. 67(3) and (5).
319. *Ibid.*, s. 66(5) and s. 67(6).
320. *See* Commerce Commission, *Mergers and Acquisitions Guidelines* (2013) http://www.comcom.govt.nz/business-competition/guidelines-2/mergers-and-acquisitions-guidelines/ (accessed 10 Aug. 2017).
321. Commerce Act 1986 ss 74A-74C. The undertakings regime was inserted into the Commerce Act by the Commerce Amendment Act 2018.
322. Commerce Act 1986 s 74C

respect to the carrying out of its functions and exercise of its powers under the Commerce Act 1986,[323] and with respect to the purposes and provisions of the Commerce Act.[324] It is also required to have regard to the economic policies of Government when these are transmitted to it in writing by the responsible Minister.[325]

147. In practice, the Commerce Commission regularly publishes media releases and fact sheets. It issues a range of Guidelines which provide information on its approach to the exercise of its functions and on procedure.[326] The Commission also provides information to government and provides its views on matters such as proposals for competition law reform.[327]

II. Government Direct Enforcement Activities

148. Enforcement of the Commerce Act 1986 is the responsibility of the Commerce Commission, which is New Zealand's competition enforcement and regulatory agency.

III. Other Administrative Agencies Applying Antitrust Rules

149. New Zealand does not have other agencies applying antitrust rules. Antitrust rules are applied by the Commerce Commission.

IV. Administrative Fines

150. The Commerce Commission does not have the power to impose administrative fines. There is provision for proceedings for pecuniary penalties, but these are a civil remedy imposed by a court, rather than by the Commerce Commission.[328] The standard of proof is that applying in civil proceedings, which is a balance of probabilities standard.[329] Pecuniary penalties are payable to the Crown.

151. In addition to the pecuniary penalties provisions, the Commerce Act 1986 also provides for offences in limited circumstances. Offences involve criminal

323. *Ibid.*, s. 25(a).
324. *Ibid.*, s. 25(b).
325. *Ibid.*, s. 26.
326. *See* https://comcom.govt.nz/business (accessed 9 May 2019).
327. *See* for example the Commerce Commission's *Letter to the Minister of Commerce and Consumer Affairs 2 June 2016*, available from New Zealand Ministry of Business, Innovation and Employment, *Targeted Review of the Commerce Act 1986,* https://www.mbie.govt.nz/business-and-employment/business/competition-regulation-and-policy/reviews-of-the-commerce-act-1986/targeted-review-of-the-commerce-act-2015/ (accessed 9 May 2019).
328. The Commerce Act 1986 s. 79A-s 80 provides for pecuniary penalties for restrictive trade practices, s. 83 provides for pecuniary penalties for business acquisitions.
329. Commerce Act 1986 s. 79A.

liability and the penalty is a fine imposed by the court. They apply only in limited circumstances in the competition law context, and they include conduct such as knowingly misleading the Commerce Commission or refusing to produce a document to the Commission when required to do so.[330]

V. Administrative Injunctions and Other Restrictive Orders

152. The Commerce Act 1986 does not provide for the Commerce Commission to make administrative injunctions. Injunctions are issued by the courts.

153. From 2001 to 2018 the Commerce Act provided for a regime empowering the Commerce Commission to make cease and desist orders. The cease and desist regime was added to the Commerce Act in 2001. It has been rarely used. The Commerce Amendment Act repealed the cease and desist regime from 26 October 2018.[331] The provisions were replaced with provisions empowering the Commerce Commission to accept undertakings, which are enforceable in the High Court.[332]

VI. Interim Measures

154. The Commerce Commission or any other person may seek court injunctions to restrain contravening conduct.[333] The courts may also grant interim injunctions.[334]

§2. Civil Enforcement

155. Civil enforcement actions may be brought by the regulator, the Commerce Commission. Only the Commerce Commission may bring an action seeking pecuniary penalties.[335]The Commission or a private party may bring a civil action seeking an injunction or damages.[336]

I. Competent Civil Courts

156. The Commerce Act 1986 provides for the jurisdiction of the courts in relation to civil enforcement of the competition law provisions. The High Court has jurisdiction in relation to contraventions of the restrictive trade practices provisions

330. *Ibid.*, s. 103.
331. Commerce Amendment Act 2018 s 12.
332. Commerce Act 1986 ss 74A-74C.
333. *Ibid.*, ss 81 and 84.
334. *Ibid.*, s. 88.
335. *Ibid.*, s. 80.
336. *Ibid.*, ss 81–82A.

and business acquisitions provisions.[337] It also has jurisdiction to enforce undertakings[338] and hear and determine appeals from determinations of the Commerce Commission.[339] High Court decisions may be appealed to the Court of Appeal. Decisions of the Court of Appeal may be appealed to the highest court, the New Zealand Supreme Court.

157. The Commerce Commission has published *Enforcement Criteria*[340]and *Enforcement Response Guidelines*[341] to outline the approach of the Commission to choosing enforcement options and whether it will pursue court action in any given case.

II. Sanctions

A. *Nullity*

158. Nullity is not a common term in New Zealand competition law. The Commerce Act does provide that provisions of contracts that contravene the Act are not enforceable. Section 27(4) provides that no provision of a contract 'that has the purpose, or has or is likely to have the effect, of substantially lessening competition in a market is enforceable'.[342] The Act specifies that it is the provision, not the contract, that is unenforceable.[343] Similarly, no person, either on their own or on behalf of an associated person, may carry out or enforce the terms of a covenant that has the purpose, or has or is likely to have the effect, of substantially lessening competition in a market.[344] No covenant 'that has the purpose, or has or is likely to have the effect of substantially lessening competition in a market is enforceable'.[345] The prohibitions on giving effect to and enforcement of anti-competitive provisions do not apply where the Commerce Commission has granted authorisation.[346]

159. The new cartel provisions also prohibit the enforcement of provisions that contravene the Act. No person may give effect to a cartel provision, as defined.[347] In addition, section 30C provides that no cartel provision is enforceable, unless it is covered by one of the Act's exceptions to the cartel prohibition.[348]

337. *Ibid.*, s. 75(1)(a) and (b).
338. Commerce Act 1986 s75(1)(aa)
339. *Ibid.*, s. 75(1)(e).
340. Commerce Commission New Zealand, *Enforcement Criteria*, http://www.comcom.govt.nz/the-commission/commission-policies/enforcement-criteria/ (accessed 9 May 2019).
341. Commerce Commission New Zealand, *Enforcement Response Guidelines* (October 2013), http://www.comcom.govt.nz/the-commission/commission-policies/enforcement-response-guidelines/ (accessed 9 May 2019).
342. Commerce Act 1986 s. 27(4).
343. *See Ibid.*, s. 89(6).
344. *Ibid.*, s. 28(2).
345. *Ibid.*, s. 28(4).
346. *Ibid.*, s. 58A.
347. *Ibid.*, ss 30 and 30A.
348. *Ibid.*, s. 30C.

160. Section 89 of the Commerce Act provides for other orders in relation to the restrictive trade practices provisions. These orders include varying or cancelling a contract where the contract was entered into in contravention of the Act, or where the contract contains a provision which, if given effect to, would contravene the Act. The court may also require any person who is party to the contract to make restitution to or pay compensation to any other party to the contract.[349] There is a similar provision for covenants.[350]

161. The court may make an order for divestiture or assets or shares where the business acquisitions provisions are contravened. Section 47 of the Commerce Act prohibits the acquisition of assets of a business or shares if the acquisition would have, or would be likely to have, the effect of substantially lessening competition in a market.[351] The prohibition does not apply if the assets or shares are acquired in accordance with a clearance or authorisation and the authorisation is in force.[352] If the court, on application of the Commerce Commission, is satisfied that a person has contravened the business acquisition prohibition, the court may order divestiture of assets or shares.[353] An application for a divestiture order must be made within two years from the date of contravention.[354] Orders for divestiture may also be made where a party to an acquisition has made an undertaking to the Commission to dispose of assets or shares, and has contravened that undertaking.[355] In this situation, application for a divestiture order must be made within twelve months from the date on which the obligation under the undertaking was required to be met.[356]

The Commerce Commission or any other person may also seek court injunctions to restrain contravening conduct.[357]

B. Damages

162. In New Zealand competition law, remedies in civil actions include both damages and pecuniary penalties. Both are civil law remedies, and the civil standard of proof applies, meaning that liability must be established on the balance of probabilities.[358] Both damages and pecuniary penalties are imposed after a civil trial under civil procedure rules. However they have important differences. Pecuniary penalties have some similarities to criminal fines. They are payable to the Crown, courts consider a number of factors in imposing a penalty and deterrence is an

349. *Ibid.*, s. 89(2).
350. *Ibid.*, s. 89(3).
351. *Ibid.*, s. 47(1).
352. *Ibid.*, s. 69.
353. *Ibid.*, s. 85.
354. *Ibid.*, s. 85(2).
355. *Ibid.*, s. 69A and s. 85B.
356. *Ibid.*, s 85B(2).
357. *Ibid.*, ss 81 and 84.
358. *Ibid.*, s. 79A.

important consideration. Damages are awarded after a civil trial and are generally to compensate a party who has suffered loss or damage. However there is also provision for exemplary damages.

1. Pecuniary Penalties

Pecuniary penalties relating to restrictive trade practices

163. Section 80 of the Commerce Act 1986 provides for court imposition of pecuniary penalties in relation to restrictive trade practices. Section 80 applies to actions brought by the competition regulator, the Commerce Commission. It provides for the court to order a pecuniary penalty if the court is satisfied that a person has engaged in contravening conduct under the restrictive trade practices provisions. Contravening conduct giving rise to pecuniary penalties includes:[359]

- Contravention of any of the provisions in Part 2 of the Act (the restrictive trade practices provisions).
- Attempting to contravene such a provision.
- Aiding, abetting, counselling or procuring any other person to contravene such a provision
- Inducing, or attempting to induce, any other person, whether by threats or promises or otherwise, to contravene such a provision.
- Being in any way, directly or indirectly, knowingly concerned in, or party to, the contravention by any other person of such a provision.
- Conspiring with any other person to contravene such a provision.

164. The penalty for an individual can be up to NZD 500,000 in respect of each act or omission. In any other case, the penalty in respect of each act or omission can be up to the greater of NZD 10 million, or either 3 times the value of any commercial gain resulting from the contravention if it can be readily ascertained, or 10% of turnover if the commercial gain cannot readily be ascertained.[360] 'Turnover' is defined as meaning 'the total gross revenues (exclusive of any tax required to be collected) received or receivable by a body corporate in an accounting period as a result of trading by that body corporate within New Zealand'.[361]

165. In determining an appropriate penalty, the court is required to have regard to all relevant matters. In particular, the court must have regard to any exemplary damages awarded under section 82A and, for a body corporate, to the nature and extent of any commercial gain. [362] Section 80 of the Act was amended in 2001 to substantially increase the penalties. Before the 2001 amendment, section 80 provided that the court should have regard to all relevant matters, including:

359. *Ibid.*, s. 80(1).
360. *Ibid.*, s. 80(2B).
361. *Ibid.*, s. 2.
362. *Ibid.*, s. 2A.

(a) The nature and extent of the act or omission.
(b) The nature and extent of any loss or damage suffered by any person as a result of the act or omission.
(c) The circumstances in which the act or omission took place.
(d) Whether or not the person has previously been found by the Court in proceedings under this Part of this Act to have engaged in any similar conduct.

166. The courts have taken the view that the reference to all relevant matters in the current section 80(2A) includes all of the factors listed in the pre-2001 section 80.[363] Case law on penalties indicate the approach of the courts in setting penalties. The courts have repeatedly stated that general and specific deterrence is the primary objective in imposing a penalty.[364] Penalties must be sufficient to ensure anti-competitive conduct is not profitable.[365] Courts will first determine an appropriate starting point and then consider the aggravating and mitigating factors. In identifying an appropriate starting point, the relevant factors include the nature of the market, the nature and seriousness of the conduct, the deliberateness of the conduct, the duration of the conduct, the seniority of employees or officers involved, the extent of any benefit derived, the extent of any loss or damage suffered, the market share or degree of market power held by the defendant, the role of the defendant and the size and resources of the defendant.[366]

167. Section 80 also specifies the limitation period. Where a defendant admits to contravening conduct, it is common for the Commerce Commission and the defendant to reach agreement as to appropriate penalty, and then seek to have the Court impose that figure as the penalty. The courts have accepted this process, and the role of the court is then to assess whether the proposed penalty is within the proper range. [367]

168. Commerce Commission actions seeking pecuniary penalties may be commenced within 3 years after the contravention was discovered or ought reasonably to have been discovered, and must be commenced within ten years of the contravention.[368]

169. Section 80(2) provides that the court must order an individual who has engaged in any such conduct to pay a pecuniary penalty, unless the court considers that there is good reason for not making that order. There is therefore a presumption

363. *Telecom Corporation of New Zealand Ltd v. Commerce Commission* [2012] NZCA 344 at [13]. *See also Commerce Commission v First Gas Ltd* [2019] NZHC 231, Footnote 8.
364. *See* for example *Commerce Commission v. Lodge Real Estate* [2016] NZHC 1494, at [10], *Telecom Corporation of New Zealand Ltd v. Commerce Commission* [2012] NZCA 344 at [53].
365. *Commerce Commission v. Lodge Real Estate* & Ors [2017] NZHC 1875, at [16].
366. *Commerce Commission v. Lodge Real Estate* [2016] NZHC 1494, at [10]–[29].
367. *See Commerce Commission v. Lodge Real Estate* & Ors [2017] NZHC 1875, at [14], *Commerce Commission v. Alstom Holdings SA & Ors* [2009] NZCCLR 22 at [18].
368. Commerce Act 1986 s. 80(5).

that an individual engaging in contravening conduct will be required to pay a pecuniary penalty. In addition, for price-fixing conduct, there is a restriction on body corporates indemnifying individuals. A body corporate must not indemnify any director, employee, or agent, or former director, employee, or agent, of the body corporate or of any of its interconnected bodies corporate in respect of any pecuniary penalty imposed on that individual in respect of the price-fixing prohibition.[369] Any indemnity for litigation costs is also prohibited.[370] The section provides that any such indemnities are void, [371] and there is provision for pecuniary penalties to be imposed for contravention of the indemnity prohibition.[372]

Pecuniary penalties relating to business acquisitions

170. There is also provision for the imposition by the court of pecuniary penalties relating to business acquisitions.[373] Under section 83, the court may impose a penalty for contravention of the business acquisitions prohibitions provisions. The section extends to secondary conduct including attempts to contravene, aiding abetting counselling or procuring another person to contravene, inducing or attempting to induce another person to contravene.[374] It also covers a person who has been in any way, directly or indirectly, knowingly concerned, or party to, the contravention, and conspiring with any person to contravene.[375]

171. The amount of a penalty for contravention of the business acquisitions provisions is a maximum of NZD 500,000 for an individual and NZD 5 million otherwise.[376] The limitation period is three years from the date of contravention.[377] The section specifies that in setting a penalty, the court shall have regard to all relevant matters, including the nature and extent of the act or omission, the nature and extent of any loss or damage suffered, the circumstances in which the act or omission took place, and whether or not the person had been previously found to have engaged in similar conduct.[378]

2. Damages

172. In addition to pecuniary penalties, civil courts may award damages for contravention of the restrictive trade practices or business acquisitions provisions.[379]

369. *Ibid.*, s. 80A(1).
370. *Ibid.*, s. 80A(1).
371. *Ibid.*, s. 80A(2).
372. *Ibid.*, s. 80B.
373. *Ibid.*, s. 83.
374. *Ibid.*, s. 83(1).
375. *Ibid.*, s. 83(1).
376. *Ibid.*, s. 83(1A).
377. *Ibid.*, s. 83(5).
378. *Ibid.*, s. 83(2). *See also Commerce Commission v New Zealand Bus Ltd (No 2)* (2006) 3 NZCCLR 854 (HC), *Commerce Commission v First Gas Ltd* [2019] NZHC 231.
379. *Ibid.*, ss 82 and 84A.

These provisions impose liability for any loss or damage caused by conduct that contravenes the relevant provisions. Section 82 relates to restrictive trade practices and provides for damages awards for any loss or damage resulting from contravention of the restrictive trade practices provisions. It also extends to liability for aiding, abetting, counselling or procuring a contravention, inducing a contravention, being in any way directly or indirectly, knowingly concerned in, or party to, a contravention, and conspiring in a contravention.[380] Unlike the pecuniary penalties provisions, attempts to contravene are not included. The limitation period is three years after the contravention was discovered or ought reasonably to have been discovered, up to a maximum of ten years after the conduct.[381]

173. Exemplary damages are also available for breach of the restrictive trade practices provisions.[382] These damages are intended to punish the defendant and are only awarded where the nature of the conduct justifies it. They are available even where a pecuniary penalty has been imposed for the same conduct.[383] In making a decision on exemplary damages, the court is required to have regard to whether a pecuniary penalty has been imposed on the defendant and if so, the amount of the pecuniary penalty.[384]

174. Damages are also available in relation to contraventions of the business acquisitions provisions. Section 84A provides for damages for any loss or damage caused by conduct that contravenes the prohibition on acquisitions that would have, or would be likely to have, the effect of substantially lessening of competition in a market.[385] Liability also extends to secondary conduct, specifically aiding, abetting, counselling or procuring the contravention, inducing the contravention, being in any way directly or indirectly, knowingly concerned in, or party to, the contravention, or conspiring in the contravention.[386] The limitation period is three years from the time the cause of action arose.[387]

C. Interim Measures

175. Interim injunctions are provided for in the Commerce Act and are available in relation to restrictive trade practices and business acquisitions provisions. Section 81 provides that the Commission or any person may apply for the grant of an injunction restraining conduct that would contravene the restrictive trade practices provisions. It also extends to secondary conduct.[388] Section 84 provides that the

---

380. *Ibid.*, s. 82(1).
381. *Ibid.*, s. 82(2).
382. *Ibid.*, s. 82A.
383. *Ibid.*, s. 82A(1).
384. *Ibid.*, s. 82A(2).
385. The prohibition is in the Commerce Act 1986 s. 47. Damages may also be awarded in relation to contravention of s. 47B.
386. *Ibid.*, s. 84A(1).
387. *Ibid.*, s. 84A(2).
388. *Ibid.*, s. 81.

Commission or any person may apply for an injunction in relation to a contravention of the business acquisitions provisions.[389]

176. Under section 88, the courts may grant interim injunctions where an application is made for the grant of an injunction.[390] Where an application is made to the court for the grant of an injunction restraining a person from engaging in conduct of a particular kind, the court may, if in the opinion of the court it is desirable to do so, grant an interim injunction restraining the person from engaging in conduct of that kind.[391] This applies whether or not the person has previously engaged in conduct of that kind and whether or not there is an imminent danger of substantial damage to any person if the person engages in conduct of that kind.[392] The section also provides that, in deciding whether to grant an interim injunction, the court must give any weight that the court considers appropriate to the interests of consumers or, as the case may be, acquirers.[393]

177. If the Commerce Commission applies for an interim injunction, the court must not require the Commission to give an undertaking as to damages as a condition of granting the injunction.[394] In making its decision on the Commission's application for an interim injunction, the court must not take into account the fact that the Commission is not required to give an undertaking as to damages.[395]

§3. Criminal Enforcement

I. Criminal Sanctions for Antitrust Violations

178. New Zealand generic competition law does not currently include significant criminal offences or criminal sanctions. The restrictive trade practices and business acquisitions provisions are enforced through the civil courts. Sanctions include pecuniary penalties, but these are a civil rather than criminal remedy.

179. However, the New Zealand Parliament has passed legislation that introduces criminal sanctions for cartel conduct, and these provisions will come into force on 8 April 2021.[396]The New Zealand government began considering proposals for criminalisation of cartel conduct in 2010, as part of a broader reform of the

389. *Ibid.*, s. 84(1).
390. *Ibid.*, s. 88.
391. *Ibid.*, s. 88(3)(b).
392. *Ibid.*, s. 88(3).
393. *Ibid.*, s. 88(3A).
394. *Ibid.*, s. 88A(1).
395. *Ibid.*, s. 88A(2).
396. Commerce (Criminalisation of Cartels) Amendment Act 2019

cartel provisions in the Commerce Act 1986[397]. The resulting cartel bill as initially introduced included criminal sanctions for cartel conduct.[398] Then on 8 December 2015, the Minister of Commerce and Consumer Affairs announced that criminalisation of cartel conduct would not proceed and criminal sanctions for cartel behaviour would be removed from the bill.[399] The bill was finally passed in August 2017 without the criminal provisions. A new Government took a different view, and the Commerce (Criminalisation of Cartels) Amendment Act was passed in 2019, introducing criminal sanctions to come into force two years from date of assent.

180. The Commerce Act 1986 also includes a limited number of other competition law offences.

- Section 80E provides that it is an offence to act in contravention of a court order prohibiting a person from being a director, promoter or involved in the management of a body corporate.[400] The penalty is imprisonment for up to five years or a fine up to NZD 200,000.
- Section 99A provides for an offence in relation to information required by the Australian Competition and Consumer Commission. The section empowers the New Zealand Commerce Commission to receive information on behalf of the ACCC.[401] Where the ACCC requires a person in New Zealand to supply information, non-compliance constitutes an offence. The penalty is a fine up to NZD 10,000 for an individual or NZD 30,000 in any other case.[402]
- Section 100 empowers the Commerce Commission in the course of investigations to make orders prohibiting publication, communication or giving of evidence in relation to information, documents or evidence.[403] The section also provides that it is an offence to contravene such an order, with potential penalties up to NZD 4,000 for an individual and NZD 12,000 for a body corporate.

---

397. *See* Ministry of Economic Development *Cartel Criminalisation: Discussion Document* (January 2010) https://www.mbie.govt.nz/business-and-employment/business/competition-regulation-and-policy/reviews-of-the-commerce-act-1986/cartels-and-collaborative-activities-2017/submissions-on-the-cartel-criminalisation-discussion-document-2010/ (accessed 9 May 2019). *See also* David King, *Criminalisation of Cartel Behaviour,* (Ministry of Economic Development Occasional Paper 10/01) (January 2010).
398. The Commerce (Cartels and Other Matters) Amendment Bill was introduced in 2011, and the Commerce (Cartels and Other Matters) Amendment Act was passed in 2017. *See* https://www.mbie.govt.nz/business-and-employment/business/competition-regulation-and-policy/reviews-of-the-commerce-act-1986/cartels-and-collaborative-activities-2017/how-the-cartel-reform-came-to-be/ (accessed 9 May 2019).
399. Paul Goldsmith, *Amendments to Cartels Bill*, (press release) (8 Dec. 2015). *See also* Paul Goldsmith, Minister of Commerce and Consumer Affairs, *Removal of the Criminal Offence for Cartels from the Commerce (Cartels and Other Matters) Amendment Bill* (Cabinet Committee Paper), and Cabinet Economic Growth and Infrastructure Committee, *Minute of Decision,* Available from https://www.mbie.govt.nz/business-and-employment/business/competition-regulation-and-policy/reviews-of-the-commerce-act-1986/cartels-and-collaborative-activities-2017/how-the-cartel-reform-came-to-be/ (accessed 9 May 2019).
400. A court may make such an order under s. 80C of the Commerce Act 1986 where the court has found a contravention of the cartel prohibition in s. 30.
401. Commerce Act 1986 s. 99A(1).
402. *Ibid.*, s. 99A(3).
403. *Ibid.*, s. 100(1).

– There are also offences in the Commerce Act that relate to regulated goods and services, separate from generic competition law.[404]

181. Other than the offences created above, competition law violations are generally civil matters.

182. The Commerce Commission has published *Criminal Prosecutions Guidelines* to provide guidance as to the circumstances in which it will initiate criminal prosecution, and the principles and practices applicable to a criminal prosecution.[405]

II. Other Application of Criminal Law to Relevant Conducts

183. In New Zealand, competition law is set out in the Commerce Act 1986. Other criminal law does not apply.

The Commerce Commission is able to bring an action under the Crimes Act 1961, but in a competition law context such an action would only relate to more generic offences such as supplying misleading information.[406]

III. Role of Prosecutors

184. The Commerce Commission has published *Criminal Prosecutions Guidelines* which outline the principles and practices applicable to a criminal prosecution.[407] The *Criminal Prosecutions Guidelines* apply to all criminal prosecutions and potential prosecutions under the Commerce Act 1986, including appeals against court decisions.[408] They do not cover civil proceedings. The *Solicitor-General's*

404. Commerce Act s. 86B, s. 87B and s. 103 are examples.
405. *See* Commerce Commission New Zealand, *Criminal Prosecutions Guidelines* (October 2013) 3, http://www.comcom.govt.nz/the-commission/commission-policies/criminal-prosecution-guidelines/ (accessed 9 May 2019). *See also* Commerce Commission New Zealand, *Enforcement Response Guidelines* (October 2013), http://www.comcom.govt.nz/the-commission/commission-policies/enforcement-response-guidelines/ (accessed 9 May 2019).
406. *See* Commerce Commission New Zealand, *Criminal Prosecutions Guidelines* (October 2013) 4, http://www.comcom.govt.nz/the-commission/commission-policies/criminal-prosecution-guidelines/ (accessed 9 May 2019).
407. *Ibid.*, 3. *See also* Commerce Commission New Zealand, *Enforcement Response Guidelines* (October 2013), http://www.comcom.govt.nz/the-commission/commission-policies/enforcement-response-guidelines/ (accessed 10 May 2019).
408. Commerce Commission New Zealand, *Criminal Prosecutions Guidelines* (October 2013) 3, http://www.comcom.govt.nz/the-commission/commission-policies/criminal-prosecution-guidelines/ (accessed 10 May 2019).

Prosecution Guidelines[409] also apply, and the Commerce Commission *Criminal Prosecutions Guidelines* are subject to those guidelines.[410]

185. As with all Commerce Commission prosecutions, competition law prosecutions are conducted by Crown solicitors throughout New Zealand, and sometimes by Queen's Counsel, on behalf of the Commerce Commission. Under the *Criminal Prosecutions Guidelines* and the *Solicitor-General's Prosecution Guidelines,* the test for whether to initiate a prosecution is first to assess whether there is sufficient evidence to provide a reasonable prospect of conviction and second whether criminal prosecution is required in the public interest.[411] The decision to prosecute is made by a majority of members of the Commerce Commission.[412] Decisions to appeal a criminal prosecution decision are also made by a majority of Commerce Commission members, and any proposed appeal must also be referred by the Crown solicitor to the Solicitor-General, and must be approved by the Solicitor-General.[413]

IV. Competent Criminal Courts

186. As noted above, there are very few criminal offences in New Zealand competition law, and the offences that exist are somewhat peripheral. For the offences that exist, jurisdiction is divided between the District Court and the High Court.

187. The District Court has jurisdiction to hear and determine proceedings for offences against sections 86B, 87B, 100 and 103.[414] Sections 86B, 87B and 103 relate to regulated goods and services, rather than competition law. Section 100 empowers the Commerce Commission in the course of investigations to make orders prohibiting publication, communication or giving of evidence in relation to information, documents or evidence.[415] The section provides that it is an offence to contravene such an order.

---

409. Crown Law, *Solicitor-General's Prosecution Guidelines* (2013), http://www.crownlaw.govt.nz/publications/prosecution-guidelines/ (accessed 2 Oct. 2017).

410. Commerce Commission New Zealand, *Criminal Prosecutions Guidelines* (October 2013) 3, http://www.comcom.govt.nz/the-commission/commission-policies/criminal-prosecution-guidelines/ (accessed 10 May 2019).

411. *Ibid.*, 4–6.

412. Specifically, the decision is made by a majority of members of the Commerce Commission sitting as the relevant Division under s. 16 of the Commerce Act 1986.

413. Commerce Commission New Zealand, *Criminal Prosecutions Guidelines* (October 2013) 7, http://www.comcom.govt.nz/the-commission/commission-policies/criminal-prosecution-guidelines/ (accessed 10 May 2019). This process for Solicitor-General approval is in accordance with the Criminal Procedure Act 2011.

414. Commerce Act 1986 s. 76.

415. *Ibid.*, s. 100(1).

188. The High Court has jurisdiction in proceedings for offences under section 80E, which provides that it is an offence to act in contravention of a court order prohibiting a person from being a director, promoter or involved in the management of a body corporate.[416]

416. A court may make such an order under s. 80C of the Commerce Act 1986 where the court has found a contravention of the cartel prohibition in s. 30.

Part II. Application of the Prohibitions

Chapter 1. Restrictive Agreements

§1. Horizontal Agreements

189. Horizontal agreements are covered in Part 2 of the Commerce Act, in sections 27–34. These provisions include a general prohibition on anti-competitive agreements, including horizontal and vertical agreements. This general prohibition on anti-competitive agreements employs a rule of reason-style competition test, prohibiting agreements that have the purpose, effect or likely effect of substantially lessening competition in a market.[417] Section 27 provides that:

(1) No person shall enter into a contract or arrangement, or arrive at an understanding, containing a provision that has the purpose, or has or is likely to have the effect, of substantially lessening competition in a market.
(2) No person shall give effect to a provision of a contract, arrangement or understanding that has the purpose, or has or is likely to have the effect, of substantially lessening competition in a market.

190. Section 27 applies to agreements made before or after the commencement of the Commerce Act.[418] It also provides that no provision of a contract, whether made before or after the commencement of the Act, that has the purpose, or has or is likely to have the effect, of substantially lessening competition in a market is enforceable.[419] The phrase 'give effect to' used in section 27(2) in relation to a provision of a contract, arrangement or understanding includes doing an act or thing in pursuance of or in accordance with that provision and enforcing or purporting to enforce that provision.[420]

191. Section 28 is a similar provisions to section 28, but applying to covenants. Section 28 provides that:[421]

(1) No person, either on his own or on behalf of an associated person, shall –

417. *Ibid.*, s. 27.
418. *Ibid.*, s. 27(3).
419. *Ibid.*, s. 27(4).
420. *Ibid.*, s. 2(1).
421. *Ibid.*, s. 28(1)–(2).

(a) require the giving of a covenant; or
(b) give a covenant –
that has the purpose, or has or is likely to have the effect, of substantially lessening competition in a market.

(2) No person, either on his own or on behalf of an associated person, shall carry out or enforce the terms of a covenant that has the purpose, or has or is likely to have the effect, of substantially lessening competition in a market.

192. Section 28 applies to covenants given before or after the commencement of the Act.[422] There is an additional deeming provision that effectively extends the meaning of 'require the giving of the covenant' to cover an invitation to enter into a contract containing a covenant, offering to enter into a contract containing a covenant, or making it known that the person will not enter into a contract of a particular kind unless the contract contains a covenant of a particular kind or in particular terms.[423] It also provides that no covenant, whether given before or after the commencement of the Act, that has the purpose, or has or is likely to have the effect of substantially lessening competition in a market is enforceable.[424] Additional provisions extend the prohibition to threatening to engage, or to engaging, in conduct, because a person has not complied or fails to comply with the terms of the covenant.[425] There is also an additional provision extending the interpretation of 'associated person'.[426]

193. Sections 27 and 28 are very broad, they cover horizontal and vertical agreements, there is no requirement that the parties to an agreement are in competition with each other, and the effect may take place in any market, not necessarily the market in which the parties to the agreement compete. However, liability is not per se, it requires a rule of reason-style competition analysis with evidence of a purpose, effect or likely effect of substantially lessening competition in a market. There is a growing body of relevant case law, particularly on section 27:

Section 27
An action under section 27 requires establishing three key elements. These are:
The existence of a contract, arrangement or understanding
Market definition
Purpose, effect or likely effect of substantially lessening of competition in the market.
Contract, arrangement or understanding

422. *Ibid.*, s. 28(3).
423. *Ibid.*, s. 28(6).
424. *Ibid.*, s. 28(4).
425. *Ibid.*, s. 28(5).
426. *Ibid.*, s. 28(7).

194. The meaning of 'contract' is relatively clear from contract law. In the context of the Commerce Act, the meaning of 'contract' includes 'a lease of, or a licence in respect of, any land or a building or part of a building'.[427]

195. The meaning of the terms 'arrangement' and 'understanding' have been considered by the courts. These terms are included to capture agreements that are less formal than a contract and are not defined in the Commerce Act.

196. New Zealand courts have taken an approach to arrangements and understandings that is similar to the approach taken by courts in Australia and the United Kingdom. In one early New Zealand case, the Privy Council (New Zealand's highest court at that time) said that the term 'arrangement' should be construed in its ordinary popular sense, and that it did not necessarily involve some discreditable or conspiratorial element. 'Arrangement' was a perfectly ordinary English word and in the context of section 27 involved no more than a meeting of minds between two or more persons, not amounting to a formal contract, but leading to an agreed course of action.[428]

197. New Zealand courts have often referred to the United Kingdom case of *Re British Basic Slag Ltd's Agreements.*[429] In that case Wilmer L J said that:[430]

> For when each of two or more parties intentionally arouses in the others an expectation that he will act in a certain way, it seems to me that he incurs at least a moral obligation to do so. An arrangement as so defined is therefore something 'whereby the parties to it accept mutual rights and obligations'.

198. The New Zealand courts' approach to arrangements and understandings has consequently generally focussed on concepts of mutual communication and obligation.[431] Courts have also tended to equate arrangements and understandings, although understandings are generally understood as less formal than arrangements, and it has been suggested that an arrangement may arise from negotiations and an understanding may arise from observed conduct.[432]

---

427. *Ibid.*, s. 2(6).
428. *NZ Apple & Pear Board v. Apple Fields* [1991] 1 NZLR 257, 261.
429. *Re British Basic Slag Ltd's Agreements* [1962] 3 All ER 247, [1963] 2 All ER 807.
430. *Re British Basic Slag Ltd's Agreements* [1963] 2 All ER 807, 819 (CA).
431. *See* for example the case of *Auckland Regional Authority v. Mutual Rental Cars (Auckland Airport) Ltd* [1987] 2 NZLR 647, 661–662 and *Commerce Commission v. Caltex New Zealand Ltd* (1999) 9 TCLR 305, 314–5.
432. *Auckland Regional Authority v. Mutual Rental Cars (Auckland Airport) Ltd* [1987] 2 NZLR 647, 662.

199. In the 2003 decision in *Giltrap City Ltd v. Commerce Commission*, the New Zealand Court of Appeal considered the concepts of communication and obligation, and concluded that the test for arrangement could be put more simply. The Court said that:[433]

> We do not consider it appropriate to be tied in any determinative way to the concepts of mutuality, obligation and duty. While the concept of moral obligation is helpful in that it will often reflect the effect of an arrangement or understanding under s 27, the flexible purpose of the section is such that it is best to focus the ultimate inquiry on the concepts of consensus and expectation. A finding that there was a consensus giving rise to an expectation that the parties would act in a certain way necessarily involves communication among the parties of the assumption of a moral obligation.

200. The Judges therefore preferred to use the concepts of consensus and expectation, but they have not necessarily rejected communication and moral obligation. They expressly require communication, and can be interpreted as generally requiring obligation. The Judges went on to discuss the concepts of consensus and expectation in the context of section 27. They said that there must be a consensus between those said to have entered in the arrangement, and said:[434]

> Their minds must have met – they must have agreed – upon the subject matter. The consensus must engender an expectation that at least one person will act or refrain from acting in the manner the consensus envisages. In other words, there must be an expectation that the consensus will be implemented in accordance with its terms. If no specific action or inaction is envisaged on anyone's part, it would be difficult to find an arrangement under s 27, if only for want of the existence of the necessary purpose or effect of substantially lessening competition.

201. The Judges then set out a test for the existence of an arrangement or understanding, using the concepts of consensus and expectation. They said that:[435]

> [T]he question whether a particular person entered into an arrangement or arrived at an understanding under s 27 should be answered by asking whether that person was part of a consensus giving rise to an expectation that some proscribed action or inaction take place. If they were, they will have entered into an arrangement. If they were not, they will not have entered into any arrangement.

433. Judgment of Gault P and Tipping J in *Giltrap City Ltd v. Commerce Commission* [2004] 1 NZLR 608, 613 (CA).
434. *Giltrap City Ltd v. Commerce Commission* [2004] 1 NZLR 608, 613 (CA).
435. *Giltrap City Ltd v. Commerce Commission* [2004] 1 NZLR 608, 614 (CA).

202. In a separate judgment, McGrath J emphasised the importance of moral obligation, and expressed a concern that the new test should not be interpreted as not requiring moral obligation.[436] He said that moral obligation was important to ensure that conscious parallelism was not caught by the provision. He said that the concepts of consensus and expectation still carried the notion of a moral (non-legal) obligation, and he said that in his view this remained 'an important touchstone for determining whether there is an arrangement or understanding under s 27'.[437] Subsequent cases have applied the consensus and expectation test.[438]

203. The Judges in *Giltrap* also discussed the potential for liability as a secondary party. A person who is not a party to the arrangement may nevertheless have contravened s27 by being a secondary party in the sense of being knowingly concerned in, inducing, or encouraging entry into a proscribed consensus by others.[439] An attempt to enter into an arrangement or arrive at an understanding may also give rise to liability.[440]

Proof of the existence of an arrangement or understanding

204. New Zealand courts have also addressed the question of proving the existence of an arrangement or understanding. The civil standard of proof applies, proof is on the balance or probabilities. New Zealand courts have noted that arrangements and understandings are rarely provable by direct evidence and that failure of a defendant to explain reasons for its conduct will be a relevant factor.[441] In *Commerce Commission v. Caltex New Zealand Ltd,* the Commerce Commission in its argument relied on inferences to be drawn from facts to establish the existence of the arrangement or understanding.[442] The Court then considered the appropriate standard to adopt in relation to inferences. In considering the approach to proof, the Court quoted the following passage from *R v. Associated Northern Collieries*:[443]

> Community of purpose may be proved by independent facts, but it need not be. If the other defendant is shown to be committing other acts, tending to the same end, then though primarily each set of acts is attributable to the person whose acts they are, and to him alone, there may be such a concurrence of time, character, direction and result as naturally to lead to the inference that these separate acts were the outcome of pre-concert, or some mutual contemporaneous engagement, or that they were themselves the manifestations of mutual

436. Judgment of McGrath J in *Giltrap City Ltd v. Commerce Commission* [2004] 1 NZLR 608, 625–6 (CA).
437. Judgment of McGrath J in *Giltrap City Ltd v. Commerce Commission* [2004] 1 NZLR 608, 625 (CA).
438. *See* for example *Commerce Commission v. Ophthalmological Society of NZ Ltd* (2004) 10 TCLR 994, 1024–1026.
439. The Judges referred here to s. 80(1)€.
440. Commerce Act 1986 s. 80(1)(b).
441. *Auckland Regional Authority v. Mutual Rental Cars (Auckland Airport) Ltd* [1987] 2 NZLR 647, 664.
442. *Commerce Commission v. Caltex New Zealand Ltd* (1999) 9 TCLR 305, 313–4.
443. *R v. Associated Northern Collieries* (1911) 14 CLR 387, 499 (HCA).

consent to carry out a common purpose, thus forming as well as evidencing a combination to effect the one object towards which the separate acts are found to converge.

205. The Judge in *Caltex* said that reference to facts which are such as 'naturally to lead to the inference' was an approach which commended itself to all parties. The Judge also said that in reaching conclusions and drawing inferences the Court 'should be mindful of the seriousness of the allegations having regard to the penalties involved'.[444] On the facts in the *Caltex* case, the Court applied the *Northern Collieries* test and found such a concurrence of time, character, direction and result as naturally to lead to the inference that there was an understanding, based on the combined effect of ten key matters of fact.[445]

206. The question of proof as to whether a person is party to an arrangement or understanding was considered in the *Giltrap City* case. In that case, the defendant, Mr MacKenzie, was present but silent at a meeting in which an arrangement was made. He argued that he did not enter into the arrangement. The Court of Appeal considered the approach to proof, and adopted the same approach that is taken in contract law, saying that the correct touchstone was 'outward appearance rather than inner thoughts'.[446]. The Court said that:[447]

> The existence of the necessary consensus is therefore to be judged by reference to what reasonable people would infer from the conduct of the person whose participation in the consensus is in issue ... the consensus must of course be such that it engenders an expectation in the minds of the participants that at least one person will act in a proscribed manner ... Here the essential question is whether Mr MacKenzie so conducted himself that reasonable people, appraised of all the relevant circumstances, would take the view that he was part of the consensus.

Purpose, Effect or Likely Effect

207. In addition to the contract, arrangement or understanding element, section 27 also requires a plaintiff to establish that a provision has the purpose, or has or is likely to have the effect, of substantially lessening competition in a market. These elements have been considered by New Zealand courts.

Purpose

444. *Commerce Commission v. Caltex New Zealand Ltd* (1999) 9 TCLR 305, 314.
445. *Ibid.*, 332–4.
446. *Giltrap City Ltd v. Commerce Commission* [2004] 1 NZLR 608, 618 (CA), Gault P and Tipping J.
447. *Ibid.*

208. Under section 27, parties to a contract, arrangement or understanding may be liable if the agreement contains a provision shown to have the purpose of substantially lessening competition in a market. It is the purpose of the provision, not of the agreement, that matters for section 27.[448] Purpose has been held to imply object or aim.[449] A purpose can be one of a number of purposes, so long as it is a substantial purpose.[450] The purpose may be the purpose of one party alone, it need not be a common purpose.[451]There has been some argument about the test for purpose and whether it was objective or subjective, but the courts have generally taken the view that a plaintiff may establish anti-competitive purpose objectively, and that this will be the more ordinary approach. However a plaintiff may also provide subjective evidence, and it should also be open to the defendant to attempt to rebut by subjective evidence.[452]

Likely Effect

209. Under section 27, parties to a contract, arrangement or understanding may be liable if the agreement contains a provision shown to have the likely effect of substantially lessening competition in a market. Likely effect of provisions in a number of agreements may be aggregated for this purpose.[453]

210. There has been consideration by the courts as to the meaning of 'likely' in the context of 'likely effect. It has been held that likely effect refers to 'a real and substantial risk that the stated consequence will happen',[454] or a 'real chance'.[455]

Effect

211. Under section 27, parties to a contract, arrangement or understanding may be liable if the agreement contains a provision shown to have the effect of substantially lessening competition in a market. 'Effect' refers to actual effect in this context. Effects of provisions in a number of agreements may be aggregated for this purpose.[456]

Substantially lessening competition in a market

---

448. *See Commerce Commission v. Ophthalmological Society of NZ Ltd* (2004) 10 TCLR 994, 1029.
449. *Union Shipping New Zealand Ltd v. Port Nelson* [1990] 2 NZLR 662, 707.
450. Commerce Act 1986 s. 2(5).
451. *Commerce Commission v. Port Nelson Ltd* (1995) 5 NZBLC 103,762, 103,773 McGechan J. *See also Port Nelson Ltd v. Commerce Commission* (1996) 5 NZBLC 104,142, 104,151 (CA).
452. *Commerce Commission v. Port Nelson Ltd* (1995) 5 NZBLC 103,762, 103,777 McGechan J. *See also Port Nelson Ltd v. Commerce Commission* (1996) 5 NZBLC 104,142, 104,151 (CA), *ANZCO Foods Waitara Ltd v. AFFCO NZ Ltd* [2006] 3 NZLR 351.
453. Commerce Act 1986 s. 3(5).
454. *Port Nelson Ltd v. Commerce Commission* (1996) 5 NZBLC 104,142, 104,150 (CA).
455. *Commerce Commission v. Woolworths Ltd* (2008) 12 TCLR 194, 209.
456. Commerce Act 1986 s. 3(5).

212. The remaining element in establishing liability under section 27 is that the purpose, effect or likely effect of the provision must be of substantially lessening of competition in a market. 'Substantial' means real or of substance.[457] This is interpreted as meaning 'not insubstantial or nominal'.[458] 'Lessening' of competition includes 'hindering or preventing' of competition.[459]

213. In assessing substantial lessening of competition in any particular case, the New Zealand courts have adopted the approach of the Australian Federal Court in *Dandy Power Equipment v. Mercury Marine*.[460] This approach uses a future focused counter-factual test. The court will consider the nature and extent of the market, the probable nature and extent of competition which would exist therein but for the conduct in question, the way the market operates and the nature and extent of the contemplated lessening. As Smithers J said in *Dandy Power Equipment*[461]

> To apply the concept of substantially lessening competition in a market, it is necessary to assess the nature and extent of the market, the probable nature and extent of competition which would exist therein but for the conduct in question, the way the market operates, and the nature and extent of the contemplated lessening. To my mind one must look at the relevant significant portion of the market, ask oneself how and to what extent there would have been competition therein but for the conduct, assess what is left and determine whether what has been lost in relation to what would have been, is seen to be a substantial lessening of competition. I prefer not to substitute other adverbs for 'substantially'. 'Substantially' is a word the meaning of which in the circumstances in which it is applied must, to some extent, be of uncertain incidence and a matter of judgment. There is no precise scale by which to measure what is substantial. I think … the word is used in a sense importing a greater rather than a lesser degree of lessening. Accordingly, in my opinion, competition in a market is substantially lessened if the extent of competition in the market which has been lost, is seen by those competent to judge to be substantial lessening of competition. Has competitive trading in the market been substantially interfered with? It is then that the public as such will suffer.

457. *Ibid.*, s. 2(1A).
458. *Commerce Commission v. Port Nelson Ltd* (1995) 5 NZBLC 103,762, 103,780–1 McGechan J.
459. Commerce Act 1986 s. 3(2). *See also Commerce Commission v. Port Nelson Ltd* (1995) 5 NZBLC 103,762, 103,781 McGechan J.
460. *Dandy Power Equipment v. Mercury Marine* (1982) 44 ALR 173.
461. *Ibid.*, 191–192, quoted in *Auckland Regional Authority v. Mutual Rental Cars (Auckland Airport) Ltd* [1987] 2 NZLR 647,674–675. *See also Tru Tone Ltd v. Festival Records Marketing Ltd* [1988] 2 NZLR 352, 362, *Commerce Commission v. Ophthalmological Society of NZ Ltd* (2004) 10 TCLR 994, 1029, and *ANZCO Foods Waitara Ltd v. AFFCO NZ Ltd* [2006] 3 NZLR 351, 404.

214. A court will consider the likely state of future competition in market with and without the conduct.[462] 'Competition' is defined as meaning 'workable or effective competition'.[463] In assessing competition, a court will consider the relevant elements, as listed below. The first five elements are from the decision of the Australian Trade Practices Tribunal in *Re Queensland & Co-Operative Milling Associates Ltd* – Proposed Merger; *Re Defiance* – Proposed Mergers 1 and 2.[464] The sixth, behaviour in the market, was added by the New Zealand Court of Appeal in *Tru Tone Ltd v. Festival Records Marketing Ltd.*[465] These elements are regularly referred to in New Zealand cases.[466] The elements are as follows:

(i) number and size distribution of independent sellers: degree of market concentration;
(ii) height of barriers to entry;
(iii) product differentiation and sales promotion;
(iv) vertical relationships with customers and suppliers, extent of vertical integration;
(v) formal stable and fundamental arrangements between firms which restrict their ability to function as independent entities; and
(vi) behaviour in the market.

215. In making a substantially lessening of competition assessment, a court will consider the net effect on competition, balancing the procompetitive effects (including efficiencies) against the anticompetitive effects.[467] 'Substantial' is defined as meaning 'real or of substance'.[468] Lessening must be 'substantial' in the sense of meaningful or relevant to the competitive process.[469] Lessening of competition includes hindering or preventing of competition.[470] Short-term effects are unlikely to be substantial, and effects on an individual competitor are unlikely to be important.[471] There is a provision allowing courts to combine provisions of agreements for the purposes of section 27.[472]

216. An assessment as to whether conduct will have the purpose, effect or likely effect of substantially lessening competition in a market will also require definition

---

462. *ANZCO Foods Waitara Ltd v. AFFCO NZ Ltd* [2006] 3 NZLR 351, 404.
463. Commerce Act 1986 s. 3(1). *See* discussion in Adhar, 'The Meaning of "Competition" and the Commerce Act 1986' (1986) 6 Otago LR 319. *See also Re Queensland & Co-Operative Milling Associates Ltd* – Proposed Merger; *Re Defiance* – Proposed Mergers 1 and 2 (1976) 8 ALR 481, 514–516. *See also Auckland Regional Authority v. Mutual Rental Cars (Auckland Airport) Ltd* [1987] 2 NZLR 647, 671.
464. *Re Queensland & Co-Operative Milling Associates Ltd* – Proposed Merger; *Re Defiance* – Proposed Mergers 1 and 2 (1976) 8 ALR 481, 514–516.
465. *Tru Tone Ltd v. Festival Records Marketing Ltd* [1988] 2 NZLR 352, 363.
466. *See ANZCO Foods Waitara Ltd v. AFFCO NZ Ltd* [2006] 3 NZLR 351, 403.
467. *ANZCO Foods Waitara Ltd v. AFFCO NZ Ltd* [2006] 3 NZLR 351, 405.
468. Commerce Act 1986 s. 2(1A).
469. *Ibid.*, 404.
470. *Ibid.*, s. 3(2).
471. *Ibid.*, 404.
472. *Ibid.*, s. 3(5).

of the relevant market. 'Market' is defined as 'a market in New Zealand for goods or services as well as other goods or services that, as a matter of fact and commercial common sense, are substitutable for them'.[473] Market definition is therefore a question of fact in any particular case, and courts are required to consider both substitutability and commercial common sense, which are not regarded as being in conflict.[474] New Zealand courts have followed Australian case law on market definition. A market is 'the field of actual and potential transactions between buyers and sellers amongst whom there can be strong substitution, at least in the long run, if given a sufficient price incentive'.[475] Boundaries of the market are drawn by reference to the alleged conduct.[476] Market definition is a tool for competition analysis, not an end in itself.[477] In the case of *Tru Tone Ltd*, the New Zealand Court of Appeal said that 'market' is 'ordinarily regarded as a multi-dimensional concept with dimensions of product, functional level, space and time'.[478]

217. In summary, section 27 of the Commerce Act is a broad provision prohibiting a range of anti-competitive agreements, including cartel agreements. In addition to this general prohibition, there are specific provisions applying to cartel conduct, including price fixing. It should, however, be borne in mind that agreements that are not covered by the specific cartel provisions may still be prohibited agreements under section 27.

I. Cartels

A. Price Fixing

218. The New Zealand Commerce Act has had a longstanding prohibition on horizontal price-fixing agreements. This provision, the former section 30 of the Commerce Act, constituted a per se prohibition on horizontal price-fixing agreements. However this provision has recently been replaced by new cartel provisions as part of a process of cartel law reform. As from 15 August 2017 a new price-fixing regime applies.[479] Horizontal price-fixing is now prohibited by the new cartel provisions.

---

473. *Ibid.*, s. 3(1A).
474. *Telecom v. Commerce Commission* (1991) 4 TCLR 473, 499.
475. *Re Queensland & Co-Operative Milling Associates Ltd* – Proposed Merger; *Re Defiance* – Proposed Mergers 1 and 2 (1976) 8 ALR 481,517. *See also Brambles NZ Ltd v. Commerce Commission* (2003) 10 TCLR 868, 892.
476. *Telecom v. Commerce Commission* (1991) 4 TCLR 473, 499–500.
477. *Brambles NZ Ltd v. Commerce Commission* (2003) 10 TCLR 868, 892.
478. *Tru Tone Ltd v. Festival Records Marketing Ltd* [1988] 2 NZLR 352, 359. The Commerce Commission has produced Guidelines outlining its approach to market definition, drawing on the case law. *See* Commerce Commission, *Mergers and Acquisitions Guidelines* (2013), 23-29 http://www.comcom.govt.nz/business-competition/guidelines-2/mergers-and-acquisitions-guidelines/ (accessed 10 May 2019).
479. Commerce (Cartels and Other Matters) Amendment Act 2017 s. 7 repealed the former ss 30–34 and replaced with new ss 30–33 under the heading 'Cartel provisions'.

219. The cartel provisions do not currently contain criminal provisions. The New Zealand government began considering proposals for criminalisation of cartel conduct in 2010, as part of a broader reform of the cartel provisions in the Commerce Act 1986[480]. The resulting cartel bill as initially introduced included criminal sanctions for cartel conduct.[481] Then on 8 December 2015 the Minister of Commerce and Consumer Affairs announced that criminalisation of cartel conduct would not proceed and criminal sanctions for cartel behaviour would be removed from the bill.[482] The bill was finally passed in August 2017 without the criminal provisions, and New Zealand, unlike many cognate jurisdictions, did not have laws imposing criminal sanctions on cartel conduct. However, a new Government took a different view, and the Commerce (Criminalisation of Cartels) Amendment Act was passed in 2019, introducing criminal sanctions to come into force 2 years from date of assent, on 8 April 2021.[483]

220. The new cartel provisions have not yet been considered by the courts, and so judicial guidance as to their interpretation is not available. However, New Zealand courts have taken a relatively robust approach to price-fixing cases in the past, and it seems likely that this will continue.[484]

221. The new cartel provisions prohibit cartel provisions in agreements[485] and provide that no cartel provision is enforceable.[486] Section 30 provides that:

No person may –

480. *See* Ministry of Economic Development *Cartel Criminalisation: Discussion Document* (January 2010) https://www.mbie.govt.nz/business-and-employment/business/competition-regulation-and-policy/reviews-of-the-commerce-act-1986/cartels-and-collaborative-activities-2017/submissions-on-the-cartel-criminalisation-discussion-document-2010/ (accessed 9 May 2019). *See also* David King, *Criminalisation of Cartel Behaviour*, (Ministry of Economic Development Occasional Paper 10/01) (January 2010).
481. The Commerce (Cartels and Other Matters) Amendment Bill was introduced in 2011, and the Commerce (Cartels and Other Matters) Amendment Act was passed in 2017. *See* https://www.mbie.govt.nz/business-and-employment/business/competition-regulation-and-policy/reviews-of-the-commerce-act-1986/cartels-and-collaborative-activities-2017/how-the-cartel-reform-came-to-be/ (accessed 9 May 2019).
482. Paul Goldsmith, *Amendments to Cartels Bill*, (press release) (8 Dec. 2015). *See also* Paul Goldsmith, Minister of Commerce and Consumer Affairs, *Removal of the Criminal Offence for Cartels from the Commerce (Cartels and Other Matters) Amendment Bill* (Cabinet Committee Paper), and Cabinet Economic Growth and Infrastructure Committee, *Minute of Decision*, Available from https://www.mbie.govt.nz/business-and-employment/business/competition-regulation-and-policy/reviews-of-the-commerce-act-1986/cartels-and-collaborative-activities-2017/how-the-cartel-reform-came-to-be/ (accessed 9 May 2019).
483. Commerce (Criminalisation of Cartels) Amendment Act 2019
484. *See* for example *Commerce Commission v Caltex New Zealand Ltd* (1999) 9 TCLR 305, *Giltrap City Ltd v Commerce Commission* [2004] 1 NZLR 608, 618 (CA), *Commerce Commission v Lodge Real Estate Ltd* [2018] NZCA 523. (Note however that the Lodge Real Estate decision is under appeal to the Supreme Court. *See Lodge Real Estate Ltd v Commerce Commission* [2019] NZSC 28).
485. Commerce Act 1986 s. 30.
486. *Ibid.*, s. 30C(1).

(a) enter into a contract or arrangement, or arrive at an understanding, that contains a cartel provision; or
(b) give effect to a cartel provision.

222. Section 30A provides a definition of 'cartel provision' and related terms. It defines a cartel provision as follows:[487]

> A cartel provision is a provision, contained in a contract, arrangement, or understanding, that has the purpose, effect, or likely effect of 1 or more of the following in relation to the supply or acquisition of goods or services in New Zealand:
>
> (a) price fixing:
> (b) restricting output:
> (c) market allocating.

223. The section then defines each of the terms 'price fixing', 'restricting output' and 'market allocating'.[488] 'Price fixing' is defined as follows:[489]

> In this Act, price fixing means, as between the parties to a contract, arrangement, or understanding, fixing, controlling, or maintaining, or providing for the fixing, controlling, or maintaining of, –
>
> (a) the price for goods or services that any 2 or more parties to the contract, arrangement, or understanding supply or acquire in competition with each other; or
> (b) any discount, allowance, rebate, or credit in relation to goods or services that any 2 or more parties to the contract, arrangement, or understanding supply or acquire in competition with each other.

224. Agreements restricting output are also prohibited under the cartel provisions. Restricting output may be regarded as a means of price fixing, as an agreement on output will generally have the effect of fixing the price. In the Commerce Act, 'restricting output' is defined as:[490]

> In this Act, restricting output means preventing, restricting, or limiting, or providing for the prevention, restriction, or limitation of, –

487. *Ibid.*, s. 30A(1).
488. *Ibid.*, s. 30A(2)–30A(4).
489. *Ibid.*, s. 30A(2).
490. *Ibid.*, s. 30A(3).

(a) the production or likely production by any party to a contract, arrangement, or understanding of goods that any 2 or more of the parties to the contract, arrangement, or understanding supply or acquire in competition with each other; or
(b) the capacity or likely capacity of any party to a contract, arrangement, or understanding to supply services that any 2 or more parties to the contract, arrangement, or understanding supply or acquire in competition with each other; or
(c) the supply or likely supply of goods or services that any 2 or more parties to a contract, arrangement, or understanding supply in competition with each other; or
(d) the acquisition or likely acquisition of goods or services that any 2 or more parties to a contract, arrangement, or understanding acquire in competition with each other.

225. 'Market allocating' is also included in the cartel provision. Market allocation agreements can also be seen as having an effect similar to price fixing, as they eliminate price competition by dividing customers.[491] In the Commerce Act, 'market allocation' is defined as:[492]

> In this Act, market allocating means allocating between any 2 or more parties to a contract, arrangement, or understanding, or providing for such an allocation of, either or both of the following:
>
> (a) the persons or classes of persons to or from whom the parties supply or acquire goods or services in competition with each other;
> (b) the geographic areas in which the parties supply or acquire goods or services in competition with each other.

226. Additional interpretation provisions extend the reach of the cartel prohibition. The definition of parties to an agreement includes interconnected body corporates.[493] Similarly, where the cartel provisions refer to parties supplying or acquiring goods or services in competition with each other, this extends to situations where one or both of the parties' interconnected corporate bodies are in competition with each other.[494] The definition of 'persons in competition with each other for the supply or acquisition of goods or services' also includes a reference to:

i. persons who are, or are likely to be, in competition with each other in relation to the supply or acquisition of those goods or services; and

491. Market allocation is further discussed below at §1. Horizontal agreements, I. Cartels, B Market/Client Allocation.
492. Commerce Act 1986 s. 30A(4).
493. *Ibid.*, s. 30B(a).
494. *Ibid.*, s. 30B(b).

ii. persons who, but for a cartel provision relating to those goods or services, would, or would be likely to, be in competition with each other in relation to the supply or acquisition of those goods or services.[495]

227. The effect of these extensions is that parties to an agreement will be covered by the cartel prohibitions whether the party itself, or one of its interconnected corporate bodies, is a party. In addition, the provisions will apply if the parties themselves are not in competition with each other, but body corporates interconnected with the parties are in competition. They will also apply if the parties are not in competition but are likely to be in competition, or would be in competition but for the effect of the cartel provision.

228. The creation of the new cartel prohibitions was a significant change to the existing cartel legislation. The new provisions continue the pre-existing per se prohibition on price-fixing, but extend it explicitly to restricting output and market allocation. The new provisions provide a much fuller explanation of what constitutes prohibited cartel conduct, reflecting the definition used by the OECD.[496] The new definition extends beyond price fixing to expressly include output restrictions and market allocation agreements, although many of these agreements would have been caught as price fixing agreements under the previous legislation. Nevertheless, the new provision has the potential to be broader than the former per se prohibitions. It means that cartel provisions as defined are per se unlawful without a substantial lessening of competition test, unless they are covered by an exemption or subject to a clearance. In addition, Commerce Act liability extends to attempts to contravene, to aiding, abetting, counselling, procuring, inducing or attempting to induce another person to contravene.[497] Conduct such as attempting to enter into a prohibited agreement will therefore also be covered and give rise to liability.

Exceptions to Cartel Provisions

229. There are new exceptions to the cartel prohibition, replacing the existing, narrower, exceptions to section 30. Where a cartel provision in an agreement is covered by one of these exceptions, the effect is that the cartel prohibitions do not apply,

495. *Ibid.*, s. 30B(c).

496. *See* OECD, *Cartels and Anti-competitive Agreements* http://www.oecd.org/competition/cartels/ (accessed 10 Jul. 2018). The OECD defines a hard core cartel as 'an anticompetitive agreement, anticompetitive concerted practice, or anticompetitive arrangement by competitors to fix prices, make rigged bids (collusive tenders), establish output restrictions or quotas, or share or divide markets by allocating customers, suppliers, territories, or lines of commerce'. The hard core cartel category 'does not include agreements, concerted practices, or arrangements that (i) are reasonably related to the lawful realisation of cost-reducing or output-enhancing efficiencies, (ii) are excluded directly or indirectly from the coverage of a Member country's own laws, or (iii) are authorised in accordance with those laws'. *See* OECD, *Recommendation of the Council concerning Effective Action against Hard Core Cartels* (1998) [C/M(98)7/PROV] [IA(2)] http://www.oecd.org/daf/competition/2350130.pdf (accessed 10 Jul. 2018).

497. Commerce Act 1986 s. 80(1).

but it is still possible for the agreement to be covered by other provisions, particularly the broad prohibition on anti-competitive agreements in section 27.

230. The most important exception is the new exemption for collaborative activity, included to mitigate any risk that section 30 may capture pro-competitive conduct.[498] This exception replaces the existing joint venture exception, but is much wider. Section 31 provides an exception for 'collaborative activity' if, at the time the agreement was entered into or arrived at, or at the time of giving effect to the cartel provision, the parties were involved in a collaborative activity and the cartel provision was reasonably necessary for the purpose of the collaborative activity.[499] The term 'collaborative activity' is defined as follows:[500]

> In this Act, collaborative activity means an enterprise, venture, or other activity, in trade, that –
>
> (a) is carried on in co-operation by 2 or more persons; and
> (b) is not carried on for the dominant purpose of lessening competition between any 2 or more of the parties.

231. This definition of collaborative activity therefore requires two main elements. The first is carrying on an enterprise, venture or other activity in trade, in cooperation. There are no cases on the provisions as yet to provide guidance. However, one commentator has suggested that this could apply to 'consortia, partnerships, strategic alliances, syndicated lending arrangements, lender work-out arrangements for insolvent borrowers, litigation settlement agreements, franchisors and franchisees under a franchise agreement and other kinds of collaborative activity between competitors'.[501] It has also been suggested that it would extend to such activities as 'arrangements for cost sharing and capacity allocation on shared infrastructure, joint buying (buyers clubs), research and development joint ventures, and committees for establishing technology standards'.[502]

232. The Commerce Commission has produced *Competitor Collaboration Guidelines* for the new legislation.[503] In an introduction to the *Competitor Collaboration Guidelines*, the Chair of the Commerce Commission expressed the view that

498. *See* Commerce Commission New Zealand, *The Commerce (Cartels and Other Matters) Amendment Bill Submission to Commerce Select Committee* (4 Sep. 2012) [17].

499. Commerce Act 1986 s. 31.

500. *Ibid.*, s. 31(4).

501. Caron Beaton-Wells 'The Harper Review: Qualified Hope for Australian Competition Law' (2015) 48:4 *Australian Economic Review* 417, 424.

502. John Land and Aaron Schiff, 'Analysing Collaborative Activities' [2014] *New Zealand Law Journal* 230, 230, *See also* John Land, 'Joint Ventures and the Collaborative Activity Exemption' [2014] *New Zealand Law Journal* 190.

503. Commerce Commission New Zealand, *Competitor Collaboration Guidelines* (January 2018). http://www.comcom.govt.nz/business-competition/guidelines-2/competitor-collaboration-guidelines/ (accessed 10 Jul. 2018).

it is reasonable to have exceptions to mitigate any overreach, but that equally the exemptions should not be interpreted in a way that undermines the fundamental per se nature of the cartel prohibition.[504]

233. On the first element of carrying on an enterprise, venture or other activity in trade, in cooperation, the Commerce Commission *Competitor Collaboration Guidelines* specify that the parties must be carrying on a commercial activity in cooperation, and that the parties must be 'combining their businesses, assets or operations in some way in a commercial activity, or otherwise operating a commercial activity jointly'.[505] The *Competitor Collaboration Guidelines* also stated that 'the parties should be able to identify and to explain how they intend to combine their businesses, assets or operations in a commercial activity, or otherwise operate in a commercial activity jointly'.[506] A simple agreement between competitors without the carrying on in cooperation element would not therefore be sufficient on the Commerce Commission's interpretation.

234. The second element of the collaborative activity definition requires that the activity is not carried on for the dominant purpose of lessening competition between any 2 or more of the parties. The requirement here is that it not be for the dominant purpose of lessening competition. Any effect or likely effect of lessening competition is not a consideration. There is therefore no requirement that a defendant show that the collaborative activity will not have the effect or likely effect of lessening competition. Purpose is the only relevant consideration in applying this aspect of the exemption. On one view this is appropriate as section 27 already includes a substantial lessening competition test to which the conduct would be subject if the collaborative activity exemption applies.[507] However on another view, the onus in establishing the exception is on the defendant, whereas under section 27 the onus will be on the plaintiff, an arguably significant difference in the context of a detailed consideration of the application of the test. In relation to determining purpose, the Commerce Commission Competitor Collaboration Guidelines refer to dominant

504. Mark Berry, 'Introduction' in Commerce Commission New Zealand, *Competitor Collaboration Guidelines* (January 2018), 3. http://www.comcom.govt.nz/business-competition/guidelines-2/competitor-collaboration-guidelines/ (accessed 10 Jul. 2018).

505. Commerce Commission New Zealand, *Competitor Collaboration Guidelines* (January 2018). http://www.comcom.govt.nz/business-competition/guidelines-2/competitor-collaboration-guidelines/ (accessed 10 Jul. 2018) 30, at [102]. The Commission refers to *Commerce Commission v. Visy Board Pty Ltd* [2012] NZCA 383.

506. Commerce Commission New Zealand, *Competitor Collaboration Guidelines* (January 2018). http://www.comcom.govt.nz/business-competition/guidelines-2/competitor-collaboration-guidelines/ (accessed 10 Jul. 2018), 31 at [107].

507. Caron Beaton-Wells and Brent Fisse discussed this in their submission on the cartels bill, saying that there is no justification for replacing the limitation with a SLC test: the general prohibition under s 27 already provides a SLC-based safeguard. *See* Caron Beaton-Wells and Brent Fisse, *Submission For The Ministry Of Economic Development (NZ) Commerce (Cartels and Other Matters) Amendment Bill* (1 Aug. 2011), 8. Available from https://www.mbie.govt.nz/business-and-employment/business/competition-regulation-and-policy/reviews-of-the-commerce-act-1986/cartels-and-collaborative-activities-2017/exposure-draft-bill-material-and-submissions-2011/ (accessed 10 May 2019).

purpose as the 'prevailing objective' of the collaborative activity.[508] The Commerce Commission took the view that there was no bright line determining when an objective is the dominant objective.[509] The test for purpose was primarily objective, and in assessing purpose the Commission would look at the parties' conduct and any other relevant circumstance.[510]

235. Under section 31, the parties must not only establish a collaborative activity, but must also show that the cartel provision is reasonably necessary for the purpose of the collaborative activity.[511] The test for reasonably necessary is objective[512] and the provision requires that it be assessed at the time of entering into or giving effect to the contract, arrangement or understanding.[513] The Commerce Commission in its *Competitor Collaboration Guidelines* notes that 'reasonably necessary' does not require that the cartel provision be essential, and a 'but for' test would not apply.[514] A determination of 'reasonably necessary' would require consideration of why the parties have included the cartel provision, consideration of the scope of the provision, and an assessment of other available options.[515] In developing the new provision, consideration was given to introducing an ancillary restraints defence based on the United States jurisprudence. However this option was rejected because of potential uncertainty of scope.[516] The preferred option of a collaborative activity exemption was intended to be 'sufficiently broad to cover both joint ventures and ancillary restraints'.[517] In relation to ancillary restraints it has however been suggested that, although the inquiry is as to whether the provision is 'reasonably necessary' rather than 'necessary' or 'essential', the Commission is

508. Commerce Commission New Zealand, *Competitor Collaboration Guidelines* (January 2018). http://www.comcom.govt.nz/business-competition/guidelines-2/competitor-collaboration-guidelines/ (accessed 10 Jul. 2018) 32, at [110].
509. *Ibid.*, at [115].
510. Commerce Act 1986 s. 31(5). Commerce Commission New Zealand, *Competitor Collaboration Guidelines* (January 2018). http://www.comcom.govt.nz/business-competition/guidelines-2/competitor-collaboration-guidelines/ (accessed 10 Jul. 2018) 32–33, at [113]–[119].
511. Commerce Act 1986 s. 31(1)(b) and s. 31(2)(b).
512. Commerce Commission New Zealand, *Competitor Collaboration Guidelines* (January 2018). http://www.comcom.govt.nz/business-competition/guidelines-2/competitor-collaboration-guidelines/ (accessed 10 Jul. 2018) 34, at [121], referring to *Mana v. Fleming* [2007] NZCA 324.
513. Commerce Act 1986 s. 3(1).
514. Commerce Commission New Zealand, *Competitor Collaboration Guidelines* (January 2018). http://www.comcom.govt.nz/business-competition/guidelines-2/competitor-collaboration-guidelines/ (accessed 10 Jul. 2018) 34, at [124].
515. Commerce Commission New Zealand, *Competitor Collaboration Guidelines* (January 2018). http://www.comcom.govt.nz/business-competition/guidelines-2/competitor-collaboration-guidelines/ (accessed 10 Jul. 2018) 35–36, [128]–[133].
516. Ministry of Economic Development, *Cartel Criminalisation: Exposure Draft Commerce (Cartels and Other Matters) Amendment Bill Explanatory Material* (June 2011) 15 [49]. Available from https://www.mbie.govt.nz/business-and-employment/business/competition-regulation-and-policy/reviews-of-the-commerce-act-1986/cartels-and-collaborative-activities-2017/exposure-draft-bill-material-and-submissions-2011/ (accessed 10 May 2019).
517. Ministry of Economic Development, *Cartel Criminalisation: Exposure Draft Commerce (Cartels and Other Matters) Amendment Bill Explanatory Material* (June 2011) 15 at [46]. Available from https://www.mbie.govt.nz/business-and-employment/business/competition-regulation-and-policy/reviews-of-the-commerce-act-1986/cartels-and-collaborative-activities-2017/exposure-draft-bill-material-and-submissions-2011/ (accessed 10 May 2019).

likely to draw on United States, Canadian and European jurisprudence on the doctrine of ancillary restraints in making these assessments.[518]

236. There are additional exceptions for vertical supply contracts and for joint buying and promotion agreements. The exception for vertical supply contracts provides for an exemption to section 30. It applies to cartel provisions in contracts between supplier and customer that do not have the dominant purpose of lessening competition between any two or more of the parties.[519] Section 32 provides that:

(1) Nothing in section 30 applies to a person in relation to a cartel provision in a contract, if:
  (a) the contract is entered into between a supplier or likely supplier of goods or services and a customer or likely customer of that supplier; and
  (b) the cartel provision –
    (i) relates to the supply or likely supply of the goods or services to the customer or likely customer, including to the maximum price at which the customer or likely customer may resupply the goods or services; and
    (ii) does not have the dominant purpose of lessening competition between any 2 or more of the parties to the contract.
(2) The purpose referred to in subsection (1)(b)(ii) may be inferred from the conduct of any relevant person or from any other relevant circumstance.

237. Section 32 therefore provides for an exception to the section 30 cartel prohibition for contracts between suppliers of goods or services and customers if the cartel provision relates to supply or likely supply of goods or services or to the maximum price at which the customer may resupply the goods or services, and does not have the dominant purpose of lessening competition. This provision excepts vertical supply contracts that might otherwise be caught by the per se prohibition. It includes an exception for maximum resale prices, which the Select Committee believed were pro-competitive.[520]

238. The new cartel legislation also provides for an exception from the price fixing prohibition for joint buying and promotion agreements. Section 33 provides:

A provision in a contract, arrangement or understanding does not have the purpose, effect or likely effect of price fixing if the provision –

(a) relates to the price for goods or services to be collectively acquired, whether directly or indirectly, by some or all of the parties to the contract, arrangement or understanding; or

518. *See* discussion in L Hampton and P Scott *Guide to Competition Law*, (2013) 107.
519. Commerce Act 1986 s. 32.
520. *See also Tru Tone Ltd v. Festival Records Records Marketing Ltd* [1988] 2 NZLR 352.

(b) provides for joint advertising of the price for the resupply of goods or services acquired in accordance with paragraph (a); or
(c) provides for a collective negotiation of the price for goods or services followed by individual purchasing at the collectively negotiated price; or
(d) provides for an intermediary to take title to goods and resell or resupply them to another party to the contract, arrangement or understanding.

239. This exception for joint buying and promotion agreements therefore applies to provisions relating to price for collectively acquired goods, to joint advertising of price for resupply, to collective negotiation of price followed by individual purchasing, or to an agreement that an intermediary take title and resell or resupply to a party to the agreement.[521] The Commerce Commission in its *Competitor Collaboration Guidelines* uses as an example a group of small grocers getting together to collectively purchase a large order of tinned fruit at a volume discount. In this case the exemption may apply if the requirements are met but the grocers must remain free to sell the goods at whatever price they choose.[522]

240. The cartel reform included a new provision reversing the onus of proof in the civil regime where the defendant claims an exception under section 31, 32 or 33. In that situation, it will be for the defendant to prove on the balance of probabilities that the relevant exception applies.[523] This reversal of onus in a civil context is consistent with other areas of civil liability where the defendant has the onus of proving that a defence applies. The Commerce Commission *Competitor Collaboration Guidelines* require that parties must be able to explain why they are collaborating, and must be able to explain that the dominant purpose of their activity is benign or pro-competitive, and that if they cannot persuasively do so, it is highly likely that the Commission or court will infer that the dominant purpose is to lessen competition between the parties.[524] The new provision reversing the onus, as interpreted by the Commerce Commission, will go some way to ensuring that the courts or Commission will consider any evidence of a pro-competitive purpose of the collaboration.

241. Authorisation is not available for cartel provisions. However the 2017 amendments added a new regime of clearances relating to cartel provisions.[525] Under this new regime, the Commerce Commission is required to give a clearance for a proposed contract, arrangement or understanding if the parties are involved in a collaborative activity, the cartel provision is reasonably necessary for the purpose

521. Commerce Act 1986 s. 33.
522. Commerce Commission New Zealand, *Competitor Collaboration Guidelines* (January 2018). http://www.comcom.govt.nz/business-competition/guidelines-2/competitor-collaboration-guidelines/ (accessed 10 Jul. 2018) 26, [88]–[90].
523. Commerce Act 1986 s. 80(2C).
524. Commerce Commission New Zealand, *Competitor Collaboration Guidelines* (January 2018). http://www.comcom.govt.nz/business-competition/guidelines-2/competitor-collaboration-guidelines/ (accessed 10 Jul. 2018) 33, [116].
525. Commerce Act 1986 ss 65A–65D.

of the collaborative activity, and it will not have the effect or likely effect of substantially lessening competition in a market.[526] The effect of a clearance is that the parties do not contravene section 27 or section 30 and the provision may be enforced.[527]

B. Market/Client Allocation

242. Market allocation is explicitly included in the cartel provisions inserted into the Commerce Act 1986 in 2017. In the past, market allocation agreements were subject to the general prohibitions on restrictive agreements, and could be challenged either under the previous per se prohibition on price fixing, or under section 27 in which case they were subject to a substantially lessening competition test.

243. From 15 August 2017, a new cartel regime applied, explicitly covering market allocation agreements. The new cartel provisions prohibit cartel agreements[528] and provide that no cartel provision is enforceable.[529] Section 30 provides that:

> No person may –
>
> (a) enter into a contract or arrangement, or arrive at an understanding, that contains a cartel provision; or
> (b) give effect to a cartel provision.

244. Section 30A provides a definition of 'cartel provision' and related terms. It defines a cartel provision as follows:[530]

> A cartel provision is a provision, contained in a contract, arrangement, or understanding, that has the purpose, effect or likely effect of 1 or more of the following in relation to the supply or acquisition of goods or services in New Zealand:
>
> (a) price fixing:
> (b) restricting output:
> (c) market allocating.

526. *Ibid.*, s. 65A(2).
527. *Ibid.*, s. 65B.
528. *Ibid.*, s. 30.
529. *Ibid.*, s. 30D(1).
530. *Ibid.*, s. 30A(1).

245. The section then defines each of the terms 'price fixing', 'restricting output' and 'market allocating'.[531] In the Commerce Act, 'market allocation' is defined as:[532]

> In this Act, market allocating means allocating between any 2 or more parties to a contract, arrangement, or understanding, or providing for such an allocation of, either or both of the following:
>
> (a) the persons or classes of persons to or from whom the parties supply or acquire goods or services in competition with each other:
>
> (b) the geographic areas in which the parties supply or acquire goods or services in competition with each other.

246. This definition covers both agreements allocating customers and agreements dividing the market by geographic area. In addition, Commerce Act liability extends to attempts to contravene, to aiding, abetting, counselling, procuring, inducing or attempting to induce another person to contravene.[533] Conduct such as attempting to enter into a prohibited market allocation agreement will therefore also be covered and give rise to liability.

247. An example of a customer allocation agreement is the case of *Commerce Commission v. Eli Lilly & Co (NZ) Ltd*.[534] In that case, the two companies that were parties to the agreement, Elanco and Chemstock, were both suppliers of animal remedies. They agreed that Chemstock would not proactively sell to large customers and Elanco would either not sell to smaller customers, or it would do so only at the published price-list which would give Chemstock a competitive edge.[535] The agreement was therefore an agreement to divide the market into large and small customers and the parties acknowledged that it contravened the former price fixing provisions and was therefore prohibited per se.[536] Other cases have involved attempts to divide customers or clients and not to compete in relation to each other's customers.[537] These agreements would now be likely to be expressly covered by the prohibition on market allocating in section 30 and section 30A. There have also been cases involving geographic market allocation agreements. One example is *Commerce Commission v. Christchurch Transport Ltd*[538] in which the parties attempted to form an agreement allocating bus transport routes between them in a

531. *Ibid.*, s. 30A(2)-30A(4).
532. *Ibid.*, s. 30A(4).
533. *Ibid.*, s. 80(1).
534. *Commerce Commission v. Eli Lilly & Co (NZ) Ltd*, High Court, Auckland, CL 19/98, (30 Apr. 1999), Fisher J.
535. *Commerce Commission v. Eli Lilly & Co (NZ) Ltd*, High Court, Auckland, CL 19/98, (30 Apr. 1999), Fisher J, 1.
536. *Commerce Commission v. Eli Lilly & Co (NZ) Ltd*, High Court, Auckland, CL 19/98, (30 Apr. 1999), Fisher J, 2.
537. *See* for example *Commerce Commission v. Enviro Waste Services Ltd* [2015] NZHC 2936.
538. *Commerce Commission v. Christchurch Transport Ltd*, High Court, Christchurch CP72/98, (21 Aug. 1998), Panckhurst J.

tender process. This conduct was held to be an attempt to form an agreement in contravention of the then price fixing prohibition, but could now be covered by the express prohibition on market allocation.

248. The definition of market allocation will also cover bid rigging, in which parties competing for tenders agree to allocate the market between them. Before the amendments of 2017, market allocating agreements, including cases of bid rigging, had to be brought as price fixing cases. Examples include *Commerce Commission v. Roadmarkers Waikato (1981) Ltd.*[539] In that case an attempt was made to rig a tender for road marking services, and it was acknowledged that this amounted to an attempt to fix prices in contravention of the then section 30.[540]

249. As is the case with price fixing, additional interpretation provisions extend the reach of the cartel prohibition on market allocation. The definition of parties to an agreement includes interconnected body corporates.[541] Similarly, the definition of market allocation refers to the parties supplying or acquiring goods or services in competition with each other. Under section 30B this extends to situations where one or both of the parties' interconnected corporate bodies are in competition with each other.[542] The definition of 'persons in competition with each other for the supply or acquisition of goods or services' also includes a reference to:

i. persons who are, or are likely to be, in competition with each other in relation to the supply or acquisition of those goods or services; and
ii. persons who, but for a cartel provision relating to those goods or services, would, or would be likely to, be in competition with each other in relation to the supply or acquisition of those goods or services.[543]

250. The effect of these extensions is that parties to an agreement will be covered by the prohibition on market allocation whether the party itself, or one of its interconnected corporate bodies, is a party. In addition, the prohibition will apply if the parties themselves are not in competition with each other, but body corporates interconnected with the parties are in competition. They will also apply if the parties are not in competition but are likely to be in competition, or would be in competition but for the effect of the provision.

539. *Commerce Commission v. Roadmarkers Waikato (1981) Ltd*, High Court, Auckland, CL 1/97, (25 Jun. 1998), Elias J.
540. *Commerce Commission v. Roadmarkers Waikato (1981) Ltd*, High Court, Auckland, CL 1/97, (25 Jun. 1998), Elias J, 4.
541. Commerce Act 1986 s. 30B(a).
542. *Ibid.*, s. 30B(b).
543. *Ibid.*, s. 30B(c).

251. The exceptions to the cartel prohibition[544] also apply to market allocation agreements. These exceptions are for collaborative activity,[545] vertical supply contracts[546] and for joint buying and promotion agreements.[547] Where a cartel provision in an agreement is covered by one of these exceptions, the effect is that the cartel prohibitions do not apply, but it is still possible for the agreement to be covered by other provisions, particularly the broad prohibition on anti-competitive agreements in section 27.

C. Production/Innovation Limitation

252. Agreements containing production or innovation limitations would be assessed under either the per se cartel provisions in sections 30–33, or under the general prohibition in section 27, in which case a substantial lessening of competition test applies. The cartel provisions, in force from 15 August 2017, now include an express prohibition on output agreements.

253. The cartel provisions prohibit cartel agreements[548] and provide that no cartel provision is enforceable.[549] Sections 30 and 30A are the relevant provisions, and provisions 'restricting output' are covered.

254. In the Commerce Act, 'restricting output' is defined as follows:[550]

> In this Act, restricting output means preventing, restricting, or limiting, or providing for the prevention, restriction or limitation of, –
>
> (a) the production or likely production by any party to a contract, arrangement, or understanding of goods that any 2 or more of the parties to the contract, arrangement, or understanding supply or acquire in competition with each other; or
> (b) the capacity or likely capacity of any party to a contract, arrangement, or understanding to supply services that any 2 or more parties to the contract, arrangement, or understanding supply or acquire in competition with each other; or
> (c) the supply or likely supply of goods or services that any 2 or more parties to a contract, arrangement, or understanding supply in competition with each other; or
> (d) the acquisition or likely acquisition of goods or services that any 2 or more parties to a contract, arrangement, or understanding acquire in competition with each other.

544. Discussed under 'A. Price Fixing' above.
545. Commerce Act 1986 s. 31.
546. *Ibid.*, s. 32.
547. *Ibid.*, s. 33.
548. *Ibid.*, s. 30.
549. *Ibid.*, s. 30C(1).
550. *Ibid.*, s. 30A(3).

255. Agreements limiting production are therefore expressly included, as are agreements on supply or acquisition of goods or services. Agreements restricting output can also be regarded as a means of price fixing, as an agreement on output will generally have the effect of fixing the price. Agreements limiting innovation are not expressly included under the cartel provision and are not clearly covered by price fixing. Such agreements may fall to be assessed under section 27, unless they also constitute price fixing, restricting output or market allocation.

256. As is the case with price fixing, additional interpretation provisions extend the reach of the cartel prohibition on restricting output. The definition of parties to an agreement includes interconnected body corporates.[551] Similarly, the definition of restricting output refers to the parties supplying or acquiring goods or services in competition with each other. Under section 30B this extends to situations where one or both of the parties' interconnected corporate bodies are in competition with each other.[552] The definition of 'persons in competition with each other for the supply or acquisition of goods or services' also includes a reference to:

i. persons who are, or are likely to be, in competition with each other in relation to the supply or acquisition of those goods or services; and
ii. persons who, but for a cartel provision relating to those goods or services, would or would be likely to, be in competition with each other in relation to the supply or acquisition of those goods or services.[553]

257. The effect of these extensions is that parties to an agreement will be covered by the prohibition on restricting output whether the party itself, or one of its interconnected corporate bodies, is a party. In addition, the prohibition will apply if the parties themselves are not in competition with each other, but body corporates interconnected with the parties are in competition. They will also apply if the parties are not in competition but are likely to be in competition, or would be in competition but for the effect of the provision.

258. The exceptions to the cartel prohibition[554] also apply to agreements restricting output. These exceptions are for collaborative activity,[555] vertical supply contracts[556] and for joint buying and promotion agreements.[557] Where a cartel provision in an agreement is covered by one of these exceptions, the effect is that the cartel prohibitions do not apply, but it is still possible for the agreement to be covered by other provisions, particularly the broad prohibition on anti-competitive agreements in section 27.

551. *Ibid.*, s. 30B(a).
552. *Ibid.*, s. 30B(b).
553. *Ibid.*, s. 30B(c).
554. Discussed under 'A. Price Fixing' above.
555. *Ibid.*, s. 31.
556. *Ibid.*, s. 32.
557. *Ibid.*, s. 33.

D. Group Boycott

259. New Zealand competition law no longer contains a specific provision applying to collective or group boycotts. Until August 2017, section 29 prohibited contracts, arrangements or understandings containing exclusionary provisions, but the section was repealed on 15 August 2017. Group boycotts now fall to be assessed under section 27, applying a substantial lessening of competition test.[558]

E. Collusion on Other Objects

260. The New Zealand Commerce Act does not include additional provisions applying to collusion. Horizontal collusive agreements will be assessed under either the cartel provisions in section 30 or the provisions applying to practices substantially lessening competition in sections 27 and 28.

II. Information Exchange Practices

261. There are no provisions in the Commerce Act 1986 specifically targeted at information exchange practices. Such practices will be subject to assessment under either the cartel provisions or the provisions applying to practices substantially lessening competition in sections 27 and 28.

262. Simple information exchange will not automatically contravene competition law. Establishment of a contract, arrangement or understanding is necessary before contravention can be established. An arrangement or understanding may be found where there is evidence of information sharing, especially if the information shared relates to price, output and tendering processes or might constitute market allocation. In such situations, evidence of information sharing combined with other evidence suggesting collusive conduct may lead a court to find that an arrangement or understanding exists. An example of this can be seen in the case of *Commerce Commission v. Caltex New Zealand Ltd*, in which the Commerce Commission relied on inferences to be drawn from facts to establish the existence of an arrangement or understanding between petrol companies.[559] The petrol companies had all run a promotion in which customers received a free car wash when they bought NZD 20 worth of petrol, and they had all ceased the promotion on the same day. The court found an understanding based on ten factors, one of which was the fact that the intentions of one of the companies had been signalled to another. Other factors included opportunities for discussion, incentive to cease the promotion but a disincentive to move unilaterally, and the fact that all ceased the promotion on the same day.[560]

558. *See* discussion of the s. 27 prohibition at §1. Horizontal Agreements above.
559. *Commerce Commission v. Caltex New Zealand Ltd* (1999) 9 TCLR 305.
560. *Commerce Commission v. Caltex New Zealand Ltd* (1999) 9 TCLR 305, 324.

263. Sharing or exchange of information may therefore be a factor in finding the existence of an arrangement or understanding, if combined with other evidence of collusion. If the arrangement or understanding contains a cartel provision as defined, then it will be covered by the cartel provisions, (which are discussed in detail above under the heading 'Cartels').[561] It will constitute a cartel provision if it has the purpose, effect or likely effect of price fixing, restricting output or market allocating, as defined, in relation to the supply or acquisition of goods or services in New Zealand by parties in competition with each other. [562] The parties will then potentially contravene the cartel provisions. Ancillary liability is also a possibility, attempts to form such an understanding can also contravene.[563] Exceptions to the cartel prohibition[564] may apply to information sharing practices in some circumstances. These exceptions are for collaborative activity,[565] vertical supply contracts[566] and for joint buying and promotion agreements.[567] Where a cartel provision in an agreement is covered by one of these exceptions, the effect is that the cartel prohibitions do not apply, but it is still possible for the agreement to be covered by other provisions, particularly the broad prohibition on anti-competitive agreements in section 27.

264. Section 27 may also be applied to information exchange practices. If an arrangement or understanding is found to exist, it will then be for a court to assess whether that arrangement or understanding has the purpose, effect or likely effect of substantially lessening competition in a market.[568] Attempts to enter into an agreement or arrive at an understanding will also give rise to liability.[569]

III. Cooperation Agreements

265. Horizontal cooperation agreements are also subject to examination under the cartel provisions or under sections 27 and 28 which are the provisions applying to practices substantially lessening competition. If the per se cartel provisions apply, then an agreement will contravene unless it can be shown that an exception applies. If an exception does apply, the cartel provisions are not contravened, but the agreement may still contravene section 27 or section 28.

Cartel provisions

561. *See* above under '§1. Horizontal agreements: I. Cartels'.
562. Commerce Act 1986 ss 30 and 30A.
563. *Ibid.*, s. 80(1)(b).
564. Discussed under 'A. Price Fixing' above.
565. Commerce Act 1986 s. 31.
566. *Ibid.*, s. 32.
567. *Ibid.*, s. 33.
568. *Ibid.*, s. 27. There is a detailed discussion of the requirements of s. 27 above under '§1. Horizontal agreements'.
569. *Ibid.*, s. 80(1)(b).

266. A cooperation agreement is very likely to be found to constitute a contract, arrangement or understanding, proof is unlikely to be an issue. If the agreement contains a cartel provision as defined, then it will be covered by the cartel provisions.[570] It will constitute a cartel provision if it has the purpose, effect or likely effect of price fixing, restricting output or market allocating, as defined, in relation to the supply or acquisition of goods or services in New Zealand by parties in competition with each other. [571] The parties will then potentially contravene the cartel provisions. Ancillary liability is also a possibility, attempts to form such an understanding can also contravene.[572] Exceptions to the cartel prohibition[573] may apply to cooperation agreements in some circumstances. These exceptions are for collaborative activity,[574] vertical supply contracts[575] and for joint buying and promotion agreements.[576] Where a cartel provision in an agreement is covered by one of these exceptions, the effect is that the cartel prohibitions do not apply, but it is still possible for the agreement to be covered by other provisions, particularly the broad prohibition on anti-competitive agreements in section 27.

267. Application of the cartel exceptions will depend upon the nature of the cooperation agreement.[577] There is certainly potential for the section 31 collaborative activity exception to apply. This exception will apply to joint venture agreements but is much wider.

268. Cooperation agreements can be expected to qualify as 'collaborative activity' as defined. This definition of collaborative activity therefore requires two main elements. The first is carrying on an enterprise, venture or other activity in trade, in cooperation. The second element of the collaborative activity definition requires that the activity is not carried on for the dominant purpose of lessening competition between any 2 or more of the parties. The requirement here is that it not be for the dominant purpose of lessening competition. Any effect or likely effect of lessening competition is not a consideration. There is therefore no requirement that a defendant show that the collaborative activity will not have the effect or likely effect of lessening competition. Purpose is the only relevant consideration in applying this aspect of the exception.

269. Under section 31, the parties must not only establish a collaborative activity, but must also show that the cartel provision is reasonably necessary for the purpose of the collaborative activity.[578] The test is objective and the provision requires

570. *See* above under '§1. Horizontal agreements: I. Cartels'.
571. Commerce Act 1986 ss 30 and 30A.
572. *Ibid.*, 80(1)(b).
573. Discussed under 'A. Price Fixing' above.
574. Commerce Act 1986 s. 31.
575. *Ibid.*, s. 32.
576. *Ibid.*, s. 33.
577. The exceptions to the cartel provisions are discussed in detail above under '§1. Horizontal agreements: I. Cartels'.
578. Commerce Act 1986 s. 31(1)(b) and s. 31(2)(b).

that it be assessed at the time of entering into the contract, arrangement or understanding.[579] Parties to a cooperation agreement would have to show that the cartel provision was reasonably necessary for the purpose of their collaborative activity, and this may pose difficulties in some situations.

270. There is also an exception for vertical supply contracts, and this may apply to some cooperation agreements. Vertical agreements typically do not constitute cartel provisions. However, the cartel provisions may apply where there is also a horizontal element, for example where one or more parties operate at different supply chain levels. In such cases, the exception for vertical supply contracts may exempt the parties from liability under the cartel provisions. Section 32 provides that:

> (1) Nothing in section 30 applies to a person in relation to a cartel provision in a contract, if:
> (a) the contract is entered into between a supplier or likely supplier of goods or services and a customer or likely customer of that supplier; and
> (b) the cartel provision –
> (i) relates to the supply or likely supply of the goods or services to the customer or likely customer, including to the maximum price at which the customer or likely customer may resupply the goods or services; and
> (ii) does not have the dominant purpose of lessening competition between any 2 or more of the parties to the contract.
>
> (2) The purpose referred to in subsection (1)(b)(ii) may be inferred from the conduct of any relevant person or from any other relevant circumstance.

271. Section 32 therefore provides for an exception to the section 30 cartel prohibition for contracts between suppliers of goods or services and customers if the cartel provision relates to supply or likely supply of goods or services or to the maximum price at which the customer may resupply the goods or services, and does not have the dominant purpose of lessening competition. This provision exempts vertical supply contracts that might otherwise be caught by the per se prohibition. It includes an exception for maximum resale prices. The exception does not cover arrangements or understandings. The agreement must constitute a contract, and contain a cartel provision. The onus is on the parties to the contract to prove that the exception applies, on the balance of probabilities.[580]

272. There is also an exception from the cartel provisions for joint buying and promotion agreements. Section 33 provides:

> A provision in a contract, arrangement, or understanding does not have the purpose, effect or likely effect of price fixing if the provision –

579. *Ibid.*, s. 3(1).
580. *Ibid.*, s. 80(2C).

(a) relates to the price for goods or services to be collectively acquired, whether directly or indirectly, by some or all of the parties to the contract, arrangement, or understanding; or
(b) provides for joint advertising of the price for the resupply of goods or services acquired in accordance with paragraph (a); or
(c) provides for a collective negotiation of the price for goods or services followed by individual purchasing at the collectively negotiated price; or
(d) provides for an intermediary to take title to goods and resell or resupply them to another party to the contract, arrangement, or understanding.

273. This exception for joint buying and promotion agreements potentially applies to a range of cooperation agreements. It applies to provisions relating to price for collectively acquired goods, to joint advertising of price for resupply, to collective negotiation of price followed by individual purchasing, or to an agreement that an intermediary take title and resell or resupply to a party to the agreement.[581] It covers not only contracts, but also arrangements and understandings. The onus is on the defendant to prove that the exception applies, on the balance of probabilities.[582]

274. Parties to a cooperation agreement to which the cartel provisions apply cannot seek authorisation of that agreement but may apply for a clearance. Authorisation is not available for cartel provisions but the 2017 amendments added a new regime of clearances for cartel provisions.[583] Under this new regime, the Commerce Commission is required to give a clearance for a proposed contract, arrangement or understanding if the parties are involved in a collaborative activity, the cartel provision is reasonably necessary for the purpose of the collaborative activity, and it will not have the effect or likely effect of substantially lessening competition in a market.[584] The effect of a clearance is that the parties do not contravene section 27 or section 30 and the provision may be enforced.[585]

Section 27

275. Horizontal cooperation agreements are also subject to examination under sections 27 and 28 which are the provisions applying to practices substantially lessening competition.[586] If the per se cartel provisions apply, then an agreement will contravene unless it can be shown that an exception applies. If an exception does apply, the cartel provisions are not contravened, but the agreement may still contravene section 27 or section 28.

581. *Ibid.*, s. 33.
582. *Ibid.*, s. 80(2C).
583. *Ibid.*, ss 65A-65D.
584. *Ibid.*, s. 65A(2).
585. *Ibid.*, s. 65B.
586. These provisions are discussed in detail above under '§1. Horizontal agreements: I. Cartels'.

276. The general prohibition on anti-competitive agreements employs a substantial lessening of competition test, prohibiting agreements that have the purpose, effect or likely effect of substantially lessening competition in a market.[587] Section 27 provides that:

> (1) No person shall enter into a contract or arrangement, or arrive at an understanding, containing a provision that has the purpose, or has or is likely to have the effect, of substantially lessening competition in a market.
> (2) No person shall give effect to a provision of a contract, arrangement, or understanding that has the purpose, or has or is likely to have the effect, of substantially lessening competition in a market.

277. Section 27 applies to agreements made before or after the commencement of the Act.[588] It also provides that no provision of a contract, whether made before or after the commencement of the Act, that has the purpose, or has or is likely to have the effect, of substantially lessening competition in a market is enforceable.[589] The phrase 'give effect to' used in section 27(2) in relation to a provision of a contract, arrangement or understanding includes doing an act or thing in pursuance of or in accordance with that provision and enforcing or purporting to enforce that provision.[590]

278. Section 28 is a similar provisions to section 27, but applying to covenants. Section 28(1) provides that:

> No person, either on his own or on behalf of an associated person, shall
>
> (a) require the giving of a covenant; or
> (b) give a covenant
>
> that has the purpose, or has or is likely to have the effect, of substantially lessening competition in a market.[591]

279. Carrying out or enforcing such a covenant is also prohibited.[592] The provisions apply to covenants whether given before or after the commencement of the Act.[593]

280. Sections 27 and 28 are very broad, they cover horizontal and vertical agreements, there is no requirement that the parties to the agreement are in competition with each other, and the effect may take place in any market, not necessarily the

---

587. *Ibid.*, s. 27.
588. *Ibid.*, s. 27(3).
589. *Ibid.*, s. 27(4).
590. *Ibid.*, s. 2(1).
591. *Ibid.*, s. 28(1).
592. *Ibid.*, s. 28(2).
593. *Ibid.*, s. 28(3).

market in which the parties to the agreement compete. However liability is not per se, it requires a rule of reason-style analysis with evidence of purpose, effect or likely effect of substantially lessening competition in a market.

281. A cooperation agreement will contravene section 27 if it is shown to constitute a contract, arrangement or understanding containing a provisions that has the purpose, effect or likely effect of substantially lessening competition in a market. There is obvious potential for this to cover a range of possible agreements.

A. *Research and Development*

282. Research and development cooperation agreements will be subject to the provisions discussed above. If the agreement contains a cartel provision as defined, the exception for collaborative activity is likely to apply if the agreement is genuinely for research and development. If the agreement does not contain a cartel provision, or if it does, but the collaborative activity exception applies, then the agreement may still require assessment under section 27.

B. *Specialisation*

283. Joint ventures allowing for specialisation will be regulated as with other cooperation agreements. If they contravene the cartel prohibitions they will be illegal per se unless an exception applies.

284. Joint ventures allowing for specialisation will also be subject to a competition assessment under section 27.

C. *Standardisation*

285. Joint ventures for industry standardisation will also be regulated under the cartel provisions and under section 27, as discussed above.

D. *Joint Production*

286. Cooperation agreements for joint production will also be regulated under the cartel provisions and section 27. The exception for collaborative activity may apply to agreements allowing for joint production. Parties relying on the exception would need to show that they were involved in a joint commercial activity satisfying the definition of collaborative activity.[594] They would also need to show that the

594. *Ibid.*, s. 31(4).

activity is not carried on for the dominant purpose of lessening competition,[595] and that the cartel provision is reasonably necessary for the purpose of the collaborative activity.[596]

E. Joint Purchasing

287. Cooperation agreements for joint purchasing will also be regulated under the cartel provisions and section 27. There is an exception to the cartel provisions for joint buying and promotion, although it only applies to price-fixing and not to other forms of cartel provision. Section 33 provides:

> A provision in a contract, arrangement or understanding does not have the purpose, effect or likely effect of price fixing if the provision –
>
> (a) relates to the price for goods or services to be collectively acquired, whether directly or indirectly, by some or all of the parties to the contract, arrangement, or understanding; or
> (b) provides for joint advertising of the price for the resupply of goods or services acquired in accordance with paragraph (a); or
> (c) provides for a collective negotiation of the price for goods or services followed by individual purchasing at the collectively negotiated price; or
> (d) provides for an intermediary to take title to goods and resell or resupply them to another party to the contract, arrangement, or understanding.

288. This exception for joint buying and promotion agreements therefore potentially applies to a range of cooperation agreements. It applies to provisions relating to price for collectively acquired goods, to joint advertising of price for resupply, to collective negotiation of price followed by individual purchasing, or to an agreement that an intermediary take title and resell or resupply to a party to the agreement.[597] It covers not only contracts, but also arrangements and understandings. The onus is on the defendant to prove that the exception applies, on the balance of probabilities.[598]

---

595. Commerce Act 1986 s. 31(4). In relation to parties not having the dominant purpose, the Commerce Commission gives an example of two computer manufacturers with different capabilities and resources combining to offer more affordable computer products. *See* Commerce Commission New Zealand, *Competitor Collaboration Guidelines* (January 2018), http://www.comcom.govt.nz/business-competition/guidelines-2/competitor-collaboration-guidelines/ (accessed 10 Jul. 2018) 33, [117].
596. Commerce Act 1986 s. 31(1)(b) and s. 31(2)(b).
597. Commerce Act 1986 s. 33. In its *Guidelines*, the Commerce Commission gives examples of joint buying that would and would not be covered by the exception. *See* Commerce Commission New Zealand, *Competitor Collaboration Guidelines* (January 2018). http://www.comcom.govt.nz/business-competition/guidelines-2/competitor-collaboration-guidelines/ (accessed 10 Jul. 2018) 27, [92].
598. Commerce Act 1986 s. 80(2C).

289. Because the exception in section 33 only applies to price-fixing, a joint purchasing agreement that is covered by section 33 may still contravene the cartel provisions if, for example, it also constitutes market allocation and the collaborative activity exception does not apply. Also, if it is exempted under section 33, it will still be subject to substantial lessening of competition assessment under section 27.

F. Joint Selling

290. Cooperation agreements for joint selling will also be regulated under the cartel provisions and section 27. The cartel provisions may apply to a joint selling agreement, however the exception for collaborative activity may apply.[599]

§2. Vertical Agreements

291. New Zealand competition law applies to vertical agreements as well as horizontal agreements.

Sections 27 and 28

292. The broadest provisions applying to vertical agreements are in sections 27 and 28.[600] Section 27 is a broad general prohibition on contracts, arrangements or understandings containing provisions that have the purpose, effect or likely effect of substantially lessening competition.[601] Section 28 is a similar provisions to section 28, but applying to covenants. Both employ a substantial lessening of competition test, prohibiting agreements that have the purpose, effect or likely effect of substantially lessening competition in a market.[602] Section 27 provides that:

> (1) No person shall enter into a contract or arrangement, or arrive at an understanding, containing a provision that has the purpose, or has or is likely to have the effect, of substantially lessening competition in a market.
> (2) No person shall give effect to a provision of a contract, arrangement, or understanding that has the purpose, or has or is likely to have the effect, of substantially lessening competition in a market.

293. Section 27 applies to agreements made before or after the commencement of the Act.[603] It also provides that no provision of a contract, whether made before

599. The Commerce Commission gives an example of how the s. 31 exception might apply to joint selling. *See* Commerce Commission New Zealand, *Competitor Collaboration Guidelines* (January 2018). http://www.comcom.govt.nz/business-competition/guidelines-2/competitor-collaboration-guidelines/ (accessed 10 Jul. 2018) 37, [135].
600. Sections 27 and 28 are discussed above under §1. Horizontal agreements.
601. Commerce Act 1986 s. 27.
602. *Ibid.*, s. 27.
603. *Ibid.*, s. 27(3).

or after the commencement of the Act, that has the purpose, or has or is likely to have the effect, of substantially lessening competition in a market is enforceable.[604] The phrase 'give effect to' used in section 27(2) in relation to a provision of a contract, arrangement, or understanding includes doing an act or thing in pursuance of or in accordance with that provision and enforcing or purporting to enforce that provision.[605]

294. Section 28 is a similar provisions to section 28, but applying to covenants. Section 28 provides that:[606]

> (1) No person, either on his own or on behalf of an associated person, shall –
> (a) require the giving of a covenant; or
> (b) give a covenant –
> that has the purpose, or has or is likely to have the effect, of substantially lessening competition in a market.
> (2) No person, either on his own or on behalf of an associated person, shall carry out or enforce the terms of a covenant that has the purpose, or has or is likely to have the effect, of substantially lessening competition in a market.

295. Section 28 applies to covenants given before or after the commencement of the Act.[607] There is an additional deeming provision that effectively extends the meaning of requiring the giving of the covenant to cover an invitation to enter into a contract containing a covenant, offering to enter into a contract containing a covenant, or making it known that the person will not enter into a contract of a particular kind unless the contract contains a covenant of a particular kind or in particular terms.[608] It also provides that no covenant, whether given before or after the commencement of the Act, that has the purpose, or has or is likely to have the effect of substantially lessening competition in a market is enforceable.[609] Additional provisions extend this to threatening to engage or engaging in conduct because a person has not complied or fails to comply with the terms of the covenant.[610] There is also an additional provision extending the interpretation of 'associated person'.[611]

296. These provisions are very broad, they cover horizontal and vertical agreements, there is no requirement that the parties to the agreement are in competition with each other, and the effect may take place in any market, not necessarily the

604. *Ibid.*, s. 27(4).
605. *Ibid.*, s. 2(1).
606. *Ibid.*, s. 28(1)–(2).
607. *Ibid.*, s. 28(3).
608. *Ibid.*, s. 28(6).
609. *Ibid.*, s. 28(4).
610. *Ibid.*, s. 28(5).
611. *Ibid.*, s. 28(7).

market in which the parties to the agreement compete. However liability is not per se, it requires evidence of purpose, effect or likely effect of substantially lessening competition in a market.

297. An action under section 27 requires establishing three key elements. These are:

(1) The existence of a contract, arrangement or understanding.
(2) Market definition.
(3) Purpose, effect or likely effect of substantially lessening of competition in a market.

Resale price maintenance

298. In addition to the general prohibitions in section 27 and 28, the Commerce Act also contains a specific regime prohibiting resale price maintenance. In New Zealand competition law, resale price maintenance applies to goods and not to services. Resale price maintenance is per se unlawful, meaning that it is prohibited without a need to establish a purpose, effect or likely effect of substantially lessening competition in a market.[612] The prohibition applies to resale price maintenance by suppliers[613] and resale price maintenance by others.[614] Recommended prices are permitted so long as they are not enforced.[615]

299. The statutory regime prohibiting resale price maintenance is detailed. The regime first establishes that resale price maintenance by suppliers is prohibited. Section 37 provides as follows:[616]

> 37 Resale price maintenance by suppliers prohibited
>
> (1) No person shall engage in the practice of resale price maintenance.
> (2) For the purposes of this section, a person engages in the practice of resale price maintenance if that person (in this section referred to as the supplier) does any of the acts referred to in subsection
> (3) The acts referred to for the purposes of subsection (2) are
>   (a) the supplier making it known to another person that the supplier will not supply goods to the other person unless the other person agrees not to sell those goods at a price less than a price specified by the supplier:
>   (b) the supplier inducing, or attempting to induce, another person not to sell, at a price less than a price specified by the supplier, goods supplied to the other person by the supplier or by a third person who, directly or indirectly, has obtained the goods from the supplier:

612. *Ibid.*, ss 37–42.
613. *Ibid.*, s. 37.
614. *Ibid.*, s. 38.
615. *Ibid.*, s. 39.
616. *Ibid.*, s. 37.

(c) the supplier entering or offering to enter into an agreement, for the supply of goods to another person, where one of the terms is or would be that the other person will not sell the goods at a price less than a price specified, or that would be specified, by the supplier:

(d) the supplier withholding the supply of goods to another person for the reason that the other person

(i) has not agreed to the condition mentioned in paragraph (a); or

(ii) has sold, or is likely to sell, goods supplied to him by the supplier, or goods supplied to him by a third person who, directly or indirectly, has obtained the goods from the supplier, at a price less than a price specified by the supplier as the price below which the goods are not to be sold:

(e) the supplier withholding the supply of goods to another person for the reason that a third person who, directly or indirectly, has obtained, or wishes to obtain, goods from the other person

(i) has not agreed not to sell those goods at a price less than a price specified by the supplier; or

(ii) has sold or is likely to sell goods supplied or to be supplied to that third person, by the other person, at a price less than a price specified by the supplier as the price below which the goods are not to be sold.

(4) For the purposes of subsection (3),

(a) where the supplier makes it known, in respect of any goods, that the price below which those goods are not to be sold is a price specified by another person in respect of those goods, or in respect of goods of a like description, that price shall be deemed to have been specified, in respect of the first-mentioned goods, by the supplier:

(b) where a set form, method, or formula is specified by or on behalf of the supplier and a price may be ascertained by calculation from, or by reference to, that set form, method, or formula, that price shall be deemed to have been specified by the supplier:

(c) where the supplier makes it known, in respect of any goods, that the price below which those goods are not to be sold is a price ascertained by calculation from or by reference to a set form, method, or formula specified by another person in respect of those goods, or in respect of goods of a like description, that price shall be deemed to have been specified, in respect of the first-mentioned goods, by the supplier:

(d) where the supplier makes a statement to another person of a price that is likely to be understood by that person as the price below which goods are not to be sold, that price shall be deemed to have been specified by the supplier as the price below which the goods are not to be sold:

(e) anything done by a person acting on behalf of, or by arrangement with, the supplier shall be deemed to have been done by the supplier.

(5) For the purposes of this section, sale includes advertise for sale, display for sale, and offer for sale, and sell, selling, and sold have corresponding meanings.

300. In summary, section 37 defines and prohibits resale price maintenance by suppliers.[617] A key concept in the provisions is 'specified price'. If there is no specified price then a supplier is free to refuse supply. Section 39 provides that prices may be recommended.[618] A supplier can refuse supply if there is a recommended price, provided that the recommended price does not become a specified price. Section 37(4) sets out circumstances in which a price shall be deemed to be a specified price.[619]

301. Resale price maintenance as defined includes withholding the supply of goods for the reason that the person has not agreed to the specified price, or has sold or is likely to sell at a price below the specified price.[620] There is no general obligation to supply, but withholding supply will be a contravention if it is for a resale price maintenance reason. The reason can be one of a number of reasons so long as it is a substantial reason.[621] Section 40 deems a number of things to be withholding supply.[622] These include refusing or failing to supply, refusing to supply except on disadvantageous terms, supply with less favourable treatment, and causing or procuring another person to withhold supply.[623] 'Supply' is defined in section 2 to include, in relation to goods, 'supply (or resupply) by way of gift, sale, exchange, lease, hire, or hire purchase'.[624] Genuine agency transactions will not be covered. There is an evidentiary provision in section 42 which provides for circumstances in which there will be a presumption that supply has been withheld for a resale price maintenance reason.[625]

302. In addition to the provisions applying to resale price maintenance by suppliers, there are also provisions prohibiting resale price maintenance by others.[626] Section 38 provides:

> Resale price maintenance by others prohibited
>
> (1) No person (in this section referred to as the third party) shall
>
> (a) make it known to another person that the third party proposes to engage in conduct, whether alone or in concert with any other person, that will hinder or prevent the supply of any goods to, or the acquisition of any goods from, that person unless that person agrees not to sell those goods at a price less than the price specified by the third party; or

617. *Ibid.*, s. 37. *See also Commerce Commission v. Hewlett Packard* (1993) 5 TCLR 136, *Commerce Commission v. Aquanaut Pty Ltd* HC Auckland (CIV 2002 404 1562) 18 June 2004.
618. Commerce Act 1986 s. 39.
619. *Ibid.*, s. 37(4).
620. *Ibid.*, s. 37(3)(d) and (e).
621. *Ibid.*, s. 2(5).
622. *Ibid.*, s. 40.
623. *Ibid.*, s. 40(a)–(d).
624. *Ibid.*, s. 2.
625. *Ibid.*, s. 42.
626. *Ibid.*, ss 38 and 42.

(b) engage in conduct, whether alone or in concert with any other person, that will hinder or prevent the supply of goods to, or the acquisition of goods from, another person for the purpose of inducing that person not to sell those goods at a price less than a price specified by the third party.

(2) For the purposes of subsection (1),

(a) where the third party makes it known, in respect of any goods, that the price below which those goods are not to be sold is a price specified by another person in respect of those goods, or in respect of goods of a like description, that price shall be deemed to have been specified in respect of the first-mentioned goods, by the third party:

(b) where a set form, method, or formula is specified by or on behalf of the third party and a price may be ascertained by calculation from, or by reference to, that set form, method, or formula, that price shall be deemed to have been specified by the third party:

(c) where the third party makes it known, in respect of any goods, that the price below which those goods are not to be sold is a price ascertained by calculation from or by reference to a set form, method, or formula specified by another person in respect of those goods, or in respect of goods of a like description, that price shall be deemed to have been specified, in respect of the first-mentioned goods, by the third party:

(d) where the third party makes a statement to another person of a price that is likely to be understood by that person as the price below which goods are not to be sold, that price shall be deemed to have been specified by the third party as the price below which the goods are not to be sold:

(e) anything done by a person acting on behalf of, or by arrangement with, the third party shall be deemed to have been done by the third party.

(3) For the purposes of this section sale includes advertise for sale, display for sale and offer for sale, and sell, selling, and sold have corresponding meanings.

303. Section 38 therefore applies to resale price maintenance conduct by third parties and makes such conduct illegal per se.[627] Section 41 is also applicable. Section 41 provides for circumstances in which the supply of goods or acquisition of goods is deemed to be prevented.[628] The section deems supply or acquisition to be prevented if it is refused except on disadvantageous or less favourable terms.

304. In summary, vertical agreements for resale price maintenance by suppliers are per se unlawful in New Zealand competition law. Resale price maintenance by third parties is also per se unlawful. It applies to conduct in which a minimum price for resale is specified, it does not cover maximum prices, although these may contravene other provisions. Resale price maintenance in New Zealand also applies

---

627. *See also Ibid.*, s. 2 which widens the references to conduct.
628. *Ibid.*, s. 41.

only to goods and not to services. The policy is that the practice of resale price maintenance restricts competition among retailers. Although there have been a number of reforms to New Zealand competition law in recent years, there has been no serious proposal to remove the per se prohibition on resale price maintenance.

305. Resale price maintenance may be authorised. Authorisation applications are determined by the Commerce Commission applying a public benefit test.[629] The Commission will grant an authorisation if the practice 'will in all the circumstances result, or be likely to result, in a benefit to the public which would outweigh the lessening in competition that would result, or would be likely to result'.[630]

I. Distribution

A. Exclusive Distributorship

306. An exclusive distributorship involves a manufacturer or distributor granting exclusive rights to sell a product within a specified geographic area or in relation to a class of goods. Vertical exclusive distributorships are not unlawful per se in New Zealand competition law. As vertical restraints they do not typically involve parties in competition with each other and the cartel provisions will not apply.

307. Exclusive distributorships will however be assessed under a section 27 substantial lessening of competition analysis. An exclusive distributorship agreement will be unlawful if it is found to have the purpose, effect or likely effect of substantially lessening competition in a market.[631] Authorisation may be available, as with other section 27 conduct.

308. Each case would need to be assessed on its own facts. As with any vertical restraint, an exclusive distributorship is a restraint on commercial freedom, and they can interfere with competition especially if a party has market power. Generally, a manufacturer may allocate exclusive territories to its distributors and this will not interfere with interbrand competition. It may actually have competitive benefits by, for example, preventing free riding. However, the situation may be different if there is monopoly or significant market power such that other branded substitute products are not available.

B. Exclusive Dealing

309. Exclusive dealing is a practice whereby a manufacturer requires that its distributors sell only the product of the manufacturer. A distributor may not stock the

629. *Ibid.*, s. 58.
630. *Ibid.*, s. 61(6).
631. *Ibid.*, s. 27. A detailed discussion of the elements of s. 27 is above under §1. Horizontal agreements.

manufacturer's product and also competitive products. Vertical exclusive dealing requirements are not unlawful per se in New Zealand competition law. As vertical restraints they do not typically involve parties in competition with each other and the cartel provisions will not apply.

310. Exclusive dealing will however be assessed under a section 27 substantial lessening of competition test. An exclusive dealing agreement will be unlawful if it is found to have the purpose, effect or likely effect of substantially lessening competition in a market.[632] Authorisation may be available, as with other section 27 conduct.

311. There is authority that simple vertical exclusive dealing clauses are acceptable in New Zealand competition law. The New Zealand High Court considered the issue of exclusive dealing clauses and the application of section 27 in the 1990 case of *Fisher & Paykel Ltd v. Commerce Commission.*[633] Fisher & Paykel was for many years New Zealand's largest manufacturer and distributor of whiteware, comprising refrigerators, freezers, washing machines, dryers and dishwashers. The company had established a strong market position in a context of import restrictions, which were removed in 1987. Fisher & Paykel had a long-standing practice of imposing exclusive dealing clauses (EDCs) on its distributors, so that retailers of Fisher & Paykel product were not permitted to stock or sell products from competing manufacturers. The EDC was terminable on 90 days' notice and was designed to protect intensive manufacturer support of dealer training and promotional activities from free riding by other manufacturers.

312. In 1986 the Commerce Act was passed and Fisher & Paykel applied to the Commerce Commission seeking a determination as to whether its EDC had the effect of substantially lessening competition in the market for the distribution and sale to retailers of whitegoods, in contravention of section 27. In 1989 the Commerce Commission issued its majority decision that the EDC had the effect of substantially lessening competition in the market and contravened section 27. It also determined that the anti-competitive effect of the EDC was not outweighed by any public benefit which would justify granting authorisation.[634] Fisher & Paykel appealed to the High Court.

313. The High Court overturned the decision of the Commerce Commission, finding that the EDC did not contravene section 27. The High Court took a net approach to assessing the effect on competition, weighing both the pro-competitive and anti-competitive effects of the practice. The High Court said that Fisher & Paykel had significant market power but was significantly constrained by its competitors. In the absence of artificial barriers to entry, an EDC could have positive pro-competitive effects so long as a significant component, in this case retail space,

632. *Ibid.*
633. *Fisher & Paykel Ltd v. Commerce Commission.* [1990] 2 NZLR 731.
634. Commerce Act 1986 s. 58.

was not foreclosed. On the evidence, the Court found that no significant retail space had been foreclosed, and gave weight to the fact that the EDC was terminable without penalty at 90 days' notice.[635]

314. The High Court also considered the issue of authorisation. The Court said that, if it had found that the EDC did contravene section 27, it would not have found that the EDC was authorisable.[636] The public benefits contended for were not sufficient to outweigh the substantially lessening of competition. In the event, of course, the Court found no breach of section 27.

315. The *Fisher & Paykel* case remains authority that an EDC may be found on its facts to be pro-competitive and not in contravention of section 27. However it is not authority that all EDCs will be viewed favourably by the courts. Any particular EDC would need to be assessed under section 27, using the approach previously outlined.[637] This approach uses a future focused counter-factual test. The court will consider the nature and extent of the market, the probable nature and extent of competition which would exist therein but for the conduct in question, the way the market operates and the nature and extent of the contemplated lessening.[638] A court will consider the likely state of future competition in a market with and without the conduct.[639] In making a substantially lessening of competition assessment, a court will consider the net effect on competition, balancing the procompetitive effects (including efficiencies) against the anticompetitive effects.[640]

C. Selective Distribution

316. Vertical selective distribution agreements, for example agreements limiting the number of distributors, are also not per se unlawful in New Zealand competition law. As vertical restraints they do not typically involve parties in competition with each other and the cartel provisions will not apply. There are no other specific per se provisions applying to these agreements.

317. Selective distribution agreements will be assessed under a section 27 substantial lessening of competition analysis. Each case would need to be assessed on its own facts. A selective distribution agreement would be unlawful if it was found

635. *Fisher & Paykel Ltd v. Commerce Commission.* [1990] 2 NZLR 731, 766–767.
636. In terms of Commerce Act 1986 s. 58.
637. *See* detailed discussion of s. 27 above under the §1. Horizontal agreements.
638. *See Dandy Power Equipment v. Mercury Marine* (1982) 44 ALR 173, 191–192, quoted in *Auckland Regional Authority v. Mutual Rental Cars (Auckland Airport) Ltd* [1987] 2 NZLR 647, 674–675. *See also Tru Tone Ltd v. Festival Records Marketing Ltd* [1988] 2 NZLR 352, 362, *Commerce Commission v. Ophthalmological Society of NZ Ltd* (2004) 10 TCLR 994, 1029, and *ANZCO Foods Waitara Ltd v. AFFCO NZ Ltd* [2006] 3 NZLR 351, 404.
639. *ANZCO Foods Waitara Ltd v. AFFCO NZ Ltd* [2006] 3 NZLR 351, 404.
640. *ANZCO Foods Waitara Ltd v. AFFCO NZ Ltd* [2006] 3 NZLR 351, 405.

to have the purpose, effect or likely effect of substantially lessening competition in a market.[641] Authorisation may be available, as with other section 27 conduct.

D. Franchising

318. Franchising is not unlawful under New Zealand competition law, and franchise agreements have not given rise to significant case law. However, there is potential for particular provisions in franchising agreements to be found to contravene the Commerce Act. In particular, provisions relating to retail pricing, quantity requirements and tying arrangements may be subject to competition law scrutiny.

319. If a franchisor requires that franchisees sell goods at a specified minimum price, this would contravene the resale price maintenance provisions in the Commerce Act 1986 and be unlawful per se.[642] Recommended price lists are acceptable under the resale price maintenance provisions, but will contravene if the prices are enforced and therefore become specified.[643]

320. There is also potential for franchise agreements to contain provisions that contravene the cartel provisions.[644] Any agreement on price to which more than one franchisee was a party could potentially constitute a cartel provision and contravene the per se prohibition. A restraint of trade clause in a franchise agreement might also be caught as a cartel provision, but could potentially be covered by the collaborative activity exception,[645] but the restraint of trade provision must have been reasonably necessary to achieve the aims of the collaborative activity.[646]

321. Franchise agreements may also contain provisions that would constitute market allocation and if these agreements involved a horizontal element then these provisions could also be viewed as cartel provisions and per se unlawful. This might also be an issue where a franchisor also owns franchisees, so that they are interconnected body corporates[647] and will therefore be taken as also parties to the agreement under section 30B.

322. There is also potential for provisions in franchise agreements to contravene section 27 if they are found to have the purpose, effect or likely effect of substantially lessening competition in a market. In most cases, it would be expected that a

641. Commerce Act 1986 s. 27. A detailed discussion of the elements of s. 27 is above under §1. Horizontal agreements.
642. *See* Commerce Act 1986 ss 37–42. These provisions are discussed above under §2. Vertical agreements.
643. *Ibid.*, ss 37 and 39.
644. *Ibid.*, ss 30–33. *See* detailed discussion above under §1. Horizontal agreements.
645. *Ibid.*, s. 31.
646. *See* discussion in Commerce Commission New Zealand, *Competitor Collaboration Guidelines* (January 2018). http://www.comcom.govt.nz/business-competition/guidelines-2/competitor-collaboration-guidelines/ (accessed 10 Jul. 2018) 36, [134]–[135].
647. In terms of Commerce Act 1986 s. 2(7).

franchise agreement would not be found to have the purpose, effect or likely effect of substantially lessening competition in a market. However, franchisors would need to consider the effect of section 3(5) which provides that:

> For the purposes of section 27, a provision of a contract, arrangement or understanding shall be deemed to have or to be likely to have the effect of substantially lessening competition in a market if that provision and
>
> (a) the other provisions of that contract, arrangement or understanding; or
> (b) the provisions of any other contract, arrangement or understanding to which that person or any interconnected body corporate is a party
>
> taken together, have or are likely to have the effect of substantially lessening competition in that market.

323. The effect of this provision is that a number of agreements to which one person is a party may be combined for section 27 analysis. This would apply to franchisors, so that a series of franchise agreements with a common franchisor could be considered together for section 27 analysis. The agreements would only contravene if a purpose, effect or likely effect of substantially lessening competition could be established. This would generally be unlikely but unusual facts might give rise to a contravention.

II. Technology Licencing

A. *Patent Licencing*

324. The Commerce Act does not contain extensive provisions specifically relating to the licencing of technology and intellectual property rights. Technology licencing agreements are covered by the provisions applying to restrictive practices. This means that any technology licence agreement, including patent licencing, will be subject to examination under the cartel provisions and/or under the resale price maintenance provisions and sections 27 and 28 which are the provisions applying to practices substantially lessening competition. If the per se cartel provisions apply, then an agreement will contravene unless it can be shown that an exception applies. If an exception does apply, the cartel provisions are not contravened, but the agreement may still contravene section 27 or section 28 unless a relevant exception applies. In the event that the agreement sets a minimum resale price, then the resale price maintenance provisions may also be contravened.[648]

325. There is also an exception specifically applicable to intellectual property licencing. Section 45 provides an exception for intellectual property rights to both the cartel provisions and the broad provisions in sections 27 and 28. It does not

648. These provisions are discussed in detail above under §1. Horizontal agreements.

apply to the monopolisation provisions, but there is also a specific intellectual property exception to monopolisation.[649] At time of writing, all of the specific intellectual property provisions in the Commerce Act are under review, with consideration being given to repeal.[650]

326. Section 45 provides as follows:

Exceptions in relation to intellectual property rights

(1) Nothing in this Part, except sections 36, 36A, 37 and 38 applies
  (a) to the entering into of a contract or arrangement or arriving at an understanding in so far as it contains a provision authorising any act that would otherwise be prohibited by reason of the existence of a statutory intellectual property right; or
  (b) to any act done to give effect to a provision of a contract, arrangement, or understanding referred to in paragraph (a).

(2) For the purposes of subsection (1), a 'statutory intellectual property right' means a right, privilege, or entitlement that is conferred, or acknowledged as valid, by or under
  (a) the Patents Act 2013; or
  (b) the Designs Act 1953; or
  (c) the Trade Marks Act 2002; or
  (d) the Copyright Act 1994; or
  (e) the Plant Variety Rights Act 1987; or
  (f) the Layout Designs Act 1994.

(3) For the purposes of subsection (2),
  (a) a person who has applied for a patent in accordance with the Patents Act 2013 and filed the complete specification in relation to the application shall, until the application is determined, be deemed to have been granted the patent to which the application relates:
  (b) a person who has made an application for the registration of a design in accordance with section 7 of the Designs Act 1953 shall, until the application is determined, be deemed to be the registered proprietor of the design:
  (c) a person who has made an application in accordance with section 32 of the Trade Marks Act 2002 for registration of a trade mark shall, until the application is determined, be deemed to be the registered proprietor of the trade mark:
  (d) a person who has made an application in accordance with section 5 of the Plant Variety Rights Act 1987 shall, until the application is determined, be deemed to have been granted the plant variety rights to which the application relates.

---

649. This is the exception in the Commerce Act 1986 s. 36(3) and is discussed in II. Chapter 2 Dominant undertakings prohibited practices.

650. *See* Ministry of Business Information and Employment, Discussion Paper: Review of Section 36 of the Commerce Act and Other Matters (January 2019), https://www.mbie.govt.nz/have-your-say/review-of-section-36-of-the-commerce-act-and-other-matters/ (accessed 10 May 2019).

327. Section 45 therefore provides an exception from section 27 and the cartel provisions of the Commerce Act for intellectual property licensing. It is not an exception from the prohibitions on resale price maintenance[651] or taking advantage of market power.[652] The section covers entering into contracts arrangements and understandings and also the doing of acts to give effect to provisions of contracts, arrangements or understandings.

328. A simple licencing agreement is unlikely to contravene the Commerce Act. However, more complex collaborative agreements involving intellectual property licencing may raise issues about the scope of the section 45 exception. Examples are patent pool agreements, agreements where the technology involved is an industry standard, or agreements where the licence also involves restraints such as tying. Any agreement in which firms that would otherwise compete in selling substitute products are instead agreeing not to compete would give rise to competition concerns. An agreement which limits the ability to licence outside of the agreement could also cause competition harm. In these situations the agreement could contravene the cartel provisions, or section 27, or potentially constitute resale price maintenance. The parties to the agreement would then be reliant on the section 45 exception. The exception applies to an agreement 'in so far as it contains a provision authorising any act that would otherwise be prohibited by reason of the existence of a statutory intellectual property right'. The language 'in so far as it contains' means that not all provisions of licensing agreements are necessarily exempted from competition scrutiny. It will cover licencing of an intellectual property right, but will not cover associated restraints that cause competition harm. Other provisions – such as price or output restraints, exclusion of competitors, exclusive grant-back clauses for improvements, or clauses allowing a patentee to terminate the license if the other party challenges the patent's validity – may still be assessed for their effects on competition under section 27 of the Commerce Act.

329. To date, there is no significant case law on section 45, and therefore no available judicial guidance on the scope of the exception in relation to intellectual property licenses. New Zealand courts can be expected to look to other jurisdictions for guidance, particularly the United States and Europe.

B. Trademark Licencing

330. Trade mark licence agreements will also be subject to examination under the cartel provisions and/or under the resale price maintenance provisions and sections 27 and 28 which are the provisions applying to practices substantially lessening competition. If the per se cartel provisions apply, then an agreement will contravene unless it can be shown that an exception applies. If an exception does

651. Commerce Act 1986 ss 37 and 38.
652. *Ibid.*, ss 36 and 36A. There is also a limited exception for intellectual property rights in relation to the taking advantage of market power provisions in s. 36(3) and s. 36A(4). This exception is under review as discussed.

apply, the cartel provisions are not contravened, but the agreement may still contravene section 27 or 28, unless an exception applies. In the event that the agreement sets a minimum resale price, then the resale price maintenance provisions may also be contravened.[653]

331. The section 45 exception for intellectual property rights, applying to both the cartel provisions and the broad provisions in sections 27 and 28, will also apply to trade mark licences.[654]

C. Know How and Trade Secret Licencing

332. Unlike some jurisdictions, the New Zealand civil law relating to know how and trade secrets is not covered by statute, the principles derive from the common law. The Commerce Act 1986 does still apply to know how and trade secret licencing, as it applies to other agreements. This means that know how and trade secret licence agreements will also be subject to examination under the cartel provisions and/or under the resale price maintenance provisions and sections 27 and 28 which are the provisions applying to practices substantially lessening competition. If the per se cartel provisions apply, then an agreement will contravene unless it can be shown that an exception applies. If an exception does apply, the cartel provisions are not contravened, but the agreement may still contravene section 27 or section 28, unless an exception applies. In the event that the agreement sets a minimum resale price, then the resale price maintenance provisions may also be contravened.[655]

333. Unlike patent and trade mark licences, know how and trade secret licences are not covered by the intellectual property exception in section 45 of the Commerce Act. Section 45 applies to statutory intellectual property rights only, being patents, designs, trade marks, copyright, plant variety rights and layout designs. Because trade secrets and know how are not statutory rights, they are not covered by the exception. This means that if an agreement falls within the Commerce Act provisions, then it will contravene unless another exception applies.

653. These provisions are discussed in detail above under §1. Horizontal agreements.
654. *See* the discussion above at A. Patent licencing.
655. These provisions are discussed in detail above under §1. Horizontal agreements.

Chapter 2. Dominant Undertakings' Prohibited Practices

334. The New Zealand Commerce Act in its current form does not use the terminology of 'dominance' or of 'undertaking'. The equivalent restrictive trade practices concept applying to single firm conduct is 'taking advantage of market power'. This is the New Zealand monopolisation law. The Commerce Act monopolisation provision, and the merger provision, both formerly used the term 'dominant', but both have now been amended. Merger law now uses a 'substantially lessening of competition' test.[656] The term 'undertaking' is also not used in New Zealand competition law. The monopolisation provision prohibits a 'person', rather than an 'undertaking' from engaging in prohibited conduct. The New Zealand monopolisation law in section 36 of the Commerce Act is currently under review and is likely to be significantly reformed.[657]

335. Section 36 of the Commerce Act 1986 prohibits the taking advantage of market power. Section 36 sets out three requirements that must be satisfied for a firm to have contravened. Section 36(2) provides that:[658]

> A person that has a substantial degree of power in a market must not take advantage of that power for the purpose of –
>
> (d) restricting the entry of a person into that or any other market; or
> (e) preventing or deterring a person from engaging in competitive conduct in that or any other market; or
> (f) eliminating a person from that or any other market.

336. Mere enforcement of a statutory intellectual property right does not constitute taking advantage of market power.[659] Note however that, at time of writing, all of the specific intellectual property provisions in the Commerce Act are under review, with consideration being given to repeal.[660] Section 36A is a similar provision to section 36, it prohibits the taking advantage of market power in trans-Tasman (New Zealand and Australia) markets.[661]

Person

656. The Commerce Amendment Act 2001 s. 9(1) amended s. 36, and s. 11 amended the merger threshold in s. 47.
657. *See* Ministry of Business Information and Employment, Discussion Paper: Review of Section 36 of the Commerce Act and Other Matters (January 2019), https://www.mbie.govt.nz/have-your-say/review-of-section-36-of-the-commerce-act-and-other-matters/ (accessed 10 May 2019).
658. Commerce Act 1986 s. 36(2).
659. *Ibid.*, s. 36(3).
660. *See* Ministry of Business Information and Employment, Discussion Paper: Review of Section 36 of the Commerce Act and Other Matters (January 2019), https://www.mbie.govt.nz/have-your-say/review-of-section-36-of-the-commerce-act-and-other-matters/ (accessed 10 May 2019).
661. *Ibid.*, s. 36A.

337. The prohibition in section 36 refers to a 'person'. In the Commerce Act, the definition of 'person' provides that the term 'includes a local authority, and any association of persons whether incorporated or not'.[662] The definition therefore covers both individuals and body corporates, and more broadly any association of persons. Additionally, section 36(5) provides that, for the purposes of section 36, 'a reference to a person includes 2 or more persons that are interconnected'.[663] A reference to a person therefore includes a reference to an interconnected body corporate. The Act provides further details on the meaning of interconnected body corporate in the statute as a whole. Section 2(7) provides that:[664]

> For the purposes of this Act, any 2 bodies corporate are to be treated as interconnected if:
>
> (a) one of them is a body corporate of which the other is a subsidiary (within the meaning of section 5 of the Companies Act 1993); or
> (b) both of them are subsidiaries (within the meaning of that section) of the same body corporate; or
> (ba) both of them are entities referred to by any of the paragraphs (other than paragraph (e) of the definition of transferor in section 2(1) of the Health Sector (Transfers) Act 1993; or
> (c) both of them are interconnected with bodies corporate that, in accordance with paragraph (a) or paragraph (b), are interconnected,
>
> and interconnected bodies corporate has a corresponding meaning.

338. Body corporates will therefore be regarded as interconnected if one is a subsidiary of the other or if they are both subsidiaries of the same body corporate, or if both of them are interconnected with such subsidiaries. In the Commerce Act context, no body corporate may be regarded as a subsidiary of the Crown.[665]

Market

339. Section 36 applies to a person that has a substantial degree of power in a market. The threshold for the prohibition is therefore substantial market power. The first step in establishing substantial market power is to identify the relevant market. The market has to be defined in order to identify the degree of market power. 'Market' is therefore an instrumental concept, and market definition is a tool and not an end in itself.[666] In a New Zealand Court of Appeal decision, Richardson J said that:[667]

662. *Ibid.*, s. 2(1). *See also* s. 2(7).
663. *Ibid.*, s. 36(5).
664. *Ibid.*, s. 2(7).
665. *Ibid.*, s. 2(7A).
666. *Telecom v. Commerce Commission* (1991) 4 TCLR 473, 500.
667. *Tru Tone Ltd v. Festival Records Marketing Ltd* [1988] 2 NZLR 352, 358.

> The identification of the relevant market is the first step towards the assessment of the current state of competition and of the nature and extent of any inhibition of competition. At each step it is a practical jury question of fact and degree.

340. New Zealand courts have drawn heavily on Australian case law on market definition, particularly the decision of the Trade Practices Tribunal in the *QCMA* case.[668] In *QCMA* the Tribunal said that 'the identification of markets must be the essential first step in assessment of present competition and likely competitive effects'.[669] It referred to 'the identification of rivalrous relationship between sellers', and said that the concept of a market was basically a very simple idea.[670] The Tribunal said that 'a market is the field of actual and potential transactions between buyers and sellers amongst whom there can be strong substitution, at least in the long run, if given a sufficient price incentive'. [671] The Tribunal then set out its approach to defining a market:

> [I]n determining the outer boundaries of the market we ask a quite simple but fundamental question: if the firm were to 'give less and charge more' would there be, to put the matter colloquially, much of a reaction? And if so, from whom? In the language of economics the question is this: From which products and which activities could we expect a relatively high demand or supply response to price change, ie a relatively high cross-elasticity of demand or cross-elasticity of supply?

341. The Tribunal's approach to markets and competition was routinely followed by New Zealand courts in the early days of the Commerce Act,[672] and is a continuing influence on case law.[673] The approach has also evident in the Commerce Commission in its *Mergers and Acquisitions Guidelines*.[674]

342. 'Market' is defined in section 3(1A) of the Commerce Act 1986, which provides that:

---

668. *Re Queensland & Co-Operative Milling Associates Ltd* – Proposed Merger; *Re Defiance* – Proposed Mergers 1 and 2 (1976) 8 ALR 481, 516–518.
669. *Ibid.*, 516.
670. *Ibid.*, 516–517.
671. *Ibid.*, 517.
672. *See* for example *Auckland Regional Authority v. Mutual Rental Cars (Auckland Airport) Ltd* [1987] 2 NZLR 647, 670, *Telecom v. Commerce Commission* (1991) 4 TCLR 473, 497–500.
673. *See* for example *Brambles NZ Ltd v. Commerce Commission* (2003) 10 TCLR 868, 892.
674. Commerce Commission, *Mergers and Acquisitions Guidelines* (2013), 23–29 http://www.comcom.govt.nz/business-competition/guidelines-2/mergers-and-acquisitions-guidelines/ (accessed 25 Aug. 2017).

> Every reference in this Act ... to the term 'market' is a reference to a market in New Zealand for goods or services as well as other goods or services that, as a matter of fact and commercial common sense, are substitutable for them.

343. The definition therefore gives weight to both commercial common sense and to substitutability. The High Court has said that it sees no source of conflict or tension in the juxtaposition of the two elements, substitutability and commercial common sense.[675] The test is not substitutability as such,[676] and a mechanical reliance upon substitution criteria in a contextual vacuum is not sufficient.[677] The market should also be defined by reference to the alleged conduct, and should not be defined so widely that it thwarts the objectives of the Commerce Act.[678] The purpose is to discover the degree of the defendant's market power.[679]

344. The High Court in *Telecom v. Commerce Commission* set out market definition principles.[680] The Court said that:[681]

> [W]e seek to identify the area or areas of close competition of relevance for the application(s). In other words, we seek to identify the constraints upon the price and production policies of firms or divisions of firms whose conduct is of relevance for the matters litigated.

345. The Court said that competition may proceed through both substitution in demand and substitution in supply in response to changing prices or in relation to changing price-product-service packages offered. The Court referred to cross-elasticities, describing a mental test which asks how buyers and sellers would likely react to a notional small percentage increase in price of the products of interest (the 'price elevation test').[682]

346. The Court in the *Telecom* case went on to say that market is a multi-dimensional concept, and to discuss those dimensions.[683] The New Zealand Court of Appeal has said that market is 'ordinarily regarded as a multi-dimensional concept with dimensions of product, functional level, space and time'.[684] In its *Mergers and Acquisitions Guidelines,* the Commerce Commission refers to five dimensions,

675. *Telecom v. Commerce Commission* (1991) 4 TCLR 473, 499.
676. *Tru Tone Ltd v. Festival Records Marketing Ltd* [1988] 2 NZLR 352, 359.
677. *Telecom v. Commerce Commission* (1991) 4 TCLR 473, 499.
678. *Ibid.*, 499–500.
679. *Queensland Wire Industries Pty Ltd v. The Broken Hill Proprietary Co. Ltd* (1989) 83 ALR 577, 582.
680. *Telecom v. Commerce Commission* (1991) 4 TCLR 473, 501–504.
681. *Ibid.*, 501.
682. *Telecom v. Commerce Commission* (1991) 4 TCLR 473, 502.
683. *Ibid.*
684. *Tru Tone Ltd v. Festival Records Marketing Ltd* [1988] 2 NZLR 352, 359.

product, geographic, supply chain level, customer and time.[685] The importance of each dimension will vary with the relevant facts. Defining the product market involves identifying the product or services between which customers and suppliers can switch. The geographic dimension is the geographic space in which substitution would take place. The functional or supply chain level is the level in the supply chain in which the transactions take place, for example in the manufacturing, distribution or retail levels. More than one supply chain level may be identified, a court will identify the levels that best expose the play of market forces, actual and potential, among buyers and sellers.[686] The time dimension refers to the time period in which that analysis is made, and it includes the period of time required for redeploying existing production and distribution capacity but not entirely new entry.[687]

347. The Commerce Commission defines markets in order to assess merger applications, but is not a decision-maker on cases of taking advantage of market power. However, the Commission sets out its approach to each market dimension in the *Mergers and Acquisitions Guidelines*,[688] and these largely reflect the statutory definition and the approach of case law, and are therefore a useful summary of the relevant principles. The Commerce Commission uses the hypothetical monopolist test as a tool, asking whether a hypothetical sole supplier would profitably increase prices by at least a small but significant amount, a small but significant non-transitory increase in price (SSNIP). The Commerce Commission generally uses 5% as the SSNIP.[689] The smallest set of profits or locations for which the SSNIP can be profitably sustained is the relevant product or geographic market. [690] The courts have expressed some caution about this test, describing it as an analytic tool that might not be appropriate in every circumstance, and emphasising the role of commercial common sense.[691]

Substantial degree of market power

348. Once the market has been defined, the next step in a section 36 analysis is an assessment of the degree of market power held by the defendant. Market power is a central concept in the monopolisation provisions. The New Zealand Commerce Act used a dominance standard for both monopolisation and mergers until 2001, but the current provisions use the term 'substantial degree of market power'.

685. Commerce Commission, *Mergers and Acquisitions Guidelines* (2013) http://www.comcom.govt.nz/business-competition/guidelines-2/mergers-and-acquisitions-guidelines/ 23 (accessed 25 Aug. 2017).
686. *Telecom v. Commerce Commission* (1991) 4 TCLR 473, 502.
687. *Ibid.*, 503.
688. Commerce Commission, *Mergers and Acquisitions Guidelines* (2013) 23–29 http://www.comcom.govt.nz/business-competition/guidelines-2/mergers-and-acquisitions-guidelines/ (accessed 25 Aug. 2017).
689. *Ibid.*, 24.
690. *Ibid.*
691. *See* for example *Brambles NZ Ltd v. Commerce Commission* (2003) 10 TCLR 868, 891–892.

349. New Zealand courts have emphasised that it is not unlawful simply to have market power, monopolies are not unlawful in themselves. It is also not unlawful to have an anti-competitive purpose. Firms with market power have a right to compete vigorously. It is only unlawful if a firm with substantial market power takes advantage of its substantial market power for a proscribed purpose.

350. Market power is the power to raise price and exclude entry, it and is the antithesis of competition.[692]

351. The assessment of market power involves an assessment of the extent to which the firm faces competitive constraints, and a firm is regarded as having substantial market power if it can profitably raise its prices above competitive levels for a sustained period.[693] A large market share may be evidence of market power, as may vertical integration, but assessment of constraints is the focus. Barriers to entry are an essential element as the threat of new entry is a powerful constraint.[694] Constraints may be from existing or potential competitors, and any countervailing power, for example from buyers or sellers, is relevant. The New Zealand courts' approach to market power can be seen in the words of the New Zealand Supreme Court, which has said that:[695]

> A firm has market power when it is not constrained in the way in which it would be constrained in a competitive market. Any firm that is substantially unconstrained by competitive pressure has substantial market power. Market power gives some advantage if it makes it easier – that is, materially facilitates – the conduct in issue. The question whether dominance or substantial market power exists implies a comparison between the position of the firm in the actual market and a firm in the same general circumstances but otherwise in a workably competitive market. The contrast inherent in the concepts of dominance or substantial degree of market power is the contrast between the actual market and a hypothetically competitive market.

Taking Advantage of Market Power

352. The second element of section 36 analysis, taking advantage of market power, has proved the most controversial. It is not unlawful simply to have market power, monopolies are not unlawful in themselves. It is also not unlawful to have an anti-competitive purpose. Firms with market power have a right to compete vigorously. It is only unlawful if a firm with substantial market power takes advantage of its substantial market power for a proscribed purpose. Mere enforcement of a

692. *Re Queensland & Co-Operative Milling Associates Ltd* – Proposed Merger; *Re Defiance* – Proposed Mergers 1 and 2 (1976) 8 ALR 481, 515.
693. This is similar to the approach taken in *Queensland Wire Industries Pty Ltd v. The Broken Hill Proprietary Co. Ltd* (1989) 83 ALR 577, 583.
694. *Queensland Wire Industries Pty Ltd v. The Broken Hill Proprietary Co. Ltd* (1989) 83 ALR 577, 583.
695. *Commerce Commission v. Telecom Corporation of New Zealand Ltd* [2011] 1 NZLR 577, 601.

statutory intellectual property right does not constitute taking advantage of market power.[696] The 'take advantage' element constitutes a bridge between the market power and the purpose. This element has proved the most difficult and controversial element in section 36. As originally enacted, the section referred to 'use' of a dominant position, and an amendment in 2001 changed this to 'take advantage' of market power. The New Zealand courts took a restrictive approach to the former wording 'use' of a dominant position, and this restrictive approach has continued in relation to the test for take advantage. The test requires a counterfactual test which compares the conduct of the firm with market power with the conduct of a firm in a hypothetical competitive market.[697] The Parliamentary record suggests that the shift from 'use' to 'take advantage' was intended to mean that New Zealand courts would adopt a more flexible approach to the test, as in Australia.[698] However the New Zealand judicial approach has remained largely unchanged, and the New Zealand Supreme Court has emphasised the need for predictability, which would not be assisted by having a range of possible tests.[699] In the 2011 case *Commerce Commission v. Telecom*, the New Zealand Supreme Court explained its approach, saying that:[700]

> The essential point is that if the dominant firm would, as a matter of commercial judgment, have acted in the same way in a hypothetically competitive market, it cannot logically be said that its dominance has given it the advantage that is implied in the concepts of using or taking advantage of dominance or a substantial degree of market power. Conversely, if the dominant firm would not have acted in the same way in a hypothetically competitive market, it can logically be said that its dominance did give it the necessary advantage. This is because it can then be reasonably concluded that it was its dominance or substantial degree of market power that caused, enabled or facilitated its acting as it did in the actual market.

353. The Supreme Court has therefore firmly continued to require the application of the counterfactual test, and few cases are brought under section 36. This is the background to the current review of the section, in which a number of options are under discussion, including removing the taking advantage element, and the introduction of an effects test of substantially lessening competition.[701]

Anticompetitive purpose

---

696. Commerce Act 1986 s. 36(3).
697. This was the approach taken in *Telecom Corporation of New Zealand Ltd v. Clear Communications Ltd* [1995] 1 NZLR 385 (PC); (1992) 5 TCLR 166 (HC); (1993) 5 TCLR 413 (CA).
698. *Report of the Commerce Select Committee on the Commerce Amendment Bill* (2001) 13–14. The expressed intention was to adopt what was regarded as the more flexible approach in *Queensland Wire Industries Pty Ltd v. The Broken Hill Proprietary Co. Ltd* (1989) 83 ALR 577.
699. *Commerce Commission v. Telecom Corporation of New Zealand Ltd* [2011] 1 NZLR 577, 600.
700. *Ibid.*
701. *See* New Zealand Ministry of Business, Innovation and Employment, *Targeted Review of the Commerce Act 1986*, /business/competition-regulation-and-policy/reviews-of-the-commerce-act-1986/targeted-review-of-the-commerce-act-2015/ (accessed 9 May 2019).

354. The third element of section 36 is the requirement of an anticompetitive purpose. The section requires that the defendant have the purpose of:

- restricting the entry of a person into that or any other market;
- preventing or deterring a person from engaging in competitive conduct in that or any other market; or
- eliminating a person that or any other market.

355. Section 36B provides that purpose may be inferred from conduct or from any other relevant circumstances. Purpose can be distinguished from intention. 'Purpose' implies object or aim.[702] The anti-competitive purpose can be one of a number of purposes so long as it is a substantial purpose.[703] The test for purpose is not clearly established, but the New Zealand Court of Appeal has taken the view that purpose may be established or negatived using subjective or objective analysis.[704] It is, of course, not unlawful simply to have an anti-competitive purpose. The other elements of section 36 are also required.

356. Each of the prohibited purposes listed in section 36 refers to 'that or any other market'. That is, the purposes of restricting entry, preventing or deterring the engaging in competitive conduct, or eliminating a person, may be in that or any other market. This means that the defendant may have market power in one market and the purpose of affecting competition in another market. There is also no requirement that the plaintiff be a person harmed by the conduct.

§1. Exploitative Practices

I. Excessive/Unfair Pricing

357. A claim of excessive or unfair pricing would have to be tested by applying the elements of section 36 to the facts as presented. Outside of the industries subject to price regulation under Part 4 of the Commerce Act or industry specific regulation,[705] there is no general competition law prohibition on charging high prices unless this can be shown either to constitute taking advantage of substantial market power for a prohibited purpose, or to be the result of collusive conduct.

358. It is not unlawful to have a monopoly or to charge a monopoly price, even if this is not in the interests of consumers. The view is taken that charging of excessive prices will encourage new entrants and that competition in the market will eliminate monopoly prices. In a famous, and controversial, New Zealand case, the Privy Council (then New Zealand's highest court) said that Section 36 did not have

702. *Union Shipping NZ Ltd v. Port Nelson Ltd* [1990] 2 NZLR 662, 707.
703. Commerce Act 1986 s. 2(5)(b).
704. *Port Nelson Ltd v. Commerce Commission* [1996] 3 NZLR 554, 564.
705. For example under the Telecommunications Act 2001.

the purpose of eliminating monopoly profits, but was designed to produce competition which would hopefully compete out monopoly rents.[706] New Zealand courts have taken the view that monopolists are entitled to retain their monopoly position and to compete.[707] Courts have also emphasised that section 36 must be construed in such a way that monopolists know with some certainty whether or not particular conduct is lawful.[708]

359. In an excessive pricing case, the Court will assess the elements of substantial market power, taking advantage of that power and purpose. Whether or not the firm has taken advantage of market power will require application of the counterfactual test set out by the Supreme Court in the *Telecom* case.[709] It will require an assessment of whether, as a matter of commercial judgment, the firm with substantial market power would have acted in the same way in a hypothetically competitive market. If the dominant firm would not have acted in the same way in a hypothetically competitive market, it can logically be said that its dominance did give it the necessary advantage. This is because it can then be reasonably concluded that it was its dominance or substantial degree of market power that caused, enabled or facilitated its acting as it did in the actual market.

360. There is some precedent for cases of excessive pricing being found to constitute a breach. In *Queensland Wire*,[710] the High Court of Australia found under the equivalent Australian provision that excessive pricing by a firm with substantial market power constituted a refusal to supply, and in circumstances where there was no alternative source of supply, constituted taking advantage of market power for a proscribed purpose. However, the New Zealand courts approach to the meaning of 'taking advantage' means that in practice it would be very difficult to successfully bring a section 36 action for excessive pricing.

II. Discrimination

361. There are no special statutory provisions in the New Zealand Commerce Act applying to price discrimination, meaning charging different prices to different customers. A claim that price discrimination constituted taking advantage of substantial market power under section 36 would also require establishing each of the elements of the section.

---

706. *Telecom Corporation of New Zealand Ltd v. Clear Communications Ltd* (1995) 1 NZLR 385, 407–408 (PC).
707. *See Telecom Corporation of New Zealand Ltd v. Clear Communications Ltd* (1995) 1 NZLR 385, 402 (PC), *Carter Holt Harvey Building Products Ltd v Commerce Commission* [2006] 1 NZLR 145, 163.
708. *Telecom Corporation of New Zealand Ltd v. Clear Communications Ltd* (1995) 1 NZLR 385, 403, *Commerce Commission v. Telecom Corporation of New Zealand Ltd* [2011] 1 NZLR 577, 600.
709. *Commerce Commission v. Telecom Corporation of New Zealand Ltd* [2011] 1 NZLR 577, 600.
710. *Queensland Wire Industries Pty Ltd v. The Broken Hill Proprietary Co. Ltd* (1989) 83 ALR 577.

362. In general, price discrimination is not treated as automatically unlawful and may be regarded as efficient in some circumstances. However, where there is substantial market power and a proscribed purpose, price discrimination conduct may contravene if a plaintiff can establish that the firm with market power would not have acted in the same way in a hypothetically competitive market.[711]

363. Provisions other than section 36 may apply to price discrimination in some circumstances. Price discrimination may be harmful to consumers and to competition, and price discrimination generally involves vertical agreements. Price discrimination may therefore also contravene the section 27 prohibition on contracts, arrangements or understandings that have the purpose, effect or likely effect of substantially lessening competition in a market.[712]

§2. Exclusionary Practices

I. Predation

364. Predatory pricing may constitute taking advantage of substantial market power for an anticompetitive purpose in contravention of section 36 of the Commerce Act 1986.[713] Predatory pricing has been a recurring issue in section 36 cases in New Zealand. There are no specific statutory provisions in the New Zealand Commerce Act applying to predatory pricing, and no statutory guidance as to the circumstances in which it might be unlawful. A claim that a particular pricing strategy was predatory and that it constituted taking advantage of substantial market power under section 36 would require establishing each of the elements of the section.

365. The New Zealand courts approach to predatory pricing has been that low prices are not generally a contravention of section 36, although there may be liability at the time when losses are being recouped through higher prices. This approach can be seen in a line of cases.

Port Nelson

366. An early section 27 and section 36 case of alleged predatory pricing was the case of *Port Nelson Ltd v. Commerce Commission*[714] In that case the Commerce Commission brought an action against Port Nelson Ltd (PNL) which owned the land, wharves, berths and slipways at the Nelson port. PNL had a monopoly on port services including port access, berthage utilities and wharfage. However, it faced competition from an independent pilotage company (TBMPL) in providing pilotage services. PNL offered a discount to customers who used the combined services of

711. *Commerce Commission v. Telecom Corporation of New Zealand Ltd* [2011] 1 NZLR 577.
712. Commerce Act 1986 s. 27.
713. *Ibid.*, s. 36. Before the 2001 amendments, the section referred to use of a dominant position.
714. *Port Nelson Ltd v. Commerce Commission* [1996] 3 NZLR 554 (CA).

the Port, and set a low (below cost) minimum charge for pilotage services. PNL also refused to hire tugs to vessels unless PNL pilots were used. The Commerce Commission alleged that the scope discount, the low minimum charge for pilotage and the tug tie contravened section 36 of the Commerce Act. The low minimum charge for pilotage was alleged by the Commerce Commission to be substantially below the cost of providing the pilotage service, and to constitute unlawful predatory pricing.[715]

367. The case was decided under the pre-2001 legislation, so that the issue was whether these three practices constituted use of a dominant position under section 36. The High Court was bound by the Privy Council decision in *Telecom Corporation of New Zealand Ltd v. Clear Communications Ltd* which required application of the counterfactual test.[716]

368. The High Court considered the Commerce Commission's case, and found that the Port was dominant in the markets for pilotage, tug services and wharves at Port Nelson. It found that the tug tie, whereby the Port refused to hire tugs to vessels unless PNL pilots were used, did constitute use of a dominant position in the markets for pilotage and tug services for the purpose of restricting the entry of TBMPL into, preventing or deterring it from engaging in competitive conduct in, and eliminating it from, the pilotage market. It was therefore a breach of section 36. A firm not in a dominant position would probably not have refused use of tugs to ships using TBMPL pilots. However, on the facts it found that neither the 5% scope discount nor the low minimum charge for pilotage services contravened section 36. It found that the 5% discount was not proved to be use of a dominant position in wharves. It also found that the NZD 100 minimum charge for pilotage was not proved to be use of a dominant position in the market for wharfage, as a firm not in a dominant position may have acted in the same way in the same circumstances. The scope discount and minimum charge did nevertheless breach section 27 as they constituted anticompetitive agreements.[717]

369. The decision of the High Court was appealed to the Court of Appeal, and the Court of Appeal upheld the decisions of the High Court. In relation to the below cost NZD 100 minimum charge for pilotage, the Court of Appeal upheld the High Court in finding that it breached section 27 as having the purpose and likely effect of substantially lessening competition. The Court of Appeal said that:[718]

> To price a contestable service below cost can impact on competition for that service. The impact will be no different whatever the reason for the below cost pricing though, in the long term, such a practice cannot be sustained unless the loss is recovered from increased prices once competition is eliminated or

715. *Commerce Commission v. Port Nelson Ltd* (1995) 5 NZBLC 103,762, 103,766–7 (HC).
716. *Telecom Corporation of New Zealand Ltd v. Clear Communications Ltd* [1995] 1 NZLR 385 (PC).
717. *Commerce Commission v. Port Nelson Ltd* (1995) 5 NZBLC 103,762.
718. *Port Nelson v. Commerce Commission* [1996] 3 NZLR 554, 569.

unless the service is subsidised by other business for which there is no competition or perhaps by lower than market-cost equity. We agree with McGechan J that no assistance is gained by attempting to define the bounds of 'predatory' pricing. It is preferable to concentrate on the terms of the statute.

370. The Court discussed section 27 in the context of predatory pricing. The Court said that:[719]

> The section requires proof of the substantial lessening of competition – not merely aggressive competitive conduct. The purpose or (likely) effect must be more than short-term and must impact upon the competitive process in the particular market structure. The mere fact that a participant operates in the market at a loss, and even fails, will not necessarily lessen competition. But conduct that does lessen competition will contravene even in the absence of evidence of the ability ultimately to recoup the loss – though that may generally be presumed from a decision to indulge in anti-competitive conduct.

371. The Court took into account the combined, perhaps synergistic, effect of the tie, the discount and the minimum charge. The Court said that below cost pricing would not frequently give rise to competition law concerns, and that reduction of prices generally will reflect competition at work: However the combined effect of the tie and the discount the below cost charge by PNL for pilotage must be seen as exclusionary and likely to substantially lessen competition.[720] The Court also upheld the finding on purpose.[721]

372. The Court of Appeal therefore upheld the finding of the High Court on predatory pricing, but decided the issue on section 27 rather than section 36. In relation to section 36, the finding that the tug tie contravened section 36 was upheld[722] and the scope discount and below cost minimum price were in issue. The Commerce Commission challenged the High Court finding that the minimum charge and scope discount did not constitute use of a dominant position. The Court of Appeal said that in view of its findings on section 27 it did not need to consider this point. The Court of Appeal said that it was not persuaded that the findings of the High Court should be disturbed.[723] However the Court of Appeal went on to say that:[724]

> Nevertheless it should be acknowledged that there is strength in the argument that a firm not in a dominant position in port facilities, tugs and pilotage would run considerable risk in structuring a discount so that it was not available until every required service was taken. Once one service is declined there is no

719. *Ibid.*, 571.
720. *Ibid.*, 572.
721. *Ibid.*, 573.
722. *Ibid.*, 577.
723. *Ibid.*, 578–9.
724. *Ibid.*, 578–9.

incentive to take any. Similarly, where a pilotage market is contestable the risk of charging below cost in the smaller vessel sector without assurance of the ability to recover in the larger vessel sector would be real enough.

373. The *Port Nelson* case is therefore an early example of a predatory pricing case under the Commerce Act 1986. On the facts it was found to contravene section 27 rather than section 36.

Carter Holt Harvey

374. A subsequent case on predatory pricing was the case of *Carter Holt Harvey Building Products Ltd v. Commerce Commission.*[725] This was a case of predatory pricing, although a complex case in that it involved 'two-for-one' pricing by the firm, Carter Holt Harvey, in order to protect the market for a different product. The evidence was that the two-for-one pricing was substantially below cost.[726] The case was decided under the pre-2001 wording of section 36, so that the issue was whether the pricing constituted use of a dominant position. The New Zealand High Court and Court of Appeal both found that the conduct breached section 36. The case was appealed to the then highest court, the Privy Council. The Privy Council found by a 3-2 majority that the conduct did not constitute a breach of section 36. The majority held that predatory pricing is not unlawful unless it constitutes use of dominance. It reiterated that the counterfactual test set out in the *Telecom v. Clear* case was to be applied.[727] In considering predatory pricing, the Privy Council drew heavily on the reasoning of the High Court of Australia in *Boral Besser Masonry Ltd v. Australian Competition and Consumer Commission.*[728] It chose not to apply the reasoning of the decisions of the European Court of Justice in interpreting the New Zealand provision.[729] The Privy Council majority concluded that the use by a dominant firm of its financial ability to cut prices must be distinguished from its use of its position of dominance, the measure of which was its market power. It said that the financial ability to cut prices was not market power, and that cutting prices only became unlawful when the dominant firm was shown to have done so by use of its position of dominance. It said that a dominant firm uses its position of dominance when it engages in price cutting with a view to recouping its losses without loss of market share by raising prices without fear of reprisals afterwards [730]

---

725. *Carter Holt Harvey Building Products Ltd v Commerce Commission* [2006] 1 NZLR 145 (PC).
726. *Ibid.*, 154.
727. *See Carter Holt Harvey Building Products Ltd v Commerce Commission* [2006] 1 NZLR 145, 166, referring to *Telecom Corporation of New Zealand Ltd v. Clear Communications Ltd* [1995] 1 NZLR 385 (PC).
728. *Boral Besser Masonry Ltd v. Australian Competition and Consumer Commission* (2003) 195 ALR 609, 77 ALJR 623.
729. *Carter Holt Harvey Building Products Ltd v Commerce Commission* [2006] 1 NZLR 145, 168.
730. *Carter Holt Harvey Building Products Ltd v Commerce Commission* [2006] 1 NZLR 145, 166–167, referring to *Boral Besser Masonry Ltd v. Australian Competition and Consumer Commission* (2003) 195 ALR 609, 77 ALJR 623.

375. The Privy Council majority therefore took the view that, in cases of alleged predatory pricing, a dominant firm would only contravene section 36 if it engaged in price cutting with a view to recouping its losses without loss of market share or fear of reprisals. The two Judges in the minority disagreed, questioning the value of the counterfactual test in such a case, and would have found a contravention of section 36 on the facts.[731]

376. The Privy Council was replaced by the New Zealand Supreme Court as New Zealand's highest court in 2004.[732] There was some speculation that the New Zealand Supreme Court might take a different approach to section 36 from that taken by the Privy Council in cases such as *Carter Holt*. However, the New Zealand Supreme Court has continued to require the counterfactual test for taking advantage of market power, and emphasised the need for predictability, which it has said would not be assisted by having a range of possible tests.[733]

377. In New Zealand law, predatory pricing can also constitute an anti-competitive agreement and contravene section 27 of the Commerce Act 1986. To contravene, it must the predatory pricing provision must be contained in a contract, arrangement or understanding that has the purpose, effect or likely effect of substantially lessening competition.[734]

II. Tying

378. Tying involves selling a product or service on the condition that the customer purchases it together with another product or service. Bundling is similar. The sale of products and services using tying or bundling strategies is not necessarily unlawful in New Zealand, and such practices may benefit consumers and suppliers. However, in some circumstances tying practices may harm competition and may contravene section 27 of the Commerce Act as a restrictive agreement or section 36 if the Commerce Act where it constitutes taking advantage of market power.

379. For a tying practice to contravene section 36, it would need to be shown that the firm has a substantially degree of market power, that the practice constitutes taking advantage of that market power, and that the practice was undertaken for a proscribed purpose. Tying conduct may extend across more than one market, for example, a firm with market power in the market for product A may use tying to take advantage of that market power in order to restrict, prevent, deter or eliminate a competitor in the market for product B. One example is the Commerce Commission's investigation into the 2007 conduct of Aoraki/Mount Cook Alpine Village Ltd, trading as the Hermitage. The Hermitage provided accommodation to visitors

731. *Carter Holt Harvey Building Products Ltd v Commerce Commission* [2006] 1 NZLR 145, 169–173.
732. Supreme Court Act 2003.
733. *Commerce Commission v. Telecom Corporation of New Zealand Ltd* [2011] 1 NZLR 577, 600.
734. Commerce Act 1986 s. 27.

to the village and also supplied meals and drinks services at several restaurants in the village. The Hermitage commenced offering a 'Dinner, Bed and Breakfast' deal to customers. There was one other restaurant operating in the village, and that restaurant complained that the Hermitage deal prevented it from competing in the market for evening meals. The Commission's view was that the Hermitage had tied the dinner market to the hotel accommodation market in breach of section 36, and reached a settlement with the Hermitage.[735]

380. Tying in the context of section 36 was considered by the High Court and Court of Appeal in the *Port Nelson Ltd v. Commerce Commission* case. [736] The Commerce Commission brought an action against Port Nelson Ltd (PNL) which owned the land, wharves, berths and slipways at the Nelson port. PNL had a monopoly on port services including port access, berthage utilities and wharfage. However it faced competition from an independent pilotage company (TBMPL) in providing pilotage services. PNL refused to hire tugs to vessels unless PNL pilots were used. The Commerce Commission alleged that this tug tie contravened section 36 of the Commerce Act.[737] The case was decided under the pre-2001 legislation, so that the issue was whether these three practices constituted use of a dominant position under section 36. The High Court was bound by the Privy Council decision in *Telecom Corporation of New Zealand Ltd v. Clear Communications Ltd* which required application of the counterfactual test.[738]

381. The High Court found that the Port was dominant in the markets for pilotage, tug services and wharves at Port Nelson. It found that the tug tie whereby the Port refused to hire tugs to vessels unless PNL pilots were used did constitute use of a dominant position in the markets for pilotage and tug services for the purpose of restricting the entry of TBMPL into, preventing or deterring it from engaging in competitive conduct in, and eliminating it from, the pilotage market. It was therefore a breach of section 36. A firm not in a dominant position would probably not have refused use of tugs to ships using TBMPL pilots.[739]

382. The decision of the High Court was appealed to the Court of Appeal, and the Court of Appeal upheld the decision of the High Court that the tug tie contravened section 36.[740]

735. Commerce Commission New Zealand, *Where Tying Harms Competition Case Study*, (2018) https://comcom.govt.nz/business/avoiding-anti-competitive-behaviour/taking-advantage-of-market-power (accessed 10 May 2019).
736. *Port Nelson Ltd v. Commerce Commission* (1996) 5 NZBLC 104,142, [1996] 3 NZLR 554 (CA).
737. *Commerce Commission v. Port Nelson Ltd* (1995) 5 NZBLC 103,762, 103,766–7 (HC).
738. *Telecom Corporation of New Zealand Ltd v. Clear Communications Ltd* [1995] 1 NZLR 385 (PC).
739. *Commerce Commission v. Port Nelson Ltd* (1995) 6 TCLR 406, 443, 556–7.
740. *Port Nelson v. Commerce Commission* [1996] 3 NZLR 554, 577.

III. Rebates

383. Rebates are common practice, they frequently offer benefits to consumers, and will not typically breach section 36 of the Commerce Act 1986. However, as with tying, there may be circumstances in which a rebate raises competition concerns. This may arise where a customer is offered a loyalty or fidelity rebate if the customer sources their supplies exclusively from the firm offering the rebate. In such a case, the rebate may potentially contravene section 36 as taking advantage of market power, or it may contravene the provisions prohibiting restrictive agreements.

384. New Zealand has not had significant recent litigation on rebates in relation to section 36. However, rebates have been considered under the provisions covering restrictive agreements. The Court of Appeal considered the issue in 1993 in the case of *Tui Foods Ltd v. New Zealand Milk Corporation Ltd.*[741] Tui Foods (under the name Dairy Express) distributed milk and dairy products to retail outlets. Distribution was covered by a standard agreement under which retailers received a rebate of 3% on all product purchased through Dairy Express on condition that milk purchases were exclusively from Dairy Express for the duration of the offer. The plaintiff, New Zealand Milk Corporation, was a competitor of Dairy Express, and sought an interim injunction restraining Dairy Express from entering into, arriving at or giving effect to a contract, arrangement or understanding containing the rebate provision. Both the High Court and the Court of Appeal found that there was an arguable case that the rebate provision contravened section 29 of the Commerce Act which prohibited agreements containing exclusionary provisions. The Court of Appeal held that it was a highly tenable inference that the essential purpose of the rebate condition was to create an incentive for the retailer to take milk supplies exclusively from Dairy Express to the exclusion of the potential competitor.[742]

385. Section 29 of the Commerce Act was repealed in 2017.[743] This means that, in future, such a rebate would fall to be considered under section 27 which prohibits contracts, arrangements or understandings with the purpose, effect or likely effect of substantially lessening competition in a market.[744] In circumstances in which the firm offering the rebate had substantial market power, such a rebate may also be considered under section 36. In such a case, if offer of the rebate constitutes taking advantage of market power and the rebate is offered for an anticompetitive purpose then it may contravene.

741. *Tui Foods Ltd v. New Zealand Milk Corporation Ltd* [1993] 5 TCLR 406.
742. *Ibid.*, 410.
743. Section 29 of the Commerce Act 1986 was repealed from 15 August 2017 by s. 7 of the Commerce (Cartels and Other Matters) Amendment Act 2017.
744. Commerce Act 1986 s. 27.

IV. Refusal to Deal

386. There is no general prohibition on refusals to deal under the Commerce Act 1986. In general terms, firms are free to deal or not deal with whoever they wish. This general rule is, however, qualified, in that in some circumstances a refusal to deal may contravene a specific section. A refusal to deal may involve a refusal to supply or a refusal to agree to provide access to essential infrastructure. A refusal to deal in circumstances in which a competitor was not able to obtain supply or access elsewhere would raise competition concerns.

387. A refusal to deal may contravene the following sections, depending in the facts:

- Section 36, if the firm refusing to deal has market power and takes advantage of that power for a proscribed anticompetitive purpose.
- Section 27, if the refusal to deal involves an agreement containing a provision with the purpose, effect or likely effect of substantially lessening competition in a market.
- The Resale Price Maintenance provisions[745] if there is a refusal to supply goods for a resale price maintenance reason.

388. In regulated industries, supply obligations are governed by the regulatory framework rather than by generic competition law.

Section 36

389. There is limited New Zealand case law on refusals to deal in a section 36 context. However there are a number of Australian cases on the equivalent provision. One of the leading Australian cases was *Queensland Wire*, in which the High Court of Australia found under the equivalent Australian provision that excessive pricing by a firm with substantial market power constituted a constructive refusal to supply. In circumstances where there was no alternative source of supply, the Court held that this constituted taking advantage of market power for a proscribed purpose. [746] However, not every refusal to deal has been found to contravene the provision. For example, in *Melway Publishing Ltd v. Robert Hicks Pty Ltd*[747] the High Court of Australia found that a refusal to supply was a manifestation of a distributorship system that maintenance of the distributorship system, and was not necessarily taking advantage of market power. This demonstrates that supply may be refused if the defendant can demonstrate some justification for the refusal other than misuse of market power. Efficiency considerations or credit-worthiness would be possible examples of such a justification.

---

745. *Ibid.*, s. 37.
746. *Queensland Wire Industries Pty Ltd v. The Broken Hill Proprietary Co. Ltd* (1989) 83 ALR 577.
747. *Melway Publishing Ltd v. Robert Hicks Pty Ltd* (2001) 178 ALR 253.

390. Application of the New Zealand section 36 of the Commerce Act to a refusal to deal would require the establishment of each of the elements of section 36, that is, a substantial degree of market power, taking advantage of that power and an anti-competitive purpose. Section 36 refusal to deal cases are likely to involve some degree of vertical integration as the basis of market power. An anticompetitive purpose would need to be established on the facts, and the issue will then be whether the refusal to deal constitutes taking advantage of market power. The New Zealand Supreme Court continues to apply the counterfactual test for taking advantage. This was the test used by the Privy Council in cases involving telecommunications interconnection pricing disputes.[748] The New Zealand Supreme Court replaced the Privy Council but has continued to use a similar test. The Supreme Court has said that:[749]

> The essential point is that if the dominant firm would, as a matter of commercial judgment, have acted in the same way in a hypothetically competitive market, it cannot logically be said that its dominance has given it the advantage that is implied in the concepts of using or taking advantage of dominance or a substantial degree of market power. Conversely, if the dominant firm would not have acted in the same way in a hypothetically competitive market, it can logically be said that its dominance did give it the necessary advantage. This is because it can then be reasonably concluded that it was its dominance or substantial degree of market power that caused, enabled or facilitated its acting as it did in the actual market.

Section 27

391. Refusals to deal will not typically contravene section 27. Where there is no contract arrangement or understanding involved but a simple refusal to deal then section 27 will not apply. However a refusal to deal may also contravene section 27 in specific circumstances. If there is an agreement in place containing a provision that constitutes an actual or constructive refusal to deal with a person, that could contravene if at least one party had an anticompetitive purpose.

Resale Price Maintenance

392. It is more likely that a refusal to deal will contravene the Resale Price Maintenance provisions.[750] As under the other Commerce Act provisions there is no general obligation to deal with or supply a person. However, this will be different if the refusal to supply is for a resale price maintenance reason.

393. The Commerce Act contains a specific regime prohibiting resale price maintenance, applying to goods and not to services. Resale price maintenance is per

748. *Telecom Corporation of New Zealand Ltd v. Clear Communications Ltd* [1995] 1 NZLR 385 (PC).
749. *Commerce Commission v. Telecom Corporation of New Zealand Ltd* [2011] 1 NZLR 577, 600.
750. Commerce Act 1986 s. 37.

se unlawful, meaning that it is prohibited without a need to establish a purpose, effect or likely effect of substantially lessening competition in a market.[751] The prohibition applies to resale price maintenance by suppliers[752] and resale price maintenance by others.[753] The statutory regime prohibiting resale price maintenance is detailed, but in relation to refusals to supply it generally prohibits withholding supply for the reason that the person from who supply is withheld has not agreed not to sell at a price less than a specified price. Section 37 defines and prohibits resale price maintenance by suppliers.[754] A key concept in the provisions is 'specified price'. If there is no specified price then a supplier is free to refuse supply. Section 39 provides that prices may be recommended.[755] A supplier can refuse supply if there is a recommended price, provided that the recommended price does not become a specified price. Section 37(4) sets out circumstances in which a price shall be deemed to be a specified price.[756] Resale price maintenance as defined includes withholding the supply of goods for the reason that the person has not agreed to the specified price, or has sold or is likely to sell at a price below the specified price.[757]

394. There is no general obligation to supply, but withholding supply will be a contravention if it is for a resale price maintenance reason. The reason can be one of a number of reasons so long as it is a substantial reason.[758] Section 40 deems a number of things to be withholding supply.[759] These include refusing or failing to supply, refusing to supply except on disadvantageous terms, supply with less favourable treatment, and causing or procuring another person to withhold supply.[760] 'Supply' is defined in section 2 to include, in relation to goods, 'supply (or resupply) by way of gift, sale, exchange, lease, hire, or hire purchase'.[761] Genuine agency transactions will not be covered. There is an evidentiary provision in section 42 which provides for circumstances in which there will be a presumption that supply has been withheld for a resale price maintenance reason.[762]

V. Price Squeeze

395. A price or margin squeeze refers to a situation in which an input or intermediate good is priced at a level that means a downstream competitor is unable to

751. *Ibid.*, ss 37–42.
752. *Ibid.*, s. 37.
753. *Ibid.*, s. 38.
754. *Ibid.*, s. 37. *See also Commerce Commission v. Hewlett Packard* (1993) 5 TCLR 136, *Commerce Commission v. Aquanaut Pty Ltd* HC Auckland (CIV 2002 404 1562) 18 June 2004.
755. Commerce Act 1986 s. 39.
756. *Ibid.*, s. 37(4).
757. *Ibid.*, s. 37(3)(d) and (e).
758. *Ibid.*, s. 2(5).
759. *Ibid.*, s. 40.
760. *Ibid.*, s. 40(a)–(d).
761. *Ibid.*, s. 2.
762. *Ibid.*, s. 42.

compete. Typically this conduct will be that of a vertically integrated firm, operating at more than one level of the supply chain. Where a business charges a competitor high prices for an input, or for access to infrastructure that is necessary to compete in downstream markets, this may contravene section 36 of the Commerce Act 1986.[763] A successful action will require establishing that the firm doing the price squeeze has a substantial degree of market power and that the intermediate product is necessary for the competitor to compete in the downstream market.

396. The Australian High Court decision in *Queensland Wire*[764] remains a leading decision involving a price squeeze. BHP manufactured a steel product known as Y-bar that was needed in order to manufacture star picket fence posts, the posts used in by far the most popular rural fencing in Australia. BHP had a wholly owned subsidiary company that manufactured star picket posts. BHP produced 97% of Australia's steel output and was the only manufacturer of Y-bar in Australia and no significant quantities had been imported. The plaintiff, Queensland Wire Industries, manufactured and sold rural fencing, in competition with BHP. However it was not able to make star picket fence posts because it could not obtain the necessary Y-bar from BHP at a reasonable price. The High Court of Australia found this was a constructive refusal to supply. This was therefore a case in which a vertically integrated company refused supply of an intermediate good to a downstream competitor except on disadvantageous terms, limiting its ability to compete in the downstream market. The price to be charged would have involved a price squeeze. The case was decided under the equivalent provision to the New Zealand section 36. In circumstances where there was no alternative source of supply, the High Court of Australia held that the conduct constituted taking advantage of market power for a proscribed purpose. [765]

763. Commerce Commission New Zealand, *Taking Advantage of Market Power Fact Sheet* (2018) https://comcom.govt.nz/business/avoiding-anti-competitive-behaviour/taking-advantage-of-market-power (accessed 10 May 2010).

764. *Queensland Wire Industries Pty Ltd v. The Broken Hill Proprietary Co. Ltd* (1989) 83 ALR 577.

765. *Ibid.*

Chapter 3. Concentrations

397. The New Zealand Commerce Act 1986 does not refer expressly to the term concentrations. Mergers are governed by the Commerce Act provisions relating to business acquisitions. The Commerce Commission has also issued *Mergers and Acquisitions Guidelines* to explain how it assesses mergers and acquisitions. [766] The *Guidelines* are general and the Commission applies them flexibly according to the facts of each merger.[767]

The Statutory Framework

398. Part 3 of the Commerce Act 1986 deals with business acquisitions. Section 47 of the Commerce Act prohibits certain acquisitions. Section 47 provides:

> (1) A person must not acquire assets of a business or shares if the acquisition would have, or would be likely to have, the effect of substantially lessening competition in a market.
> (2) For the purposes of this section, a reference to a person includes 2 or more persons that are interconnected or associated.
> (3) For the purposes of this section, a person is associated with another person if that person is able, whether directly or indirectly, to exert a substantial degree of influence over the activities of the other.
> (4) A person is not able to exert a substantial degree of influence over the activities of another person for the purposes of subsection (3) by reason only of the fact that:
> (a) those persons are in competition in the same market; or
> (b) one of them supplies goods or services to the other.

399. Section 47 therefore prohibits a person from acquiring assets of a business or shares if the acquisition would have, or would be likely to have, the effect of substantially lessening competition in a market.[768] Under the Commerce Act assets of a business include physical and intangible assets and include goodwill, intellectual property rights and contractual rights.[769] A share is defined in the Commerce Act as meaning a share in the share capital of a company or other body corporate, whether or not it carries the right to vote at general meetings, and as including:[770]

(a) a beneficial interest in any such share:

766. *See* Commerce Commission, *Mergers and Acquisitions Guidelines* (2013) http://www.comcom.govt.nz/business-competition/guidelines-2/mergers-and-acquisitions-guidelines/ (accessed 10 Aug. 2017).
767. *Ibid.*, 10
768. Commerce Act 1986 s. 47(1).
769. *Ibid.*, s. 2(1) definition of 'assets'. *See also* Commerce Commission, *Mergers and Acquisitions Guidelines* (2013) 14. http://www.comcom.govt.nz/business-competition/guidelines-2/mergers-and-acquisitions-guidelines/ (accessed 10 Aug. 2017).
770. Commerce Act 1986 s. 2(1) definition of 'share'.

(b) a power to exercise, or control the exercise of, a right to vote attaching to any such share that carries the right to vote at meetings of the company:
(c) a power to acquire or dispose of, or control the acquisition or disposition of, any such share:
(d) a perpetual debenture and perpetual debenture stock.

400. For the purpose of the section 47 merger prohibition, 'person' includes interconnected or associated persons, including bodies corporate.[771] A person is associated if 'that person is able, whether directly or indirectly, to exert a substantial degree of influence over the activities of the other'.[772] A 'substantial degree of influence' in this context is not satisfied by reason only of the fact that they are in the same market or one supplies to the other.[773] The *Mergers and Acquisitions Guidelines*[774] state that the Commission will consider that a person has a substantial degree of influence over another person if they have the ability to bring real pressure to bear on the decision-making process of that person. If one party can substantially influence the activities of the other, it may not be appropriate to regard them as separate competitors in the market. [775] The Commission notes in the *Guidelines* that a substantial degree of influence can arise at any level of shareholding.[776] The Commission's *Guidelines* say that whether a person has a substantial degree of influence over another is a question of fact, and the Commission will consider factors including:[777]

- The nature and extent of ownership links between the companies;
- The presence of overlapping directorships;
- The rights of one company to appoint directors of another;
- The nature of other shareholder agreements and other links between the companies concerned (including family or financial links); and
- The nature and extent of the communications between the persons, and the apparent influence of one person on the key strategic decisions of the other.

401. In addition to section 47, in 2017 new sections 47A–47D were inserted into the Act.[778] These sections provide for the High Court to make a declaration if an overseas person acquires directly or indirectly a controlling interest in a New

771. *Ibid.*, s. 47(2).
772. *Ibid.*, s. 47(3).
773. *Ibid.*, s. 47(4).
774. *See* Commerce Commission, *Mergers and Acquisitions Guidelines* (2013), http://www.comcom.govt.nz/business-competition/guidelines-2/mergers-and-acquisitions-guidelines/ (accessed 10 Aug. 2017).
775. *Ibid.*, 13. The *Guidelines* refer to the case of *Commerce Commission v. New Zealand Bus Ltd* (2006) 11 TCLR 679 (HC) at [209]–[214].
776. Commerce Commission, *Mergers and Acquisitions Guidelines* (2013) 13, http://www.comcom.govt.nz/business-competition/guidelines-2/mergers-and-acquisitions-guidelines/ (accessed 10 Aug. 2017).
777. *Ibid.*.
778. Commerce (Cartels and other Matters) Amendment Act 2017 s. 11.

Zealand body corporate through acquiring assets or shares outside New Zealand, and the –acquisition of the controlling interest has the effect or likely effect of substantially lessening competition in a market in New Zealand.[779] 'Controlling interest' in this context is defined as meaning that the overseas person:[780]

(a) controls the composition of the board of the body corporate; or
(b) is in a position to exercise, or control the exercise of, more than 20% of the maximum number of votes that can be exercised at a meeting of the body corporate; or
(c) holds more than 20% of the issued shares of the body corporate, other than shares that carry no right to participate beyond an entitlement to a specified amount in a distribution of either profits or capital; or
(d) is entitled to receive more than 20% of every dividend paid on shares issued by the body corporate, other than shares that carry no right to participate beyond an entitlement to a specified amount in a distribution of either profits or capital; or
(e) is the holding company ... of the body corporate; or
(f) holds assets in circumstances where the holding of those assets results in the overseas person having effective control of the body corporate.

402. 'Overseas person' is defined as neither resident nor carrying on business in New Zealand.[781] The High Court may make orders including the requiring of disposal of shares or assets or that a New Zealand body corporate cease carrying on business in New Zealand.[782]

403. Section 47 prohibits business acquisitions that would have, or would be likely to have, the effect of substantially lessening competition in a market.[783] Parties to a proposed merger or acquisition may apply to the Commerce Commission for a clearance or authorisation.[784] Clearances are available for business acquisitions that will not, or would not be likely to have, the effect of substantially lessening competition in a market.[785] Authorisations are available for business acquisitions that will result, or will be likely to result, in such a benefit to the public that they should be permitted.[786] The effect of a clearance or authorisation is that the prohibition in section 47 or section 47A will not apply.[787] Decisions of the Commission on clearances and authorisations may be appealed to the High Court and potentially upward to the Court of Appeal and Supreme Court.

Market Definition

779. Commerce Act 1986 s. 47A(1)–(2).
780. *Ibid.*, s. 47A(5).
781. *Ibid.*, s. 47A(5).
782. *Ibid.*, s. 47B.
783. *Ibid.*, s. 47(1).
784. *Ibid.*, Part 5.
785. *Ibid.*, ss 66 and 67(3).
786. *Ibid.*, s. 67(3).
787. *Ibid.*, s. 69.

404. 'Market' is defined in section 3(1A) of the Commerce Act, which provides that:

> Every reference in this Act … to the term market is a reference to a market in New Zealand for goods or services as well as other goods or services that, as a matter of fact and commercial common sense, are substitutable for them.[788]

405. The Tribunal's approach to markets and competition was routinely followed by New Zealand courts in the early days of the Commerce Act,[789] is a continuing influence on case law,[790] and has influenced the Commerce Commission in its *Mergers and Acquisitions Guidelines*.[791] The New Zealand Court of Appeal has said that market is 'ordinarily regarded as a multi-dimensional concept with dimensions of product, functional level, space and time'.[792] In its *Mergers and Acquisitions Guidelines,* the Commerce Commission refers to five dimensions, product, geographic, supply chain level, customer and time.[793]

406. In defining the dimensions of a market, the Commerce Commission uses the hypothetical monopolist test as a tool, asking whether a hypothetical sole supplier would profitably increase prices by at least a small but significant amount, a small but significant non-transitory increase in prices of SSNIP. The smallest set of profits or locations for which the SSNIP can be profitably sustained is the relevant product or geographic market. [794] The Commission sets out its approach to each dimension in the *Mergers and Acquisitions Guidelines*,[795] which reflect the statutory definition and the approach of case law.

407. In considering a merger application, the Commission may identify more than one relevant market, for example by identifying separate markets at different levels of the supply chain. In cases involving multi-sided platforms, the Commission will consider whether to define a market for each side of the platform. For example, in a determination relating to a proposed media merger, the Commission defined markets for news and markets for advertising.[796]

---

788. Market definition is discussed in detail Part I, ch,4 §2.Relevant Market.
789. *See* for example *Auckland Regional Authority v. Mutual Rental Cars (Auckland Airport) Ltd* [1987] 2 NZLR 647, 670, *Telecom v. Commerce Commission* (1991) 4 TCLR 473, 497–500.
790. *See* for example *Brambles NZ Ltd v. Commerce Commission* (2003) 10 TCLR 868, 892.
791. Commerce Commission, *Mergers and Acquisitions Guidelines* (2013) http://www.comcom.govt.nz/business-competition/guidelines-2/mergers-and-acquisitions-guidelines/ 23–29 (accessed 25 Aug. 2017).
792. *Tru Tone Ltd v. Festival Records Marketing Ltd* [1988] 2 NZLR 352, 359.
793. Commerce Commission, *Mergers and Acquisitions Guidelines* (2013) http://www.comcom.govt.nz/business-competition/guidelines-2/mergers-and-acquisitions-guidelines/ 23 (accessed 25 Aug. 2017).
794. *Ibid.*, 24.
795. *Ibid.*, 23–29.
796. *NZME Limited and Fairfax New Zealand Limited* [2017] NZCC 8, 2 May 2017. Available from http://www.comcom.govt.nz/business-competition/mergers-and-acquisitions/authorisations/merger-authorisation-register/nzme-limited-and-fairfax-new-zealand-limited/ (accessed 12 Feb. 2018).

Substantial lessening of Competition

408. Once a market or markets are defined, the Commerce Commission is then required to assess whether a proposed merger would have, or would be likely to have, the effect of substantially lessening competition in a market.[797] The Commerce Commission *Guidelines* set out the counterfactual test for substantially lessening competition. The test is a comparison of the likely state of competition if the merger proceeds with the likely state of competition if the merger does not proceed. Both scenarios are forward-looking.[798] If competition would be substantially lessened with the merger when compared to any of the likely states of competition without the merger, then the merger will have the likely effect of substantially lessening competition.[799] The Commission makes a pragmatic and commercial assessment of what is likely to occur, taking account of factors such as market growth and technological changes.[800] The decision of the Commission may be appealed to the High Court and thence to the Court of Appeal and Supreme Court.[801]

Clearances and Authorisations

409. Parties to a proposed merger or acquisition may apply to the Commerce Commission for a clearance or authorisation.[802] Clearances are available for business acquisitions that will not, or would not be likely to have, the effect of substantially lessening competition in a market.[803] Authorisations are available for business acquisitions that will result, or will be likely to result, in such a benefit to the public that they should be permitted.[804] The effect of a clearance or authorisation is that the prohibitions in section 47 or section 47A will not apply.[805] Decisions of the Commission on clearances and authorisations may be appealed to the High Court and potentially upward to the Court of Appeal and Supreme Court.

§1. Horizontal Mergers

410. Horizontal mergers are assessed under Part 3 of the Commerce Act 1986 which deals with business acquisitions. Section 47(1) of the Act provides that a person must not acquire assets of a business or shares if the acquisition would have, or

797. Commerce Act 1986 s. 47(1).
798. Commerce Commission, *Mergers and Acquisitions Guidelines* (2013) http://www.comcom.govt.nz/business-competition/guidelines-2/mergers-and-acquisitions-guidelines/ 16–20 (accessed 10 Aug. 2017).
799. *Ibid.*, 18.
800. *Ibid.*, 19.
801. Commerce Act 1986 s. 75.
802. *Ibid.*, Part 5.
803. *Ibid.*, ss 66 and 67(3).
804. *Ibid.*, s. 67(3).
805. *Ibid.*, s. 69.

would be likely to have, the effect of substantially lessening competition in a market.[806] The Commerce Commission's *Mergers and Acquisitions Guidelines* are a guide to the approach of the Commission in assessing whether a merger or acquisition would be likely to substantially lessen competition in a market and the process for considering clearance applications. [807]

411. The Commerce Commission *Mergers and Acquisitions Guidelines* explain its approach to horizontal mergers, including mergers between competing suppliers[808] and mergers between competing buyers.[809] The *Guidelines* are detailed on mergers between competing suppliers, noting that much of the assessment is similar for mergers between competing buyers.[810]

412. The *Guidelines* refer to the potential for horizontal mergers to substantially lessen competition by giving rise to unilateral effects or coordinated effects. Unilateral effects can arise through a merger with a competitor that would otherwise provide competitive constraint. The merged firm acting on its own may give rise to an actual or likely effect of substantially lessening competition. The merger may allow the merged firm to, for example, profitably increase price above competitive levels.[811] A merger with a potential or emerging competitor may also give rise to unilateral effects.[812] Unilateral effects can occur in a range of markets, including markets in which products are homogenous, markets in which products are differentiated, and bargaining and bidding markets.[813]

413. Coordinated effects can also result from a merger and can substantially lessen competition. Coordinated effects are the result of coordinated behaviour by firms in a market, for example by collectively increasing price or reducing output. A merger may substantially lessen competition if it increases the potential for such

806. *Ibid.*, s. 47(1).
807. *See* Commerce Commission, *Mergers and Acquisitions Guidelines* (2013) http://www.comcom.govt.nz/business-competition/guidelines-2/mergers-and-acquisitions-guidelines/ (accessed 10 Aug. 2017).
808. Commerce Commission, *Mergers and Acquisitions Guidelines* (2013) Chapter 3, 21—42. http://www.comcom.govt.nz/business-competition/guidelines-2/mergers-and-acquisitions-guidelines/ (accessed 10 Aug. 2017).
809. Commerce Commission, *Mergers and Acquisitions Guidelines* (2013) Chapter 4, 43–4. http://www.comcom.govt.nz/business-competition/guidelines-2/mergers-and-acquisitions-guidelines/ (accessed 10 Aug. 2017).
810. Commerce Commission, *Mergers and Acquisitions Guidelines* (2013) 43. http://www.comcom.govt.nz/business-competition/guidelines-2/mergers-and-acquisitions-guidelines/ (accessed 10 Aug. 2017).
811. *Ibid.*, 32.
812. In this regard, the Commerce Commission refers to the example of *Commerce Commission v. Woolworths Limited* (2008) 12 TCLR 194 (CA). *See* Commerce Commission, *Mergers and Acquisitions Guidelines* (2013) 32. http://www.comcom.govt.nz/business-competition/guidelines-2/mergers-and-acquisitions-guidelines/ (accessed 10 Aug. 2017).
813. Commerce Commission, *Mergers and Acquisitions Guidelines* (2013) 32. http://www.comcom.govt.nz/business-competition/guidelines-2/mergers-and-acquisitions-guidelines/ (accessed 10 Aug. 2017).

coordinated behaviour to take place, for example by removing a particularly aggressive competitor.[814] In assessing potential coordinated effects arising from a merger, the Commerce Commission will assess whether the market is vulnerable to coordination, including evidence of prior coordinated behaviour. It will also assess whether the merger changes the conditions in the relevant market so that coordination is more likely, more complete or more sustainable.[815] The Commission identifies the following features as facilitating coordinated conduct:[816]

- homogeneous products;
- a small number of competitors and an absence of a particularly vigorous competitor or strong competition from outside the coordinating firms;
- firms repeatedly interacting through, for example, numerous transactions, through contact in other markets or other repeated interactions, for example, through industry organisations or meetings (e.g., to set technical standards);
- firms of similar size and cost structures;
- little innovation, stable demand and lack of supply shocks/volatility;
- firms that can readily observe each others' prices or volumes; and
- firms interrelated through association or cross-partial ownership.

414. Other considerations in assessing likely effect of substantially lessening competition include potential for new entry, potential for existing competitors to expand, and potential for countervailing power by buyers or suppliers. The Commission will also consider whether the merger creates efficiencies that will be passed on to customers and the impact of the firm's ownership on its incentives.[817]

415. The *Guidelines* discuss market share and concentration measures in relation to mergers between competitors.[818] The Commerce Commission uses market share and concentration indicators to identify mergers which are less likely to raise competition concerns. The *Guidelines* are clear that this is to provide an initial guide, but is not a substitute for full competition analysis.[819] The Commission's stated view is that a merger is unlikely to require a clearance where, post-merger, the three largest firms in the market have a combined market share of less than 70%, and the merged firm's combined market share is less than 40%, and/or where the three largest firms in the market have a combined market share of 70% or more, and the merged firm's combined market share is less than 20%.[820] However these indicators are not conclusive and do not substitute for a full analysis. The *Guidelines* also make clear that, where there is uncertainty about the appropriate market definition, the market definition that results in the worst case market share aggregation when applying the indicators should be adopted.[821]

814. *Ibid.*, 35-6.
815. *Ibid.*
816. *Ibid.*, 36.
817. *Ibid.*, 37–42.
818. *Ibid.*, 30–31, 44.
819. *Ibid.*, 30.
820. *Ibid.*
821. *Ibid.*

416. In measuring market shares, the Commerce Commission chooses the measure that it considers best reflects the competitive issue under consideration, taking into account the nature of the product and availability of data. The Commission states that, where relevant data is available, the starting point is to use:[822]

- revenue shares for differentiated products, as revenue share is likely to be a better indicator of market size and rival firms' competitive positions;
- production and sales capacity shares for firms with excess capacity supplying homogeneous products; and
- shares of reserves for natural resources markets where reserves are easily accessible.

417. A variety of these measures may be used, and the Commission often uses quantity sold in combination with other measures. For potential competitors in supply, the Commission includes only the output or capacity that that firm could supply easily, profitably and quickly and without significant cost. Imports are included, and when channelled through a New Zealand firm are generally added to that firm's domestic production. The Commission says that data from a number of years may be used, and that market shares that are stable over a period of years are more likely to be informative.[823] New Zealand competition law does not have a turnover threshold for merger notification, and it does not use turnover to identify mergers which are more or less likely to raise competition concerns.

§2. Vertical Mergers

418. The Commerce Commission notes that mergers between parties that are not direct competitors but who operate in related markets are less likely to result in substantially lessening of competition than a merger between competitors., because there is no direct loss of competition between firms.[824] Nevertheless, such mergers can result in substantial lessening of competition.

419. In relation to vertical mergers, (mergers between firms at different levels in a supply chain), the Commerce Commission takes the view that this may substantially lessen competition if the merger increases the merged firm's ability and/or incentive to prevent or hinder competition by either refusing to deal with competitors completely (total foreclosure) or raising prices charged to competitors (partial foreclosure).[825] Foreclosure may be of inputs or customers.[826] To foreclose, a firm generally requires market power at least one supply chain level, and will have an incentive to foreclose if it is profitable.[827]

822. *Ibid.*, 31.
823. *Ibid.*
824. *Ibid.*, 45.
825. *Ibid.*
826. *Ibid.*, 46.
827. *Ibid.*

420. The Commerce Commission will assess whether the competition lost from potentially foreclosed competitors is sufficient to have the likely effect of substantially lessening competition in light of remaining competitive constraints. Where foreclosure makes entry and expansion more difficult or otherwise reduces a competitor's ability to provide competitive constraint, a substantial lessening of competition may result.[828]

§3. MARKET/PRODUCT EXTENSION MERGERS

421. A market extension merger generally involves a merger between firms selling the same product or service in different geographic markets, for example where two firms sell the same product, with one operating in the North Island and one in the South Island. Such a merger may generate efficiencies and be pro-competitive. However there is potential for such a merger to substantially lessen competition, particularly if one firm has market power in its geographic market. A market extension merger or a series of market extension mergers may also produce market power.

422. A product extension merger will involve a merger between firms that sell different, but related, products. The products may have some degree of substitutability or they may be complements. Such a merger may give rise to efficiencies, but may also potentially substantially lessen competition, particularly if one firm has market power in its product market. Such mergers may make it possible to engage in bundling or tying conduct, meaning that competitors cannot compete by selling the same range of products of services as the merged company.

423. The Commerce Commission will use a similar approach to assessing a market or product extension merger to that used for horizontal and vertical mergers. The section 47 framework applies, prohibiting a person from acquiring assets of a business or shares if the acquisition would have, or would be likely to have, the effect of substantially lessening competition in a market.[829] The Commerce Commission will consider whether there is likely to be foreclosure which is likely to have the effect of substantially lessening competition in a market in light of remaining competitive constraints.[830]

§4. PURE CONGLOMERATE MERGERS

424. A pure conglomerate merger is a merger between unrelated firms. There are similarities to extension mergers. However a pure conglomerate merger involves a

828. *Ibid.*
829. Commerce Act 1986 s. 47(1).
830. Commerce Commission, *Mergers and Acquisitions Guidelines* (2013) 46, http://www.comcom.govt.nz/business-competition/guidelines-2/mergers-and-acquisitions-guidelines/ (accessed 10 Aug. 2017).

merger of firms that do not operate in the same market, which sell unrelated products and have no close trading relationship. Such mergers are less likely to have anti-competitive effects than horizontal mergers between competitors. Possibilities of tying and bundling are also limited where the merged firms produce entirely unrelated products. However, such a merger may substantially lessen competition if the merged entity has market power in one or more markets, or if there is some potential for the large merged firm to operate in the same market.

425. The Commerce Commission will use a similar approach in assessing a pure conglomerate merger to that used in a vertical merger or market or product extension merger. The section 47 framework applies, prohibiting a person from acquiring assets of a business or shares if the acquisition would have, or would be likely to have, the effect of substantially lessening competition in a market.[831] The Commerce Commission will consider whether there is likely to be foreclosure which is likely to have the effect of substantially lessening competition in a market in light of remaining competitive constraints.[832]

§5. Joint Ventures

426. Joint ventures are most commonly considered under the provisions that regulate anti-competitive agreements. However joint ventures are also subject to section 47, which prohibits a person from acquiring assets of a business or shares if the acquisition would have, or would be likely to have, the effect of substantially lessening competition in a market.[833]

427. If a joint venture involves the acquisition of assets or shares then it is subject to Commerce Commission consideration as to whether the acquisition will have the effect or likely effect of substantially lessening competition. Genuine joint ventures are likely to have a strong case for either a clearance or where there is a likely effect of substantially lessening competition, authorisation on grounds of public benefits (such as efficiencies) outweighing competitive detriment.

831. Commerce Act 1986 s. 47(1).
832. Commerce Commission, *Mergers and Acquisitions Guidelines* (2013) 46, http://www.comcom.govt.nz/business-competition/guidelines-2/mergers-and-acquisitions-guidelines/ (accessed 10 Aug. 2017).
833. Commerce Act 1986 s. 47(1).

Part III. Administrative Procedure

Chapter 1. Administrative Investigations Before the Antitrust Authority

§1. INITIATIVE

I. General Sectors Inquiries

428. The Commerce Commission is the competition law regulatory agency and is the administrative body responsible for enforcement as prescribed by statute. The Commerce Commission's powers are as provided for in the Commerce Act 1986. In addition, the Commerce Commission publishes *Competition and Consumer Investigation Guidelines*.[834] The *Guidelines* are provided for public education purposes and they set out in general terms the Commission's approach to investigations. In addition, in 2018, new legislation empowered the Commerce Commission to undertake a competition study if it considers it is in the public interest to do so.[835] A competition study means a 'study any factors that may affect competition for the supply or acquisition of goods or services'.[836] These studies are further discussed below.

429. There is no section of the Commerce Act that clearly lists the Commission's inquiry powers. In relation to generic competition law, a number of provisions are relevant. Section 1A provides that:[837]

> The purpose of this Act is to promote competition in markets for the long-term benefit of consumers within New Zealand.

430. Specific provisions setting out the Commission's powers are interpreted in light of this purpose statement. Section 98 provides that, where the Commission considers it necessary or desirable for the purposes of carrying out its functions and

834. Commerce Commission New Zealand, Competition and Consumer Investigation Guidelines (December 2016), http://www.comcom.govt.nz/the-commission/commission-policies/competition-and-consumer-investigation-guidelines/ (accessed 17 Jul. 2018). Note that these guidelines are currently being updated to reflect amendments to the Commerce Act 1986.

835. Commerce Act 1986 Part 3A

836. *Ibid.*, s 48

837. *Ibid.*, s. 1A.

exercising its powers under the Act, the Commission may, by notice in writing, require a person to provide information, produce documents or appear before the Commission to give evidence.[838] In this provision the powers of the Commission include the power to investigate whether an exception or exemption from the Act apply to a person or their conduct.[839] The Commission has powers to search. Section 98A sets out the search powers, providing that the Commission may authorise an employee, under a search warrant, to search a place named in the warrant.[840] Search warrants are granted by issuing officers where there are reasonable grounds to believe that it is necessary for the purpose of ascertaining whether or not a person has engaged or is engaging in conduct that contravenes the Act.[841] The power also extends to searches by the Commission in cooperation with an overseas regulator that is investigating conduct contravening its own competition law provisions.[842] The Commission has powers to receive and take evidence, including evidence that may not be admissible in a court of law.[843] It can require and take the giving of evidence on oath.[844] The Commission also has the power to prohibit disclosure of information, documents or evidence.[845] The Commission may receive information and documents on behalf of the Australian Competition and Consumer Commission,[846] and there are also provisions applying to overseas regulators generally.[847]

431. Section 25 of the Commerce Act 1986 sets out the functions of the Commission in relation to dissemination of information. It provides that:

> In addition to the functions conferred on the Commission by this Act, the Commission shall make available or co-operate in making available information with respect to
> (a) The carrying out of the functions and the exercise of the powers of the Commission under this Act; and
> (b) The purposes and provisions of this Act.

838. *Ibid.*, s. 98.
839. *Ibid.*, s. 98(2).
840. *Ibid.*, s. 98A(1).
841. *Ibid.*, s. 98A(2).
842. *Ibid.*, s. 98A(5).
843. *Ibid.*, s. (1).
844. *Ibid.*, s. 99(2)–(3).
845. *Ibid.*, s. 100.
846. *Ibid.*, s. 99A.
847. *Ibid.*, ss 99B–99P.

432. This provision allows the Commission to undertake educative and advocacy activities to promote awareness and compliance. The Commission identifies high-risk industries for targeted education programmes, and the Commission may undertake research for that purpose.[848]

433. The Commerce Commission's enforcement roles under the Commerce Act 1986 necessarily involve investigation and inquiry, and relevant powers are provided by the Act. However the Commission's investigation powers are limited. In particular, before 2018 the Commerce Act 1986 did not provide the Commerce Commission with a general power to undertake market studies. There was no provision in the Commerce Act empowering the Commerce Commission to undertake a market study on its own initiative. .

434. The extent of the Commerce Commission's ability to initiate an inquiry into competition in a market was considered by the Court of Appeal in the case of *Telecom Corporation of New Zealand Ltd v. Commerce Commission.*[849] In 1991–1992 the Commerce Commission nevertheless initiated an inquiry into competition in the telecommunications industry, and issued a report in June 1992. The report was critical of the regulatory framework and critical of the Telecom Corporation of New Zealand (Telecom), which was described as the 'the de facto regulator'. Telecom brought a court action for judicial review, arguing that the Commission did not have the power to undertake such a market study. On 17 March 1993 the New Zealand High Court issued a judgment declaring that in instituting the inquiry the Commerce Commission acted outside its powers.[850] The Commerce Commission appealed. On 15 February 1994 the New Zealand Court of Appeal dismissed the appeal.[851] The Court of Appeal considered the scheme of the Commerce Act and the powers of the Commission. The Court concluded that the Commission's functions and powers were three-fold:[852]

> It is to consider and determine applications for clearances or authorisations for restrictive trade practices and business acquisitions; it has reporting and recommendatory functions regarding the imposition of price control on particular goods and services, and where price control is in force jurisdiction to authorise prices and make other decisions (for example, to obtain or accept an undertaking under s 72); and it has the function or power of taking proceedings in

---

848. *See* New Zealand Ministry of Business, Innovation and Employment, *Targeted Review of the Commerce Act 1986, Issues Paper* (November 2015), 53, https://www.mbie.govt.nz/business-and-employment/business/competition-regulation-and-policy/reviews-of-the-commerce-act-1986/targeted-review-of-the-commerce-act-2015/ (accessed 10 May 2019).

849. *Telecom Corporation of New Zealand Ltd v. Commerce Commission* [1994] 2 NZLR 421, (1994) 5 TCLR 482.

850. *Telecom Corporation of New Zealand Ltd v. Commerce Commission* (1993) 5 TCLR 293.

851. *Telecom Corporation of New Zealand Ltd v. Commerce Commission* [1994] 2 NZLR 421, (1994) 5 TCLR 482.

852. *Ibid.*, 489–490, Cooke P. Note that these identified roles were based on the Commerce Act 1986 in its then form, there have been subsequent amendments, particularly in relation to regulated goods and services and price control.

Courts, by way of applications for penalties or injunctions or summary prosecutions, for alleged contraventions of the Act.

435. The Court said that it was in the carrying out of those functions and the exercise of those powers that the Commission had the incidental express and implied powers to carry out investigations and inquiries and to take evidence and require information. It was also in the carrying out of those functions and the exercise of those powers that it had the added function of making information available under section 25(a). The Court said that this would extend, for instance, to the publication of compilations or summaries of the Commission's decisions or of the results or Court proceedings brought by the Commission.[853]

436. The Court held that, although the Commission had wide powers and functions, these powers and functions did not extend to conducting an inquiry and publishing a report on the efficacy or otherwise of the relevant regulations. The functions and powers did not extend to making findings adverse to persons or corporations otherwise than when determining an application before the Commission, and it followed that a report publishing such findings could not be permissible.[854] The Commerce Commission was a public body, and publication of findings could damage reputations or business relationships. Such findings would also not be subject to appeal.[855] The Court of Appeal emphasised that the Commerce Commission must have power to conduct inquiries, collect information and take evidence for the purpose of exercising its prosecuting power, but this did not extend to making findings or publishing evidence or opinions about evidence.[856]

437. In 2015 the New Zealand Ministry of Business, Innovation and Employment commenced a *Targeted Review of the Commerce Act 1986*.[857] As part of the Review the Ministry considered whether the Commerce Commission should be given powers and resources to undertake market studies. There was concern that there was an institutional gap in New Zealand's competition regime regarding the ability to promote competition, and that a market studies power could fill this gap.[858] On 27 June 2017 the Government announced proposed amendments to the

853. *Telecom Corporation of New Zealand Ltd v. Commerce Commission* [1994] 2 NZLR 421, (1994) 5 TCLR 482, 489, Cooke P.

854. *Ibid.*, 489–490.

855. *Ibid.*, 490. *See also* Casey J, 495–6.

856. *Ibid. See also* Casey J, 498.

857. *See* New Zealand Ministry of Business, Innovation and Employment, *Targeted Review of the Commerce Act 1986*, https://www.mbie.govt.nz/business-and-employment/business/competition-regulation-and-policy/reviews-of-the-commerce-act-1986/targeted-review-of-the-commerce-act-2015/ (accessed 10 May 2019).

858. *Cabinet paper: Targeted Review of the Commerce Act: Initiation and Financing of Market Studies* https://www.mbie.govt.nz/business-and-employment/business/competition-regulation-and-policy/reviews-of-the-commerce-act-1986/targeted-review-of-the-commerce-act-2015/ (accessed 10 May 2019)

Commerce Act 1986 providing the Commission with a market studies power.[859] On 28 March 2018 the Government introduced a new Commerce Amendment Bill that provided for a competition studies (market studies) power. In October 2018, Commerce Amendment Act 2018 came into force, empowering the Commerce Commission to undertake studies into the competitive conditions relating to goods or services in a particular sector if it is in the public interest.[860] The Commission may commence a study on its own initiative or at the direction of the Minister.[861]

438. The above discussion applies to the situation under New Zealand's generic competition law. It should also be noted that there are specific provisions in Part 4 of the Commerce Act[862] that relate to regulated goods and services. Part 4 allows the Commerce Commission to initiate an inquiry into a market in order to assess whether regulation is required,[863] and the Commission is required to hold such an inquiry if required to do so by the Minister.[864] However these provisions apply to markets in which regulation is under consideration, the provisions do not provide for inquiries outside of the context of such regulation. The Commerce Commission does additionally have powers applicable to specific sectors under other legislation, such as the Telecommunications Act.[865]

II. Ex Officio Investigations

439. Statutory powers of the Commerce Commission in relation to investigations are discussed above. Ex Officio investigations are not a separate concept in New Zealand competition law.

III. Complaints

440. Where it receives a complaint about an alleged breach of the Commerce Act, the Commerce Commission may investigate. The Commerce Commission provides information on making a complaint on its website.[866] All complaints to the Commission are recorded and assessed. For complaints relating to a potential breach of the Commerce Act 1986, the Commission will assess it and decide on an appropriate course of action. In these situations, the Commission may exercise its investigative powers discussed above. The Commerce Commission is clear that it is not

859. Jacqui Dean, *Changes to Commerce Act will Enhance Competition: Press Release* 27 June 2017, https://www.beehive.govt.nz/release/changes-commerce-act-will-enhance-competition (accessed 9 May 2019).
860. Commerce Act 1986 s 50.
861. *Ibid.*, s 51.
862. *Ibid.*, Part 4.
863. *Ibid.*, s. 52G specifies when goods or services may be regulated.
864. *Ibid.*, s. 52H–52K.
865. Telecommunications Act 2001 s. 9A.
866. Commerce Commission New Zealand, *Make a Complaint*, http://www.comcom.govt.nz/the-commission/making-a-complaint/ (accessed 10 May 2019).

a complaint handling body and it does not investigate every report it receives. It prioritises investigations in order to use its resources most efficiently. It does not provide legal advice to individuals.[867]

441. After investigating a complaint, the Commission will decide on appropriate action. In deciding whether to undertake enforcement action, the Commission will apply its enforcement criteria. This will involve consideration of the extent of detriment, the seriousness of the conduct and the public interest.[868] The Commission reports on the results of its investigations, and in some cases the Commission decides to publish investigation reports that are of general public interest.[869]

There is also provision for the Commerce Commission to receive complaints made about the Commission, and in such cases the Commission applies its Complaints Policy.[870]

§2. Powers

I. Requests for Information

442. The Commerce Commission has investigative powers as set out in the Commerce Act 1986. In particular, it has the power to require a person to supply information, documents or evidence. Section 98 of the Commerce Act 1986 provides:[871]

> (1) Where the Commission considers it necessary or desirable for the purposes of carrying out its functions and exercising its powers under this Act, the Commission may, by notice in writing served on any person, require that person:
> (a) to furnish to the Commission, by writing signed by that person or, in the case of a body corporate, by a director or competent servant or agent of the body corporate, within the time and in the manner specified in the notice, any information or class of information specified in the notice; or
> (b) to produce to the Commission, or to a person specified in the notice acting on its behalf in accordance with the notice, any document or class of documents specified in the notice; or
> (c) to appear before the Commission at a time and place specified in the notice to give evidence, either orally or in writing, and produce any document or class of documents specified in the notice.

---

867. *Ibid.*
868. Commerce Commission New Zealand, *Enforcement Criteria*, http://www.comcom.govt.nz/the-commission/commission-policies/enforcement-criteria/ (accessed 1 Dec. 2017).
869. Published investigation reports are available on the Commerce Commission website at https://comcom.govt.nz/case-register (accessed 10 May 2019).
870. Commerce Commission New Zealand, *Complaints Policy*, http://www.comcom.govt.nz/the-commission/commission-policies/complaints-policy/ (accessed 1 Dec. 2017).
871. Commerce Act 1986 s. 98.

(2) For the purposes of subsection (1), the Commission's powers under this Act include the power to investigate whether an exception or exemption from this Act (whether under this Act or any other enactment) applies to a person or to a person's conduct.

443. Section 98 therefore gives the Commission the power to require a person to provide information, produce documents or appear before the Commission to give evidence.[872] The powers of the Commission include the power to investigate whether an exception or exemption from the Act applies to a person or their conduct.[873]

444. The Commerce Commission's *Competition and Consumer Investigation Guidelines*[874] set out the principles and process the Commission uses in undertaking an investigation. The principles as stated are:[875]

(1) We are objective, fair and impartial.
(2) We aim to be as open and transparent as we can be.
(3) We investigate in a timely way.
(4) We handle information responsibly.
(5) We are accountable for our decisions.

445. The process involves an initial screening and prioritisation stage in order to determine whether the matter warrants opening an investigation. At the investigation stage, the Commission may seek and receive information voluntarily. Under section 98, it can also issue compulsory notices requiring interviews or the supply of information.[876] The Commission gathers information from a variety of sources, such as the investigated party, other market participants, the public, experts, other third parties or information in the public domain.[877]

---

872. *Ibid.*, s. 98.
873. *Ibid.*, s. 98(2).
874. Commerce Commission New Zealand, *Competition and Consumer Investigation Guidelines* (December 2016), http://www.comcom.govt.nz/the-commission/commission-policies/competition-and-consumer-investigation-guidelines/ (accessed 17 Jul. 2018). Note that these guidelines are currently being updated to reflect amendments to the Commerce Act 1986.
875. *Ibid.*, 7–8.
876. Commerce Act 1986 s. 98. Commerce Commission New Zealand, *Competition and Consumer Investigation Guidelines* (December 2016), 16, http://www.comcom.govt.nz/the-commission/commission-policies/competition-and-consumer-investigation-guidelines/ (accessed 17 Jul. 2018). Note that these guidelines are currently being updated to reflect amendments to the Commerce Act 1986.
877. Commerce Commission New Zealand, *Competition and Consumer Investigation Guidelines* (December 2016), 16, http://www.comcom.govt.nz/the-commission/commission-policies/competition-and-consumer-investigation-guidelines/ (accessed 17 Jul. 2018). Note that these guidelines are currently being updated to reflect amendments to the Commerce Act 1986.

446. Voluntary requests for information may be made orally or in writing, including by a 'please explain' letter.[878] Compulsory requests for information are by compulsory notice under section 98, and they can require provision of information or documents as specified. The Commerce Act provides that 'document' has a broad meaning. 'Document':[879]

> means a document in any form whether signed or initialled or otherwise authenticated by its maker or not; and includes
>
> (a) any writing on any material:
> (b) any information recorded or stored by means of any tape recorder, computer, or other device; and any material subsequently derived from information so recorded or stored:
> (c) any label, marking, or other writing that identifies or describes any thing of which it forms part, or to which it is attached by any means:
> (d) any book, map, plan, graph or drawing:
> (e) any photograph, film, negative, tape, or other device in which 1 or more visual images are embodied so as to be capable (with or without the aid of some other equipment) of being reproduced.

447. The Commerce Commission has issued draft *Document Production Guidelines* with the purpose of assisting with the production of documents in response to a Commission request. [880]

448. A compulsory notice is a written notice that specifies the matter under investigation, the information required, how that information is to be provided and the timeframe.[881] A compulsory notice may also be issued requiring a person to attend a compulsory interview.[882] It is a criminal offence to refuse to comply with a compulsory notice without reasonable excuse, or to furnish information, document or evidence knowing it to be false or misleading.[883] Penalties are fines up to NZD 100,000 for an individual and NZD 300,000 for a company.[884] A person is not excused from furnishing document, evidence or information on the ground that to

878. *Ibid.*, 16–17.
879. Commerce Act 1986 s. 2.
880. Commerce Commission New Zealand, *Document Production Guidelines*, (Draft 30/06/15), Available from http://www.comcom.govt.nz/the-commission/commission-policies/document-production-guidelines/ (accessed 10 Jan. 2018).
881. Commerce Commission New Zealand, *Competition and Consumer Investigation Guidelines* (December 2016), 19, http://www.comcom.govt.nz/the-commission/commission-policies/competition-and-consumer-investigation-guidelines/ (accessed 17 Jul. 2018). Note that these guidelines are currently being updated to reflect amendments to the Commerce Act 1986.
882. Commerce Act 1986 s. 98(1)(c).
883. *Ibid.*, s. 103(1)(a) and (b).
884. *Ibid.*, s. 103(4).

do so might tend to incriminate that person.[885] Where information is obtained from a person compulsorily, there are limits on the admissibility of this evidence against that person.[886]

449. The Commerce Commission uses information received for the purposes of the investigation for which it was obtained. Information is shared within the Commission and may be used for another investigation where relevant.[887]

II. Investigating and Search Powers

450. The Commission has powers to request information as above, and to receive and take evidence, including evidence that may not be admissible in a court of law.[888] It can require and take the giving of evidence on oath.[889] The Commission also has the power to prohibit disclosure of information, documents or evidence.[890] The Commission may receive information and documents on behalf of the Australian Competition and Consumer Commission,[891] and there are also provisions applying to overseas regulators generally.[892]

451. The Commission also has powers to search premises and other places including homes. The Commission has limited powers to conduct searches without a search warrant. As with any member of the public, the Commission may rely on an implied licence to approach a business or residential premises, but the implied licence may be revoked at any time by the proprietor.[893] Searches may also be undertaken with consent.[894]

452. The Commission also has powers to search under a search warrant. Section 98A provides that:

---

885. *Ibid.*, s. 106(4).
886. Commerce Commission New Zealand, *Competition and Consumer Investigation Guidelines* (December 2016), 25, http://www.comcom.govt.nz/the-commission/commission-policies/competition-and-consumer-investigation-guidelines/ (accessed 17 Jul. 2018). Note that these guidelines are currently being updated to reflect amendments to the Commerce Act 1986.
887. *Ibid.*, 30.
888. Commerce Act 1986 s. (1).
889. *Ibid.*, s. 99(2)–(3).
890. *Ibid.*, s. 100.
891. *Ibid.*, s. 99A.
892. *Ibid.*, ss 99B-99P.
893. *Robson v. Hallett* [1967] 2 QB 939 (CA), *Tararo v. R* [2010] NZSC 157 [11]–[12]. *See also* Commerce Commission New Zealand, *Competition and Consumer Investigation Guidelines* (December 2016), 29, http://www.comcom.govt.nz/the-commission/commission-policies/competition-and-consumer-investigation-guidelines/ (accessed 17 Jul. 2018). Note that these guidelines are currently being updated to reflect amendments to the Commerce Act 1986.
894. Commerce Commission New Zealand, *Competition and Consumer Investigation Guidelines* (December 2016), 29, http://www.comcom.govt.nz/the-commission/commission-policies/competition-and-consumer-investigation-guidelines/ (accessed 17 Jul. 2018). Note that these guidelines are currently being updated to reflect amendments to the Commerce Act 1986.

(1) The Commission may, from time to time, authorise an employee of the Commission to search under a warrant issued under subsection (2) any place named in the warrant for the purpose of ascertaining whether a person has engaged in or is engaging in conduct that constitutes or may constitute a contravention of this Act, not being a contravention of section 99A.

(2) An issuing officer (within the meaning of section 3 of the Search and Surveillance Act 2012) who is satisfied, on an application made in the manner provided in subpart 3 of Part 4 of that Act by a person who is authorised under subsection (1) that there are reasonable grounds to believe that it is necessary for the purpose of ascertaining whether or not a person has engaged in or is engaging in conduct that constitutes or may constitute a contravention of this Act, not being a contravention of section 99A, for an employee of the Commission to search any place may, by warrant, authorise that employee to search a place specified in the warrant.

453. Section 98A therefore sets out the search powers. The Commission requires a search warrant in order to conduct a search. The Commission may apply for a search warrant from an issuing officer, such as a judge. Search warrants are granted by issuing officers where there are reasonable grounds to believe that it is necessary for the purpose of ascertaining whether or not a person has engaged or is engaging in conduct that contravenes the Act.[895] This also extends to searches by the Commission in cooperation with an overseas regulator that is investigating conduct contravening its own competition law provisions.[896] The Commerce Commission's practice is to apply for a search warrant where it is unable to obtain evidence in a less intrusive way, such as by voluntary request or compulsory notice.[897]

454. Once a search warrant is obtained, the Commission may authorise an employee, under the search warrant, to search a place named in the warrant.[898] The scope of the search power is limited by the Search and Surveillance Act 2012 Part 4[899] and by the terms of the warrant.[900] A search warrant and its execution must be lawful, reasonable and fair.[901] A copy of the search warrant setting out the terms of

895. Commerce Act 1986 s. 98A(2).

896. *Ibid.*, s. 98A(5).

897. Commerce Commission New Zealand, *Competition and Consumer Investigation Guidelines* (December 2016), 26, http://www.comcom.govt.nz/the-commission/commission-policies/competition-and-consumer-investigation-guidelines/ (accessed 17 Jul. 2018). Note that these guidelines are currently being updated to reflect amendments to the Commerce Act 1986.

898. Commerce Act 1986 s 98A(1).

899. *Ibid.*, s. 98A(3). *See also* Commerce Commission New Zealand, *Competition and Consumer Investigation Guidelines* (December 2016), 25, http://www.comcom.govt.nz/the-commission/commission-policies/competition-and-consumer-investigation-guidelines/ (accessed 17 Jul. 2018). Note that these guidelines are currently being updated to reflect amendments to the Commerce Act 1986.

900. Commerce Act 1986 s. 98A(2).

901. Commerce Commission New Zealand, *Competition and Consumer Investigation Guidelines* (December 2016), 25, http://www.comcom.govt.nz/the-commission/commission-policies/

the warrant is provided to the occupier. The warrant will specify the alleged contravention and what may be seized. It may provide for the Commission to seek assistance, for example in searching computer systems. It may also require the occupier to provide reasonable assistance to the warrant holder.[902] It is a criminal offence to resist, obstruct or delay an employee of the Commission acting pursuant to a warrant issues under section 98A.[903] Penalties are a fine up to NZD 100,000 for an individual and up to NZD 300,000 in any other case.[904]

455. Commission staff executing a warrant may seize items within the scope of the warrant. It may also remove any item of uncertain status in order to determine whether it may be lawfully seized, if it is not reasonably practicable to determine this at the place of search.[905] This may apply to large quantities of documents or computer files.[906] Commission staff may also seize any item found in the search if they have reasonable grounds to believe that they could have seized the item under a warrant or any other power.[907] There are particular provisions for privileged items, including items subject to legal professional privilege.[908] However privilege for a communication or information is not recognised if there is a prima facie case that the communication or information is made or received for a dishonest purpose or to enable or aid any person to commit or plan to commit what the person claiming the privilege knew or ought reasonably have known to be an offence.[909] A person making a claim of privilege may prevent the search of that material or require the return of a copy pending determination of a claim of privilege.[910] Search warrants may authorise search of materials held by a lawyer relating to a client, or held by a minister of religion, medical practitioner or clinical psychologist.[911] In these cases the search warrant may not be executed unless the professional or a representative is present.[912] Commission staff executing a warrant who have reasonable grounds to believe that anything discovered in the search may be the subject of privilege must provide a reasonable opportunity to claim privilege.[913] The Commerce Commission

---

competition-and-consumer-investigation-guidelines/ (accessed 17 Jul. 2018). Note that these guidelines are currently being updated to reflect amendments to the Commerce Act 1986.

902. Search and Surveillance Act 2012 Part 4, Commerce Commission New Zealand, *Competition and Consumer Investigation Guidelines* (December 2016), 26, http://www.comcom.govt.nz/the-commission/commission-policies/competition-and-consumer-investigation-guidelines/ (accessed 17 Jul. 2018). Note that these guidelines are currently being updated to reflect amendments to the Commerce Act 1986.
903. Commerce Act 1986 s. 103(1)(c).
904. *Ibid.*, s. 103(4).
905. Search and Surveillance Act 2012 s. 112.
906. Commerce Commission New Zealand, *Competition and Consumer Investigation Guidelines* (December 2016), 28, http://www.comcom.govt.nz/the-commission/commission-policies/competition-and-consumer-investigation-guidelines/ (accessed 17 Jul. 2018). Note that these guidelines are currently being updated to reflect amendments to the Commerce Act 1986.
907. Search and Surveillance Act 2012 s. 123.
908. *Ibid.*, Part 4, Subpart 5.
909. *Ibid.*, s. 136(2).
910. *Ibid.*, s. 142.
911. *Ibid.*, ss 143–144.
912. *Ibid.*, ss 143–144.
913. *Ibid.*, s. 145.

attempt to resolve disputes about privilege by agreement, but will refer the matter to a court if agreement is not achieved.[914] The Search and Surveillance Act 2012 sets out procedures applying to seized items.[915]

III. Cooperation with Other State Institutions

456. The Commerce Commission is an independent Crown entity. It does however work co-operatively with other agencies and organisations, and it has formal cooperation agreements with four agencies. The four agreements are:[916]

- Memorandum of Understanding between Department of Internal Affairs and Commerce Commission – 10 October 2016.
- Memorandum of Understanding between Financial Markets Authority and Commerce Commission – 31 March 2014.
- Memorandum of Understanding between Gas Industry Company Limited and Commerce Commission – 5 August 2011.
- Memorandum of Understanding between Electricity Authority and Commerce Commission – December 2010.

§3. Right of Defence

I. Content and Notification of Opening Decisions

457. New Zealand operates an adversarial court system, and the Commerce Commission may commence court action as a result of an investigation. The Commerce Commission has published *Enforcement Criteria,*[917]and *Enforcement Response Guidelines*[918] to outline the approach of the Commission to choosing enforcement options and whether it will pursue court action in any given case. Under its *Enforcement Criteria*, the Commission decides whether to commence or continue enforcement action, the most appropriate type(s) of enforcement action

914. *Ibid.*, ss 145–147, Commerce Commission New Zealand, *Competition and Consumer Investigation Guidelines* (December 2016), 28, http://www.comcom.govt.nz/the-commission/commission-policies/competition-and-consumer-investigation-guidelines/ (accessed 17 Jul. 2018). Note that these guidelines are currently being updated to reflect amendments to the Commerce Act 1986.
915. Search and Surveillance Act 2012 ss 149–163.
916. These documents are all available from the Commerce Commission website at https://comcom.govt.nz/about-us/working-with-other-agencies (accessed 10 May 2019).
917. Commerce Commission New Zealand, *Enforcement Criteria*, http://www.comcom.govt.nz/the-commission/commission-policies/enforcement-criteria/ (accessed 2 Oct. 2017).
918. Commerce Commission New Zealand, *Enforcement Response Guidelines* (October 2013), http://www.comcom.govt.nz/the-commission/commission-policies/enforcement-response-guidelines/ (accessed 9 Jan. 2018).

and the most appropriate response in each case. In making these decisions, the Commission considers the extent of the detriment; the seriousness of the conduct; and the public interest.[919]

458. The Commission will not initiate court action for every breach of the Commerce Act. The Commission prefers to encourage compliance through the use of non-enforcement options, such as education and engaging with market participants.[920] Low-level enforcement options include taking no further action, or sending a compliance advice or warning letter.[921] High level responses are reserved for situations of repeated or continued non-compliance, or where the harm is great, the conduct is serious or there is a compelling public interest.[922]

459. The Commerce Commission is also receptive to resolving non-compliance through a negotiated settlement, and this may be achieved before or after commencement of court proceedings, and settlements may be out-of-court or in-court.[923] The process involves the relevant party approaching the Commission to make a settlement proposal or initiate a plea discussion, and this can be on a 'without prejudice' basis. Commission staff will work with the parties to develop a proposal which can then be submitted to Commission members for consideration and decision. Settlements are generally recorded by formal settlement agreement, or, if in-court, by presenting the Judge with admissions and submissions. Settlements are generally made public unless there is compelling reasons not to do so.[924]

460. The Commission will not negotiate a settlement in all cases. In some cases it will consider itself unable to negotiate, for example there a court judgment is needed to provide an important public precedent or the conduct is particularly serious.[925]

461. Where court action is initiated, this will generally be a civil law action. New Zealand generic competition law does not contain significant criminal offences or criminal sanctions. Contraventions of the restrictive trade practices and business acquisitions provisions are enforced through the civil courts. Sanctions include pecuniary penalties, but these are a civil rather than criminal remedy.

---

919. Commerce Commission New Zealand, *Enforcement Criteria*, http://www.comcom.govt.nz/the-commission/commission-policies/enforcement-criteria/ (accessed 9 Jan. 2018).
920. Commerce Commission New Zealand, *Enforcement Response Guidelines* (October 2013), 4 http://www.comcom.govt.nz/the-commission/commission-policies/enforcement-response-guidelines/ (accessed 9 Jan. 2018).
921. *Ibid.*, 7–10.
922. *Ibid.*, 6.
923. *Ibid.*, 4.
924. *Ibid.*, 14.
925. *Ibid.*, 13.

462. Civil enforcement actions may be brought by the Commerce Commission, and only the Commerce Commission may bring an action seeking pecuniary penalties.[926] The Commission or a private party may bring a civil action seeking an injunction or damages.[927] Court action may also be initiated seeking an interim injunction. Interim injunctions are provided for in the Commerce Act and are available in relation to restrictive trade practices and business acquisitions provisions. Section 81 provides that the Commission or any person may apply for the grant of an injunction restraining conduct that would contravene the restrictive trade practices provisions. It also extends to secondary conduct.[928] Section 84 provides that the Commission or any person may apply for an injunction in relation to a contravention of the business acquisitions provisions.[929]

II. Proceedings: Hearings, Access to File and Briefs

463. Commencement of court action begins with the issue of proceedings by filing the appropriate pleading documents in court. It is common for the trial on the merits to be preceded by preliminary matters, for example relating to discovery of documents. Interim injunctions may also be sought.[930]

464. The Commerce Commission has published *Enforcement Criteria*[931]and *Enforcement Response Guidelines*[932] to outline the approach of the Commission to choosing enforcement options and whether it will pursue court action in any given case.

465. The conduct of court proceedings is according to the rules of the relevant court. The Commerce Act 1986 provides for the jurisdiction of the courts in relation to civil enforcement of the competition law provisions. The High Court has jurisdiction in relation to contraventions of the restrictive trade practices provisions and business acquisitions provisions.[933] It also has jurisdiction to hear and determine appeals from determinations of the Commerce Commission.[934] High Court decisions may be appealed to the Court of Appeal. Decisions of the Court of Appeal may be appealed to the highest court, the New Zealand Supreme Court.

466. Proceedings in the High Court are governed by the High Court Rules. The practice and procedure of the High Court in all civil proceedings and interlocutory

926. Commerce Act 1986 s. 80.
927. *Ibid.*, ss 81–82A.
928. *Ibid.*, s. 81.
929. *Ibid.*, s. 84(1).
930. *Ibid.*, s. 88.
931. Commerce Commission New Zealand, *Enforcement Criteria*, http://www.comcom.govt.nz/the-commission/commission-policies/enforcement-criteria/ (accessed 2 Oct. 2017).
932. Commerce Commission New Zealand, *Enforcement Response Guidelines* (October 2013), http://www.comcom.govt.nz/the-commission/commission-policies/enforcement-response-guidelines/ (accessed 2 Oct. 2017).
933. Commerce Act 1986 s. 75(1)(a) and (b).
934. *Ibid.*, s. 75(1)(e).

applications is regulated by the High Court Rules.[935] Proceedings in the High Court normally begin with the filing of a statement of claim and notice of proceeding in the appropriate court registry.[936] These documents must comply with the High Court Rules.[937] If the defendant intends to defend the proceeding, the defendant must then file a statement of defence to the plaintiff's claim within the appropriate time limit.[938] Subsequent proceedings will depend on decisions of the parties, but will also be regulated by requirements of the High Court Rules.

467. Appeals to the Court of Appeal and Supreme Court are not covered by the High Court Rules. Civil actions in the Court of Appeal are covered by the Court of Appeal (Civil) Rules.[939] Proceedings in the Supreme Court are covered by the Supreme Court Rules.[940]

468. The Commerce Commission has adopted a *Model Litigant Policy* which is a statement of civil litigation principles.[941] Under this policy, Commission lawyers and lawyers acting on behalf of the Commission are expected to act in accordance with the principles stated in the policy and to assist the Commission to comply. The policy states that the Commission will act as a model litigant in the conduct of litigation, which requires that the Commission 'act with complete propriety, fairly and in accordance with the highest professional standards'.[942] It allows the Commission to act decisively and properly to protect and advance its interests as a regulator and enforcement agency, and to take all legitimate steps in pursuing litigation or in testing claims and defending against claims.[943] Under the policy, the Commission is required to:[944]

---

935. High Court Rules 2016 Available from http://www.legislation.govt.nz/regulation/public/2016/0225/latest/DLM6959801.html (accessed 18 Jan. 2018) The High Court Rules are deemed to form part of the Senior Courts Act 2016 under s. 147 of that Act.
936. High Court Rules rr 5.22–5.25.
937. *Ibid.*, Part 5.
938. *Ibid.*, r 5.47.
939. Court of Appeal (Civil) Rules 2005, available from http://www.legislation.govt.nz/regulation/public/2005/0069/latest/DLM319746.html (accessed 10 Jan. 2018). Criminal actions are covered by the Court of Appeal (Criminal) Rules, available from http://www.legislation.govt.nz/regulation/public/2001/0371/latest/DLM95709.html (accessed 10 Jan. 2018).
940. Supreme Court Rules 2004, Available from http://www.legislation.govt.nz/regulation/public/2004/0199/latest/DLM270805.html (accessed 10 Jan. 2018). The Supreme Court Rules apply to both civil and criminal appeals.
941. Commerce Commission New Zealand, *Model Litigant Policy*, Adopted 12 February 2009. Available from https://comcom.govt.nz/about-us/our-policies-and-guidelines/model-litigant-policy (accessed 10 May 2019).
942. Commerce Commission New Zealand, *Model Litigant Policy*, Adopted 12 February 2009, [7]. Available from https://comcom.govt.nz/about-us/our-policies-and-guidelines/model-litigant-policy (accessed 10 May 2019).
943. Commerce Commission New Zealand, *Model Litigant Policy*, Adopted 12 February 2009, [9]. Available from https://comcom.govt.nz/about-us/our-policies-and-guidelines/model-litigant-policy (accessed 10 May 2019).
944. Commerce Commission New Zealand, *Model Litigant Policy*, Adopted 12 February 2009, [8]. Available from https://comcom.govt.nz/about-us/our-policies-and-guidelines/model-litigant-policy (accessed 10 May 2019).

8.1. Take and defend litigation in accordance with the Commission's statutory functions arising under a range of statutes, and at all times to act according to the Commission's purpose of promoting dynamic and responsive markets so that New Zealanders benefit from competitive prices, better quality and greater choice.
8.2. Deal with litigation promptly and efficiently and without causing unnecessary delays or expense, and to seek to have cases resolved as early as is appropriate and on such terms as are appropriate.
8.3. Apply an even-handed approach in the handling of litigation.
8.4. Consider the possibilities for, and initiate where appropriate, alternative means of avoiding or resolving litigation, including by cooperation or other agreed resolution.
8.5. Responsibly spend public funds in relation to litigation.
8.6. Not seek to take inappropriate advantage of an impecunious opponent.
8.7. Not seek to contest matters which it accepts as correct and not seek to take unmeritorious points for tactical reasons.
8.8. Not pursue appeals unless the Commission considers that it has reasonable prospects of success and /or the appeal is otherwise justified in the public interest. The filing of an appeal may be justified in the public interest where it is necessary to avoid prejudice to the interests of the Commission pending the receipt of proper consideration of legal advice, provided that a decision whether to pursue the appeal is made as soon as is practicable.

III. Statement of Objections

469. The High Court Rules set out the requirements for a defendant who wishes to defend a proceeding by filing an answer to the statement of claim. A defendant intending to defend must file a statement of defence to the plaintiff's claim within the appropriate time limit.[945] A defendant may also wish to make a counterclaim and this process is also covered by the High Court Rules.[946]

IV. Final Hearing and Decision

470. The adversarial process in New Zealand involves the court hear the evidence and arguments for both sides at trial. The court then issues its judgment. The procedures for the trial and the judgment are governed by the rules of the relevant court. The High Court Rules contain detailed rules for trial and judgment.[947]

945. High Court Rules rr 5.47–5.52.
946. *Ibid.*, rr 5.53–5.61.
947. *Ibid.*, Parts 10 and 11.

For appeals to the Court of Appeal and Supreme Court, the rules of those courts apply.[948]

948. Court of Appeal (Civil) Rules 2005, available from http://www.legislation.govt.nz/regulation/public/2005/0069/latest/DLM319746.html (accessed 10 Jan. 2018). Supreme Court Rules 2004, Available from http://www.legislation.govt.nz/regulation/public/2004/0199/latest/DLM270805.html (accessed 10 Jan. 2018).

Chapter 2. Voluntary Notifications and Clearance Decisions & Merger Control

§1. Preliminary Filing Obligations

I. Criteria and Thresholds

471. Mergers and acquisitions are prohibited if they would have, or would be likely to have, the effect of substantially lessening competition in a market.[949] Section 47(1) of the Act provides that a 'person' must not acquire assets of a business or shares if the acquisition would have, or would be likely to have, the effect of substantially lessening competition in a market.[950] 'Person' includes interconnected or associated persons, including bodies corporate.[951] A person is 'associated if 'that person is able, whether directly or indirectly, to exert a substantial degree of influence over the activities of the other'.[952] A 'substantial degree of influence' in this context is not satisfied by reason only of the fact that they are in the same market or one supplies to the other.[953]

472. In addition, in 2017 new sections 47A–47D were inserted into the Act.[954] These sections are discussed in Part II, Chapter 3 Concentrations.

473. Parties to a proposed merger or acquisition may apply to the Commerce Commission for a clearance or authorisation.[955] Clearances are available for business acquisitions that will not, or would not be likely to have, the effect of substantially lessening competition in a market.[956] Authorisations are available for business acquisitions that will result, or will be likely to result, in such a benefit to the public that they should be permitted.[957] The effect of a clearance or authorisation is that the prohibition in section 47 or 47A will not apply.[958] Decisions of the Commission on clearances and authorisations may be appealed to the High Court and potentially upward to the Court of Appeal and Supreme Court.

474. New Zealand has a voluntary merger regime, there is no statutory obligation to advise the Commerce Commission if parties are proposing to merge. Businesses can merge without applying for clearance from the Commission. However, if a merger raises competition issues and the parties proceed without a clearance or

949. Commerce Act 1986 s. 47(1).
950. *Ibid.*, s. 47(1).
951. *Ibid.*, s. 47(2).
952. *Ibid.*, s. 47(3).
953. *Ibid.*, s. 47(4).
954. Commerce (Cartels and other Matters) Amendment Act 2017 s. 11. These sections are discussed in Part II, Chapter 3 Concentrations.
955. Commerce Act 1986 Part 5.
956. *Ibid.*, ss 66 and 67(3).
957. *Ibid.*, s. 67(3).
958. *Ibid.*, s. 69.

authorisation, this may put them at risk of legal action from the Commission or others. The Commerce Commission advises businesses considering a merger to seek independent legal advice as to whether their proposed merger raises competition issues and whether they should seek a clearance.[959] The Commerce Commission may enter into pre-notification discussions before a clearance application is made, if it is satisfied that the applicant has a good faith intention to proceed with the merger. The Commission will treat the fact and content of all pre-notification discussions as confidential until the application is registered. Once an application is made, the Commission will publish a public version of the application.[960]

475. The Commerce Commission's *Mergers and Acquisitions Guidelines* are a guide to the approach of the Commission in assessing whether a merger or acquisition would be likely to substantially lessen competition in a market and the process for considering clearance applications.[961] The *Guidelines* set out the counterfactual test for substantially lessening competition. The test is a comparison of the likely state of competition if the merger proceeds with the likely state of competition if the merger does not proceed. Both scenarios are forward-looking.[962] If competition would be substantially lessened with the merger when compared to any of the likely states of competition without the merger, then the merger will have the likely effect of substantially lessening competition.[963] The Commission makes a pragmatic and commercial assessment of what is likely to occur, taking account of factors such as market growth and technological changes.[964] The decision of the Commission may be appealed to the High Court and thence to the Court of Appeal and Supreme Court.[965]

476. The *Guidelines* discuss market share and concentration measures in relation to mergers between competitors.[966] The Commerce Commission uses market share and concentration indicators to identify mergers which are less likely to raise competition concerns. The *Guidelines* are clear that this is to provide an initial

---

959. Commerce Commission New Zealand, *Mergers and Acquisitions Guidelines* (2013) 48. Available from http://www.comcom.govt.nz/business-competition/guidelines-2/mergers-and-acquisitions-guidelines/ (accessed 10 Jan. 2018). *See also* Commerce Commission New Zealand, *Mergers and Acquisitions – Applying for a Clearance*, Fact Sheet (October 2011), http://www.comcom.govt.nz/business-competition/fact-sheets-3/mergers-and-acquisitions-applying-for-a-clearance-2/ (accessed 10 Jan. 2018).
960. Commerce Commission New Zealand, *Mergers and Acquisitions Guidelines* (2013) 48-51. Available from http://www.comcom.govt.nz/business-competition/guidelines-2/mergers-and-acquisitions-guidelines/ (accessed 10 Jan. 2018).
961. *See* Commerce Commission, *Mergers and Acquisitions Guidelines* (2013) http://www.comcom.govt.nz/business-competition/guidelines-2/mergers-and-acquisitions-guidelines/ (accessed 10 Aug. 2017).
962. *Ibid.*, 16–20.
963. *Ibid.*, 18.
964. *Ibid.*, 19.
965. Commerce Act 1986 s. 75.
966. Commerce Commission, *Mergers and Acquisitions Guidelines* (2013) 30-31, 44, http://www.comcom.govt.nz/business-competition/guidelines-2/mergers-and-acquisitions-guidelines/ (accessed 10 Aug. 2017).

guide, but is not a substitute for full competition analysis.[967] The Commission's stated view is that a merger is unlikely to require a clearance where, post-merger, the three largest firms in the market have a combined market share of less than 70%, and the merged firm's combined market share is less than 40%, and/or where the three largest firms in the market have a combined market share of 70% or more, and the merged firm's combined market share is less than 20%.[968] However these indicators are not conclusive and do not substitute for a full analysis. The *Guidelines* also make clear that, where there is uncertainty about the appropriate market definition, the market definition that results in the worst case market share aggregation when applying the indicators should be adopted.[969]

II. Turnover Calculation

477. New Zealand competition law does not have a turnover threshold for merger notification and does not use turnover to identify mergers which are more or less likely to raise competition concerns.

III. Market Share Calculation

478. In measuring market shares, the Commerce Commission chooses the measure that it considers best reflects the competitive issue under consideration, taking into account the nature of the product and availability of data. The Commission states that, where relevant data is available, the starting point is to use:[970]

- revenue shares for differentiated products, as revenue share is likely to be a better indicator of market size and rival firms' competitive positions;
- production and sales capacity shares for firms with excess capacity supplying homogeneous products; and
- shares of reserves for natural resources markets where reserves are easily accessible.

A variety of these measures may be used, and the Commission often uses quantity sold as in combination with other measures. For potential competitors in supply, the Commission includes only the output or capacity that that firm could supply easily, profitably and quickly and without significant cost. Imports are included, and when channelled through a New Zealand firm they are generally added to that firm's domestic production. The Commission says that data from a number of years may be used, and that market shares that are stable over a period of years are more likely to be informative.[971]

967. *Ibid.*, 30.
968. *Ibid.*
969. *Ibid.*
970. *Ibid.*, 31.
971. *Ibid.*

IV. Other Relevant Notions

479. As discussed, New Zealand has a voluntary merger regime, and there is no statutory or other obligation to advise the Commerce Commission if parties are proposing to merge. Businesses can merge without applying for clearance from the Commission. However, if a merger raises competition issues and the parties proceed without a clearance or authorisation, this may put them at risk of legal action from the Commission or others. Because it is not compulsory to notify the Commerce Commission of mergers, the Commission monitors markets to identify potentially anticompetitive mergers where he merging firms have not sought clearance or authorisation. In these situations the Commission will investigate and may take appropriate enforcement action.[972]

§2. Structure of Proceedings

I. Preliminary Assessment and Full Investigation

480. The Commerce Commission investigates mergers that potentially raise competition concerns. Parties to a proposed merger may seek a clearance or authorisation. The Commerce Commission will grant a clearance if it is satisfied that it would not be likely to substantially lessen competition in a New Zealand market.[973] The Commission will authorise a merger if it is satisfied that the merger will result, or would be likely to result, in such a benefit to the public that it should be permitted, even though it will have, or be likely to have, the effect of substantially lessening competition in a New Zealand market.[974]

481. As discussed above, the Commerce Commission's *Competition and Consumer Investigation Guidelines*[975] set out the principles and process the Commission uses in undertaking an assessment and investigation. The process involves an initial screening and prioritisation stage in order to determine whether the matter warrants opening an investigation.

482. Clearance Process
The clearance process has four stages. These are:[976]

(1) the pre-clearance stage;

972. *Ibid.*, 10.
973. Commerce Act 1986 s. 66.
974. *Ibid.*, s. 67.
975. Commerce Commission New Zealand, *Competition and Consumer Investigation Guidelines* (December 2016), http://www.comcom.govt.nz/the-commission/commission-policies/competition-and-consumer-investigation-guidelines/ (accessed 17 Jul. 2018). Note that these guidelines are currently being updated to reflect amendments to the Commerce Act 1986.
976. Commerce Commission New Zealand, *Mergers and Acquisitions Guidelines* (2013) 48. Available from http://www.comcom.govt.nz/business-competition/guidelines-2/mergers-and-acquisitions-guidelines/ (accessed 10 Jan. 2018).

(2) the clearance application stage;
(3) the Commission investigation and determination stage; and
(4) the post-determination stage.

483. At the pre-clearance stage, the Commerce Commission advises businesses considering a merger to seek independent legal advice as to whether their proposed merger raises competition issues and whether they should seek a clearance.[977] The Commerce Commission encourages potential applicants to inform it about potential clearance applications as early as possible, by contacting the Competition Manager. It also encourages applicants to have pre-notification discussions with it before a clearance application is made, but this is not compulsory. The Commission will enter into pre-notification discussions if it is satisfied that the applicant has a good faith intention to proceed with the merger. Pre-notification discussions can reduce the time taken in the investigations stage and benefit the applicant and the Commission, although the Commission cannot give an 'informal' clearance as a result of this process. The Commission encourages at least one of the applicant's senior employees to attend pre-notification discussions, and it expects a substantially developed draft clearance application to be provided at least two working days before the meeting. The Commission will treat the fact and content of all pre-notification discussions as confidential until the application is registered.

484. The application stage requires the applicant to submit a clearance application on the prescribed form and pay the prescribed fee.[978] The Commission requires both a confidential and a public version of the application.[979] Once an application is made, the Commission will publish a public version of the application.[980]

485. At the investigation stage, the Commission may seek and receive information voluntarily. Under section 98, it can also issue compulsory notices requiring interviews or the supply of information.[981] The Commission gathers information from a variety of sources, such as the investigated party, other market participants, the public, experts, other third parties or information in the public domain.[982] Voluntary requests for information may be made orally or in writing, including by a

---

977. *Ibid. See also* Commerce Commission New Zealand, *Mergers and Acquisitions – Applying for a Clearance, Fact Sheet* (October 2011), http://www.comcom.govt.nz/business-competition/fact-sheets-3/mergers-and-acquisitions-applying-for-a-clearance-2/ (accessed 10 Jan. 2018).

978. The form is available at https://comcom.govt.nz/business/merging-or-acquiring-a-company/applying-for-a-merger-clearance (accessed 10 May 2019).

979. Commerce Commission New Zealand, *Mergers and Acquisitions Guidelines* (2013) 50, Available from http://www.comcom.govt.nz/business-competition/guidelines-2/mergers-and-acquisitions-guidelines/ (accessed 10 Jan. 2018).

980. *Ibid.*, 48-51.

981. Commerce Act 1986 s. 98. Commerce Commission New Zealand, *Competition and Consumer Investigation Guidelines* (December 2016), 16, http://www.comcom.govt.nz/the-commission/commission-policies/competition-and-consumer-investigation-guidelines/ (accessed 17 Jul. 2018). Note that these guidelines are currently being updated to reflect amendments to the Commerce Act 1986.

982. Commerce Commission New Zealand, *Competition and Consumer Investigation Guidelines* (December 2016), 16, http://www.comcom.govt.nz/the-commission/commission-policies/

'please explain' letter.[983] Compulsory requests for information are by compulsory notice under section 98, and they can require provision of information or documents as specified. A compulsory notice is a written notice that specifies the matter under investigation, the information required, how that information is to be provided and the timeframe.[984] A compulsory notice may also be issued requiring a person to attend a compulsory interview.[985] A more detailed discussion of the Commerce Commission investigatory powers is above.

The Commission prepares a range of documents as part of the assessment process. These include a statement of preliminary issues, a letter of issues and a letter of unresolved issues. For most clearance applications (other than the most straight forward) the Commerce Commission publishes a statement of preliminary issues setting out the Commission's preliminary view of the competition issues. The statement of preliminary issues is accompanied by a media release inviting responses and is published approximately 15–25 working days after registering application.[986]

486. Where after initial investigations the Commerce Commission has concerns about potential competition issues that may arise from the proposed merger, it will send a letter of issues to the applicant. The aim is to clearly outline Commission concerns and invite the applicant to respond and provide further information. If there are remaining unresolved issues after the applicant responds, the Commission is likely to send the applicant a letter of unresolved issues, which give the applicant a further opportunity to provide additional information or submissions, such as divestment undertakings.[987]

487. Another aspect of the Commission's investigation and determination stage relates to international mergers. For mergers affecting a number of jurisdictions, the Guidelines state that the Commission may contact overseas competition authorities to inform them of the application and to exchange views. There is a formal protocol for cooperation with the Australian Competition and Consumer Commission.[988] However, confidential information may not be disclosed without the consent of the party that provided the information.[989]

---

competition-and-consumer-investigation-guidelines/ (accessed 17 Jul. 2018). Note that these guidelines are currently being updated to reflect amendments to the Commerce Act 1986.

983. *Ibid.*,16–17.

984. *Ibid.*, 19.

985. Commerce Act 1986 s. 98(1)(c).

986. Commerce Commission New Zealand, *Mergers and Acquisitions Guidelines* (2013) 55. Available from http://www.comcom.govt.nz/business-competition/guidelines-2/mergers-and-acquisitions-guidelines/ (accessed 10 Jan. 2018).

987. *Ibid.*

988. Australian Competition and Consumer Commission and New Zealand Commerce Commission, *Cooperation Protocol for Merger Review* (2006), Available from http://registers.accc.gov.au/content/index.phtml/itemId/757826 (accessed 10 May 2019). *See also* Commerce Commission New Zealand, *Mergers and Acquisitions Guidelines* (2013) 56. Available from http://www.comcom.govt.nz/business-competition/guidelines-2/mergers-and-acquisitions-guidelines/ (accessed 10 Jan. 2018).

989. Commerce Commission New Zealand, *Mergers and Acquisitions Guidelines* (2013) 56. Available from http://www.comcom.govt.nz/business-competition/guidelines-2/mergers-and-acquisitions-guidelines/ (accessed 10 Jan. 2018).

488. At the post-determination stage of the clearance process the Commerce Commission issues a decision either granting of declining the clearance. The Commission advises the applicant, publishes the decision along with a media release and also publishes written reasons for the decision.[990] Confidential information, such as commercially sensitive information, will not be published.[991]

II. Time Framework

489. The Commerce Act section 66 requires that the Commerce Commission must either grant or decline a merger application within 40 days of the date of registration of the notice. It can be a longer period if the Commission and applicant agree.[992] The Commerce Commission advises that more straightforward applications may take less than 40 working days while more complex applications will take longer.[993] The Commerce Commission *Guidelines* set out an indicative timeline. Under this timeline it indicates it may publish a statement of preliminary issues by day 15, give a clearance or send a letter of issues by day 25, meet with the applicant and provide an updated tentative timeline by day 30 and grant or decline the clearance by day 40. For more complex applications, a letter of unresolved issues seeking an extension will be sent by day 40 and there will be a meeting with the applicant and updated tentative timeline by day 45.[994]

III. Right of Defence

490. The clearance process is conducted in stages, and the Commission seeks information and submissions from the applicants and others throughout the process, as outlined above. The Commission enters into pre-notification discussions[995] and seeks responses to the statement of preliminary issues, letter of issues and letter of unresolved issues.[996] The Commission may also hold a conference before making a determination.[997]

990. *Ibid.*
991. *Ibid.*, 57.
992. Commerce Act 1986 s. 66(3).
993. Commerce Commission New Zealand, *Mergers and Acquisitions Guidelines* (2013) 52. Available from http://www.comcom.govt.nz/business-competition/guidelines-2/mergers-and-acquisitions-guidelines/ (accessed 10 Jan. 2018).
994. *Ibid.*, 52.
995. *Ibid.*, 48.
996. *Ibid.*
997. Commerce Act 1986 s. 69B.

491. If the Commission's decision is to decline the merger, the applicant or a person whose assets are proposed to be acquired under the merger (the merger target) may challenge the Commission's decision in the High Court.[998] There is a right to appeal a decision of the High Court to the Court of Appeal, and with leave, to the Supreme Court.[999]

§3. Clearance and Conditional Clearance

I. Conditions and Undertakings

A. Content

492. Divestment undertakings may be accepted as part of a clearance. The Commission may accept a written undertaking to dispose of assets or shares specified in the undertaking, and the undertaking, if accepted, is deemed to form part of the clearance given.[1000] The Commerce Commission will consider whether a proposed divestment undertaking will remedy likely substantial lessening of competition in a market by resulting in sufficient competitive constraint on the merged firm so that a substantial lessening of competition is no longer likely.[1001]

493. If a clearance is granted and the divestment undertaking is contravened, the clearance is void from the date it was granted and the merger may be challenged in the High Court.[1002] The Commerce Commission may apply to the High Court for an order requiring divestment of the assets or shares in accordance with the undertaking.[1003]

494. If the divestment undertaking is contravened and the merger has not been completed, the Commerce Commission may apply for an injunction restraining completion of the merger.[1004] If the merger has proceeded, the Commerce Commission may apply for pecuniary penalties for contravention of the undertaking.[1005] Injunctions and penalties in these circumstances extend to ancillary liability, so that they apply also to attempts to contravene an undertaking and to conduct including

998. *Ibid.*, ss 75, 91, 92(c).
999. *Ibid.*, s. 97.
1000. *Ibid.*, s. 69A.
1001. Commerce Commission New Zealand, *Mergers and Acquisitions Guidelines* (2013) Attachment F, 71. Available from http://www.comcom.govt.nz/business-competition/guidelines-2/mergers-and-acquisitions-guidelines/ (accessed 10 Jan. 2018).
1002. Commerce Act 1986 s. 69AB.
1003. *Ibid.*, s. 85B. Section 85B(2) provides that the application for a divestment order must be made within 12 months from the date on which the obligation under the undertaking was required to be met.
1004. Commerce Act 1986 s. 84.
1005. *Ibid.*, s. 85A.

aiding, abetting, counselling, procuring or inducing a contravention.[1006] An applicant may apply to vary an undertaking and the Commission will accept the variation if it considers that the variation would not have materially affected its decision to give the clearance.[1007]

B. Timing

495. A divestment undertaking may be offered at any stage during the investigation, but the Commerce Commission encourages applicants to offer divestment undertakings as early as possible in the clearance application process.[1008]

§4. Relations with Other Merger Control Authorities

I. Other Authorities Within the Local Jurisdiction

496. The Commerce Commission is an independent Crown entity. It does however work co-operatively with other agencies and organisations, and it has formal cooperation agreements with four agencies.[1009]

497. For mergers, there are also other separate authorities from which approval may be required. Within New Zealand, a merger involving foreign investment may require approval from the Overseas Investment Office.

498. Overseas Investment Office

Under section 10 of the Overseas Investment Act 2005, a merger transaction requires consent of the Overseas Investment Office if it will result in an overseas investment in sensitive land or an overseas investment in significant business assets.[1010] Consent will also be required for a transaction that will result in an overseas investment in fishing quota.[1011] The Overseas Investment Act sets out criteria by which land constitutes 'sensitive land' in this context.[1012] An overseas investment requiring consent is an investment by an 'overseas person' as defined in the Overseas Investment Act.[1013] Generally this means investors who aren't New

1006. *Ibid.*, ss 84 and 85A.
1007. *Ibid.*,. An application to vary the undertaking must be made no later than 20 working days before the date on which the relevant obligation under the undertaking must be met.
1008. Commerce Commission New Zealand, *Mergers and Acquisitions Guidelines* (2013) 55 and Attachment F, 70. Available from http://www.comcom.govt.nz/business-competition/guidelines-2/mergers-and-acquisitions-guidelines/ (accessed 10 Jan. 2018).
1009. These documents are all available from the Commerce Commission website at https://comcom.govt.nz/about-us/working-with-other-agencies (accessed 10 May 2019).
1010. Overseas Investment Act 2005 s. 10.
1011. *Ibid.*, s. 10, referring to the Fisheries Act 1996 ss 56–58B.
1012. *Ibid.*, Schedule 1.
1013. *Ibid.*, s. 7.

Zealand citizens or ordinarily resident in New Zealand, or body corporates with more than 25% ownership or control. The requirements also apply to associates of overseas persons.[1014]

499. The Overseas Investment Act sets out criteria for assessment of proposed overseas investments in sensitive land, business assets and fishing quota.[1015] In general terms, investors are usually required to establish their business experience, that they are of good character and for sensitive land, demonstrate the benefits to New Zealand of their investment.[1016] The Overseas Investment Act also sets out the process for applying for consent to an overseas investment.[1017]

500. Where consent under the Overseas Investment Act is required, consent must be obtained for a transaction before the overseas investment is given effect under the transaction.[1018] It is an offence to give effect to an overseas investment for which consent is required if this is done without the consent required.[1019]

501. Under the Overseas Investment Act the decision maker is the relevant government Minister or Ministers, this may be delegated.[1020] Decisions are published by the Overseas Investment Office.[1021]

II. International Coordination

502. The Commerce Commission has entered into a number of international agreements with overseas competition agencies, and these agreements generally provide for cooperation between the agencies and information sharing. General agreements of this kind exist with Australia, Canada, United Kingdom and Taiwan competition agencies.[1022] For mergers affecting a number of jurisdictions, the *Mergers and Acquisitions Guidelines* state that the Commission may contact overseas competition authorities to inform them of the application and to exchange views. Cooperation may include coordinating processes, sharing information provided by applicants and third parties, sharing analysis and gathering information on behalf of the other agency.[1023] Sharing information does not include sharing of confidential

1014. *Ibid.*, ss 12–13.
1015. *Ibid.*, ss 16–18.
1016. *See* Land Information New Zealand, Overseas Investment, https://www.linz.govt.nz/regulatory/overseas-investment (accessed 16 Jan. 2018).
1017. Overseas Investment Act 2005 ss 21–29.
1018. *Ibid.*, s. 11.
1019. *Ibid.*, s. 42.
1020. *Ibid.*, ss 24 and 32.
1021. Decision summaries can be found at https://www.linz.govt.nz/regulatory/overseas-investment/decision-summaries-statistics (accessed 16 Jan. 2018).
1022. Details and text of the agreements can be found at https://comcom.govt.nz/about-us/working-with-other-agencies (accessed 10 May 2019).
1023. Commerce Commission New Zealand, *Mergers and Acquisitions Guidelines* (2013) 56. Available from http://www.comcom.govt.nz/business-competition/guidelines-2/mergers-and-acquisitions-guidelines/ (accessed 10 Jan. 2018).

information, confidential information may not be disclosed without the consent of the party that provided the information.[1024] The Commerce Commission may however request a waiver from parties to allow sharing of confidential information, and the Commission encourages applicants to agree to provide a waiver.[1025]

503. In addition to the general cooperation agreements between the New Zealand Commerce Commission and the Australian Competition and Consumer Commission, there is also a merger-specific protocol for Trans-Tasman mergers involving New Zealand and Australian jurisdictions. This is a formal Cooperation Protocol for Merger Review, agreed between the New Zealand Commerce Commission and the Australian Competition and Consumer Commission.[1026] The protocol is intended to facilitate cooperation and efficiency while recognising that the two agencies operate under different legislative regimes.

1024. Commerce Commission New Zealand, *Mergers and Acquisitions Guidelines* (2013) 56. Available from http://www.comcom.govt.nz/business-competition/guidelines-2/mergers-and-acquisitions-guidelines/ (accessed 10 Jan. 2018).

1025. *Ibid.*, 56.

1026. Australian Competition and Consumer Commission and New Zealand Commerce Commission, *Cooperation Protocol for Merger Review* (2006), Available from http://registers.accc.gov.au/content/index.phtml/itemId/757826 (accessed 10 May 2019). *See also* Commerce Commission New Zealand, *Mergers and Acquisitions Guidelines* (2013) 56. Available from http://www.comcom.govt.nz/business-competition/guidelines-2/mergers-and-acquisitions-guidelines/ (accessed 10 Jan. 2018).

Chapter 3. Challenging of the Administrative Decision

§1. Competent Courts

504. Decisions of the Commerce Commission may be challenged in the High Court. For general competition law, including restrictive trade practices and mergers, the Commerce Act provides that there is a right of appeal to the High Court against any determination made by the Commerce Commission under the Commerce Act.[1027] A number of parties are entitled to appeal. The Commerce Act section 92 contains provisions setting out the rights of parties to appeal under section 91. The relevant provisions provide that:

- For appeals against determinations of the Commission on applications for authorisation of restrictive trade practices under section 58 and applications for authorisation of business acquisitions under section 67, the applicant and any other person who has a direct and significant interest in the application and participated in the Commission's processes leading up to the determination.[1028]
- For appeals against determinations of the Commission revoking or amending an authorisation pursuant to section 65(1) or revoking an authorisation and substituting a further authorisation pursuant to that subsection, the person to whom the authorisation was granted.[1029]
- For appeals against determinations of the Commission relating to cartel provisions under section 65A, the person who applied for the clearance; and any other person who is a party to the contract, arrangement or understanding to which the application for clearance relates.[1030]
- For appeals against a determination of the Commission under section 66 in relation to a notice seeking a merger clearance, the person who sought the clearance; and any person whose assets, or the shares in which, are proposed to be acquired pursuant to the clearance.[1031]

505. The High Court, in deciding the appeal, may confirm, modify or reverse the Commerce Commission determination. It may also exercise any of the powers that could have been exercised by the Commission in relation to the matter.[1032] The Court also has the option of, instead of deciding the appeal, directing the Commission to reconsider the matter generally or in respect of specific matters, and in whole or in part.[1033]

1027. Commerce Act 1986 s. 91(1). There are exceptions to this general right for some provisions of the Act related to regulated goods and services, but these are not relevant to general competition law. *See* Commerce Act 1986 s. 91(1). There is a right of appeal to the High Court on a question of law against any determination of the Commission under the Commerce Act, included the provisions for regulated goods and services. *See* Commerce Act 1986 s. 91(1B).
1028. Commerce Act 1986 s. 92(a).
1029. *Ibid.*, s. 92(b).
1030. *Ibid.*, s. 92(ba).
1031. *Ibid.*, s. 92(c).
1032. *Ibid.*, s. 93.
1033. *Ibid.*, s. 94(1).

506. Once the High Court has issued its decision, there is a right of appeal to the Court of Appeal. Any party to any appeal to the High Court from a determination of the Commerce Commission may appeal to the Court of Appeal, with the leave of the High Court or the Court of Appeal.[1034] A court considering an application for leave to appeal shall have regard to whether any question of law or principle is involved, the importance of the issue to the parties, the amount of money in issue or such other matters as in the particular circumstances the court thinks fit.[1035]

§2. Time Limits

507. Appeals to the High Court from Commerce Commission determinations are required to be made within 20 working days after the date of the determination. The court may allow further time.[1036]

508. There is a further right of appeal to the Court of Appeal. Applications for leave to appeal to the Court of Appeal must be made to the court within 20 working days after the decision is given.[1037] There is a further right of appeal to the Supreme Court, with leave of that court.

509. When a Commerce Commission determination is appealed, the determination remains in full force until the appeal is decided, unless the court directs to the contrary.[1038]

§3. Scope of Judicial Review

510. Judicial review is also available for challenging decisions of the Commerce Commission, and it may be useful particularly for parties who are not entitled to appeal under the Commerce Act provisions.

1034. *Ibid.*, s. 97(1).
1035. *Ibid.*, s. 97(2).
1036. *Ibid.*, s. 91(2).
1037. High Court Rules r 20.22.
1038. Commerce Act 1986 s. 95(1).

Selected Bibliography

1. Books

Tony Dellow and Anna Parker, *Guide to Competition Law* (2nd ed, LexisNexis 2018)
Chris Noonan, *Competition Law in New Zealand* (Thomson Reuters 2017)
Matt Sumpter, *New Zealand Competition Law and Policy* (CCH 2010)

2. Legal Encyclopaedias

Robin Cooke et al. (eds.), *Laws of New Zealand: Competition.* LexisNexis, 1992–.

3. Databases

Commercial Law in New Zealand (LexisNexis database)
Gault on Commercial Law (Westlaw NZ database)

Selected Bibliography

Index

The numbers here refer to paragraph numbers.

Agreements: *see* Restrictive agreements
Arrangements: 90–94, 189, 190, 193, 195–204, 206
Authorisation: 16–18, 75–77, 139–144, 473, 474, 479, 480, 487

Bundling: *see* Tying and bundling
Business acquisitions: *see* Mergers

Cartels: 218–267, 269–272, 274, 275, 282, 283, 285, 286, 287, 289, 290
Clearances: 16–18, 61–62, 139–144, 471–503
Client allocation: *see* Market allocation
Commerce Commission: 126–147
- appeals from Commerce Commission decisions: 507–510
- complaints: 440–441
- cooperation with other state institutions: 456, 496–501
- enforcement: 126–147, 457–470
- international coordination: 502–503
- powers: 126–147, 428–440, 442–456

Competition studies: 428–438
Concentrations: 111–113, 397–427. *see also* Mergers
Contracts: 89
Cooperation agreements: 265–290
Counterfactual test: 408
Court of Appeal: 12, 156

Damages: 162–174
Dominant undertakings: 56–59. *see also* Misuse of market power

Effect and Likely effect: 209–211
Enforcement
- civil enforcement: 155–177
- criminal enforcement: 178–188
- procedure: 463–470

Excessive pricing: 357–360
Exclusive dealing: 309–315
Exclusive distributorship: 306–308

Franchising: 318–323

Group boycotts: 259
Guidelines: 24

High Court: 12, 156–157, 504–509

Information exchanges: 261–264
Innovation limitation: *see* Production limitation
Intellectual property: 324–333
International co-operation: 502–503

Joint purchasing: 287–289
Joint selling: 290
Joint ventures: 114–125, 426–427

Legal system: 10–12

Market: 81–83
Market allocation: 242–251
Market power: 84–87, 104
- taking advantage of: 105–107, 334–396

Market studies: 428–438
Mergers: 61–62, 75–76, 397–427
- clearances and authorisations: 471–503
- horizontal: 410–417
- market extension: 421–423
- notification: 474
- pure conglomerate: 424–425
- trans-tasman: 503
- vertical: 418–423

Index

Misuse of market power: 56–60, 100–110, 334–396
Monopolisation: *see* Misuse of market power

New Zealand:
- Commerce Commission: *see* Commerce Commission
- economic system: 9
- general background: 1–8
- history of competition law: 13–15
- legal system: 10–12

Output agreements: *see* Cartels, Production limitations

Patents: *see* Intellectual property
Penalties, pecuniary: 163–171
Per se prohibitions: 66–69
Precedent: 26
Predatory pricing: 364–377
Price discrimination: 361–363
Price fixing: 218–241
Price squeeze: 395–396
Production limitations: 252–258
Purpose: 96, 108–110, 208

Rebates: 383–385
Refusals to deal: 386–394
Regulated industries: 36
Remedies: 150, 162, 178
Resale price maintenance: 65, 298–305
Restrictive agreements: 42–55, 189–206
Rule of reason: 70–74

Selective distribution: 316–317
Sources of competition law: 16–26
SSNIP test: 83, 406
State owned enterprises: 38–40
Substantial lessening of competition: 97–99, 212–217
Supreme Court: 12, 156

Taking advantage of market power: *see* Misuse of market power
Technology licensing: 324–333. *see also* Intellectual property
Territorial reach: 27–35
Trade marks: *see* Intellectual property
Trade secrets: *see* Intellectual property
Tying and bundling: 378–382

Understandings: 90–94

Vertical agreements: 291–333

Made in the USA
Monee, IL
18 October 2026

66041381R10103